SLAVERY'S FUGITIVES
AND THE MAKING OF THE
UNITED STATES CONSTITUTION

SLAVERY'S FUGITIVES

AND THE MAKING OF THE

UNITED STATES CONSTITUTION

Timothy Messer-Kruse

LOUISIANA STATE UNIVERSITY PRESS

Baton Rouge

Published by Louisiana State University Press
lsupress.org

Designer: Kaelin Chappell Broaddus
Typefaces: Adobe Caslon Pro, text; Mrs Eaves, display

Portions of the introduction and chapter 1 first appeared as "The 'Carried Off'
Cover-Up: How Historians Hid the Founders' Drive to Recapture British
Fugitives from American Slavery" in *Ethnic Studies Review* 45, no. 2 (fall 2022):
27–42; portions of chapters 2 and 3 were published as "The Carried-Off and the
Constitution: How British Harboring of Fugitives from American Slavery Led
to the Constitution of 1787" in *Law and History Review* 42, no. 2 (May 2024).

Cover images: *Top, Kidnapping*, by Alexander Rider, 1817;
bottom, Treaty of Paris, by Benjamin West, 1783.

Library of Congress Cataloging-in-Publication Data

Names: Messer-Kruse, Timothy, author.
Title: Slavery's fugitives and the making of the United States Constitution
    / Timothy Messer-Kruse.
Description: Baton Rouge : Louisiana State University Press, [2024] |
    Includes bibliographical references and index.
Identifiers: LCCN 2024010651 (print) | LCCN 2024010652 (ebook) |
    ISBN 978-0-8071-8276-5 (cloth) | ISBN 978-0-8071-8315-1 (epub) |
    ISBN 978-0-8071-8333-5 (pdf)
Subjects: LCSH: Enslaved persons—Emancipation—United
    States—History—18th century. | Fugitive slaves—Legal status, laws,
    etc.—United States. | African American loyalists—Legal status, laws,
    etc.—United States. | United States—History—Revolution,
    1775–1783—Participation, African American. | United
    States—History—Revolution, 1775–1783—British forces. | United
    States—Foreign relations—Great Britain. | Great Britain—Foreign relations—
    United States. | Constitutional history—United States. |
    United States—Politics and government—1775–1783. | United
    States—Politics and government—1783–1809
Classification: LCC E446 .M53 2024 (print) | LCC E446 (ebook) | DDC
    306.3/620973—dc23/eng/20240710
LC record available at https://lccn.loc.gov/2024010651
LC ebook record available at https://lccn.loc.gov/2024010652

CONTENTS

ACKNOWLEDGMENTS

I am grateful to those who commented on this manuscript and pushed me to hone its arguments and evidence. Not only were they extraordinarily generous with their time, they approached a work with an eccentric argument with a spirit of openness and a commitment to advancing the scholarly discourse rather than a particular point of view. These days, that takes not only a broad perspective but bravery.

I am fortunate to have had the patient editorial direction of Paul Rand Dotson, who saw potential in this project at a stage when it was ragged, cold, wild, and just emerged from the woods. He never gave up on it.

I am also appreciative that Bowling Green State University granted me a semester to devote myself completely to this project. Likewise, I thank all my students who listened while I tested how these ideas sounded.

Because the thesis of this book (that patriot leaders' determination to reenslave people who had fled to the protection of the British army contributed to the making of the Constitution) will likely provoke lively and welcome debate, much of the primary source material is quoted at greater length than perhaps is necessary. In historical writing there is always a trade-off between readability and evidentiary proof (the old saying that historians are always willing to provide five sources when one is needed springs to mind), and I have chosen here to err on the documentary side. In all quotations the original and often eccentric spellings of the eighteenth century have been preserved.

SLAVERY'S FUGITIVES
AND THE MAKING OF THE
UNITED STATES CONSTITUTION

INTRODUCTION

For more than fifty years historians have been excavating evidence of the role slavery played in the founding of the United States of America. Once viewed as a minor sidebar to the nation's development, scholars' understanding of slavery's central importance to just about every corner of colonial American life has steadily accumulated. Today, historians widely agree that slavery widened the grievances that made colonists yearn for independence, acted as an accelerant when the fires of rebellion were lit, shaped the strategies both sides formulated to prosecute the war, shaped the compromises necessary to broker a united federal government, and framed the very nature of citizenship and the notions of liberty by which Americans defined themselves. To use a contractor's metaphor, slavery may not have been the architecture of the new nation, or even its building blocks, but it certainly was the mortar that cemented it all together.[1]

While scholars have made remarkable progress in identifying the multitude of ways slavery shaped the rise of the American republic and American society, many of the details of its influence remain untraced. This book explores one necessary aspect of slavery and the part it played in much larger national questions, policies, and fundamental structures of the novel democratic state. This was slavery's essential need to recapture those bold enough, strong enough, determined enough, and lucky enough to escape its dehumanizing confinement.

Unlike the Caribbean islands, where most of the men and women stolen from the homelands in Africa and trafficked by British companies ended up, the American colonies were surrounded by uncontrolled frontiers and large communities of indigenous peoples. This fact of geography presented continuous problems to enslavers and their colonial governments, and caused them to innovate new and novel means of legal and practical confinement. Once Americans won their independence, this fact impelled new definitions of just who belonged to this new experiment of a nation and who did not. It also shaped the distribution of powers between the central government and the individual states. This is the story of how the ongoing question of what role a democratic government has in ensuring the recapture and return of slave "property" molded the American republic.

Slavery's need to have some system for recapturing fugitives also shaped British colonial policies and development. Founding the colony of Georgia was initially a strategic effort to seal off escape routes to Spanish Florida, a problem ultimately solved by English diplomats swapping Florida for Havana and Manilla in 1763. As tensions with suspicious colonists in the largest and richest American colony of Virginia deepened in 1774, Governor Dunmore organized a military expedition deep into the Ohio valley whose purpose was partly to force native peoples to act as border guards and return escaped slaves. But royal administrators ultimately failed to satisfy American enslavers' demands for the confining of their human property, especially when England's highest court ruled in 1772 that escapees from slavery could not be recaptured within the territory of the British Isles.

By the eve of the Revolutionary War, European empires had been enlisting and emancipating each other's slaves for nearly a century. Across the nearly continuous colonial wars centered on control of valuable islands in the Caribbean, English, French, and Spanish armies depended on the recruitment of soldiers and sailors of color, often on terms of freeing them upon completion of their service. In the early 1700s, British authorities relied on armed slaves to staff their militias in Barbados and Bermuda, and the French raised a sizeable enslaved army in Antigua. In his campaign against Cuba in 1741, Admiral Edward Vernon mustered at least a thousand enslaved soldiers from Jamaica. When the Spanish repelled Vernon's siege of Havana, they organized a permanent artillery regiment of enslaved men. English armies made good use of enslaved soldiers in the seizure of Guadeloupe and Martinique during the Seven Years War.[2] American rebel leaders looked upon such practices with horror and distinguished themselves from their rival empires in the degree to which they shunned the recruitment of enslaved peoples.

Underlying England's and the patriots' markedly different degrees of willingness to recruit indigenous and enslaved peoples to their armies was their differing logics of colonialism. As Natsu Saito observes, "classic" external colonizing powers like England, France, and Spain were primarily structured around the exploitation of labor and resources to fuel their home economies and cultivating foreign markets for their exports. Leaders of the nascent United States, however, were pursuing a project of internal colonization, a system based not on extraction but on the displacement of natives and the permanent occupation of their lands. Between these two a central difference stands out: colonizers whose "home" was far away had more degrees of freedom in dealing with conflicts in their peripheries. When "home" and colony were one, the focus of colonization was on seizing and controlling the land itself by removing peoples in the way. Whereas the government ruling over a distant empire can define political power and privileges as being spatial—the soil of the home country conferring rights and protections denied to those abroad—a colonizing state whose home and colony overlap is forced to allocate such differential powers and rights through a process of identifying and privileging certain social groups over others. Here, then, is a key difference that likely contributed to the Americans' great reluctance to put enslaved people in a position where they could earn their freedom.[3]

While wintering at Valley Forge in early 1778, George Washington's aide-de-camp, Lieutenant Colonel John Laurens, the dashing son of South Carolina's powerful politician Henry Laurens, who was at that time serving in the Continental Congress, began pushing his commander to consider raising a regiment of enslaved soldiers to protect the deep South. Laurens wrote Washington that if he could raise "3000 such black Men as I could select in Carolina I should have no doubt of success in driving the British out of Georgia & subduing East Florida before the end of July." Washington moved to quash the idea, writing to his lieutenant that such a plan would only serve to weaken the hold on other slaves in the country because it would "render Slavery more irksome to those who remain in it—Most of the good and evil things of this life are judged of by comparison, and I fear comparison in this Case will be productive of Much discontent in those who are held in servitude."[4]

Washington's candid words exposed the fundamentally different frame of reference through which the patriots viewed the issue of slavery and emancipation compared to their imperial enemies. Britain's employment and eventual freeing of enslaved men did not threaten to alter their fundamental political or social arrangements. Aristocracy was not much impacted by growth of a free Black population, as the subjects of empire had no compelling right to representation in Parliament anyway and such freemen would naturally scatter across imperial territories literally stretching around the globe (as those freed by them in America ultimately did). But to American patriots, every Black man was potentially a subversive, a rebel, or a foreign agent. The mere fact of their existence, as Washington worried, would be "productive of Much discontent" among those left in chains. Though patriot leaders schemed and dreamed nearly continuously of shipping all Black people off to a foreign land, or perhaps some colony far to the west, they knew such plans could not be realized until the government was on solid footing.

No wonder then that after Congress approved Laurens's plan and it finally reached its crucial vote in the South Carolina legislature, it failed overwhelmingly. Laurens's plan was defeated by a much wider margin than was the previous proposal to raise an army of the enslaved that panicked plantation owners had advanced in the South Carolina assembly during a widening war with the Cherokees in 1760. That scheme to outfit a regiment of four hundred Black men on promises of their eventual freedom failed by a single vote.[5]

So entangled was slavery to their conception of the nation that when their prospects seemed bleakest, with English forces retaking Charlestown and Savannah and Lord Cornwallis capitalizing on his victory at Camden by moving south, Virginia's assembly also considered a desperate measure for recruiting additional soldiers. But unlike Laurens's plan, this bill would increase the bounty offered to each recruit to consist of an enslaved man between the ages of fourteen and forty. While provoking a vigorous and lengthy debate, apparently no legislator dared mention the alternative possibility of recruiting these Black men directly with promises of freedom for service, as the British had done. In the end this law was approved, but a reversal of American fortunes intervened before Virginia could begin implementing its complicated logistics.[6]

Even before the first shots were fired on Lexington Green, many enslaved people grasped that the brewing clash of armies would weaken the social and political fetters that reduced them to legal chattel and open opportunities to secure their freedom. As early as 1774, small groups of enslaved people, from as far south as Georgia and as far north as Massachusetts, seized the moment and rebelled against their oppressors.[7] The following year the desperate governor of Virginia, John Murray, Earl of Dunmore, chased from the capitol and taking refuge aboard the Royal frigate HMS *Fowey,* publicly announced what patriots had long rumored, that all persons who fled from slavery and joined his army would be granted their freedom. Four years later, the commander in chief of all the British forces in the American colonies, Henry Clinton, offered to harbor any "Negro who shall desert the Rebel Standard." Sir Clinton's so-called Philipsburg Proclamation was broader than Dunmore's, as those claiming sanctuary did not have to join the British army.[8]

Over the course of the Revolutionary War various English generals would exploit the labor and occasionally the military service of men, women, and children fleeing their bondage, accumulating them in their fortified cities, where many perished of yellow fever, smallpox, or want. Patriots in the meantime avoided ever making such a sweeping offer, and the Black men who fought in rebel armies were mostly free men already, and those considered property who ended up in Washington's army often mustered out in the same condition. In the end, far more African Americans fought to put down the rebels than fought with the patriots, though in the final decisive battle Washington made far better use of his Black troops than Cornwallis made of his.[9]

At the end of the war, approximately twelve thousand African American fugitives from slavery were evacuated by the British—and possibly double that number. This is where the best histories of the early years of the republic that bother to mention the flight of enslaved Americans end, with their departure for all points of the Atlantic empire: Halifax, London, the West Indies, and, for some, their eventual settlement in the African colony of Sierra Leone. But in terms of the impact of these events on the formation of American structures of government, this is actually where the story begins.[10]

After the fugitives' evacuation from New York, America's founding fathers clamored for their return, pursuing a campaign that powerfully contributed to the movement toward the convention that drafted the U.S. Constitution, to the fracturing of the patriot leadership into the first political parties, and even in a small but significant way to paving the way to renewed war with the empire from which they had just won their independence. Just as they had done when conducting the war, American patriots risked the success of their nascent republican experiment rather than allow, or even condone, the successful escape from bondage of thousands of men, women, and children. Their motives for doing so varied tremendously; some were primarily interested in their personal fortunes and wanted the return of the human property upon which their prosperity depended, others seized upon the issue of escapees as an excuse for venting their revenge on loyalists or delaying payment of the private debts they owed to British merchants. Some feared the precedent of allowing the enslaved to successfully free themselves and advocated that escapees needed to be punished to prevent their being manipulated into rebellion by meddling foreign powers. Enough supporters of the new government harbored one or more of these motives that a national consensus formed that pushed the new government to exert all its powers to try to force the British to surrender the escapees they had transported away from American shores.

When England's General Guy Carleton ignored the demands of the Americans and evacuated the Black fugitives who had been promised sanctuary, a wave of protest roiled through the young American states. Various state assemblies, led by the most populous and powerful state of them all, Virginia, responded to English laws by confiscating loyalist property and effectively canceling debts to British merchants. Virginia's law explicitly provided that it would go into force unless American slaves were returned.

The crack negotiating team assembled in Paris to hammer out the details of peace with England in 1782 was arguably the most abolitionist group of American leaders that could have been gathered at that moment. John Adams never owned people and had long opposed the practice. John Jay was soon to be the president of the New York Manumission Society. Benjamin Franklin rolled abolitionist propaganda off his press during the war. Even Henry Laurens of South Carolina was converted to the antislavery cause by his son, who tried to organize that state's only Black regiment on promises of freedom for service. Yet the treaty they wordsmithed included an article that committed the British to surrender the thousands of men and women who had fled American masters and were being sheltered in their remaining fortified camps.

Even after this treaty was signed and delivered, many American patriots refused to abide by it because they claimed the British had reneged on their promise to return the fugitive men, women, and children they claimed as property. While American diplomats were negotiating compensation for these fugitives rather than their bodily return, lawmakers in several states continued to press for the actual repatriation of fugitives from slavery. By 1785, such laws were in force from South Carolina to New York, angering the Crown and leading to Britain canceling provisional trade agreements and refusing to immediately abandon the western forts it had agreed to cede to the Americans.

State laws that conflicted with the Treaty of Paris clearly violated the Articles of Confederation, but Congress, lacking an executive branch or a federal judiciary, had no means to force states to comply with its orders. The standoff over the escapees from slavery continued to escalate as Britain responded by delaying its surrender of western forts it had promised to relinquish and took steps to curtail American commerce. At a time when a myriad of issues troubled the young republic, this impasse compounded other problems by threatening to block America's ability to expand westward, develop its commercial economy, and establish itself as a power among the courts of Europe.

Even though Congress attempted to cajole the states to comply and respect the agreement that had been reached, several of the most important states simply refused and pursued their own foreign policies. This breach exposed the weakness of the federal structure under the Articles of Confederation and powerfully pushed American leaders toward the legal revolution we now call the Constitutional Convention of 1787.

Observing these events with modern sensibilities raises questions about the character of America's leaders, the sincerity of their defining principles, and the nature of the United States itself. Ours would not be the first generation to grapple with these questions, which have divided Americans since the first decades of the republic.

In spite of the obvious importance of American determination and extraordinary actions to recapture the people who had fled their chains, references to patriot reenslavement policies have been largely absent from histories of America's founding.[11] Popular books that cover the period from the end of the war to the drafting of the U.S. Constitution, the time of the most concerted efforts to reclaim escapees under British protection, are entirely silent about these events.[12] Until very recently, even specialized academic studies of this era contained only scattered references to Article 7 of the Treaty of Paris, in which England pledged to cease "carrying away any Negroes or other property of the Americans," and generally downplayed this as a minor footnote in the larger controversy over British retention of western forts, Canadian boundary disputes, and Parliament's gradual reimposition of trade restrictions.[13]

Clearly there is a need to detail these events that shook American society and politics as the fundamental structures of American government were being erected.[14] This book charts the efforts of America's founding leaders to strengthen slavery by recapturing those who succeeded in making their escape. The advent, formulation, and course of these policies is detailed to perhaps a finer degree than might otherwise be necessary had this topic been previously explored. While organizing all these specifics, some of the connections of this topic to larger historical questions have emerged. Questions of slave recapture impacted America's earliest foreign policy with Britain, Spain, and several indigenous nations. When Britain thumbed its nose at Congress's insistence that it abide by its promise to hand over escapees, this exposed one of the chief weaknesses in the Articles of Confederation and added new energy to the drive to replace them. In part, the shape of the new constitution emerged from anxieties over the federal government's inability to police or recapture those held in slavery.

Even after the new, more empowered federal state was organized, the issue of the men, women, and children given sanctuary by Britain would not die. It flared up again when John Jay returned from England in 1794 with a treaty that failed to secure British payment for the lost slaves. Public protest around Jay's Treaty revolved around the issue of the "negroes carried off," and congressional anger over Jay's omission came within a couple votes of scuttling the entire agreement. Taking an even longer view, the issue of British harboring of escapees from American slavery contributed to the international tensions that would tumble into renewed warfare between the two empires during James Madison's administration. In the end, this study shows that slave recapture was much more than a sidebar to the process of organizing the institutions of the young republic.

In 1987, Justice Thurgood Marshall took the occasion of the bicentennial of the Constitution to rightly point out that the nation's blueprint was flawed from its inception, strengthening slavery and excluding all but a thin class of white men from the full blessings of citizenship. Marshall stunned his audience by declaring he could not celebrate that "document now yellowed with age" because he did not "find the wisdom, foresight, and sense of justice exhibited by the Framers particularly profound. To the contrary, the government they devised was defective from the start."[15]

New York Times opinion page columnist Jack Valenti said Marshall had "poked his finger in the eyes of the Founding Fathers." The chairman of the Equal Employment Opportunity Commission and a future Supreme Court justice himself, Clarence Thomas, rushed to defend the sacred document in the *Howard Law Review*, claiming that "the Founders so abhorred the institution of slavery that they would not even permit the words 'slave' or 'slavery' to appear in the document."[16] Ever since then, historical analysis of Constitution-making has been unavoidably inflected with partisan implications.

Many other scholars of the Constitution have generally supported Marshall's view of the flawed and compromised founding and have uncovered additional instances of how slavery's power loomed over Philadelphia that summer of 1787. Paul Finkelman dug out and dissected every issue and debate in that convention that bore on the future of slavery and found that the issue touched on many more clauses than ever thought. George William Van Cleve documented that the final constitutional bargain was the result of horse-trading on a treaty with Spain that pitted northern maritime and mercantile interests against southerners eager to carry slavery into the West. Robert Parkinson detailed how the task of convincing a diverse group of colonists to consider themselves one people and the British as their enemies was accomplished by harnessing their "stereotypes, prejudices, expectations, and fears about violent Indians and Africans," thus setting in motion the systematic exclusion of these "others" from the body politic through such means as the federal system and its Constitution.[17]

The events, actions, and policies this book chronicles press upon ongoing political controversies over whether the nation's revered founders intended to abet or abolish slavery, but not along the grooves already well worn by the intellectual back and forth. Highlighting the importance of patriot efforts to recapture escapees from American slavery does not prove that the founders were more interested in strengthening slavery than setting it on a path to extinction. While it may strike our modern sensibilities as ethically base, there is no inherent logical contradiction between the nation's leaders' extraordinary efforts to recapture fugitives and their belief that slavery was incompatible with both their ideals and the future of the republic for which they fought. Rather, Sean Wilentz can be correct in pointing out that the drafters of the Constitution resisted describing slaves as a form of property to preserve the possibility of future emancipation at the same time that David Waldstreicher can describe the founders' achievement as a "consensus to be silent" on slavery.[18]

Fundamentally, this study builds on William Wiecek's observation that the convention was not really a debate between those supporting or opposing slavery, because there was a "federal consensus" that slavery was legitimate in those places that would have it and that only individual states, not the federal government, could abolish it. The facts presented here reinforce that seemingly modest thesis and show that the great majority of the architects of America's federal system of national government both detested slavery and energetically upheld it where it was properly enshrined in law. While hating slavery for rotting the timbers of democracy or for breeding a dangerous population that they believed eventually would have to be subjugated, segregated, or exiled, the founders loved the law and hated anarchy more. To those whose entire edifice of national legitimacy rested on the majesty of law rather than the bloodline of His Majesty, recapturing runaways from legal slavery could be seen not as defending slavery but protecting the pillars of this new experimental government.[19]

As this book shows, the road from the Revolution to the Constitution was built, like so much else in early America, by the sweat and labor of Black people struggling for their freedom and patriots trying to confine them. These men, women, and children who secured their liberty from American slavery by resisting and fleeing and then sailing away on British ships were instrumental in forcing the founders to realize that their blueprint of government had a hole that could not be fixed without starting over.

ONE

Recapture of Slavery's Fugitives in the Early Republic

During the War of Independence, patriots devoted a surprising number of resources to recapturing those who fled from their captivity. Partly, such efforts were viewed as essential to winning the war, as the flight of an enslaved person was a double loss. Their labor, which contributed to the patriot campaign either directly, by building fortifications and hauling supplies, or indirectly, by earning the foreign exchange that purchased essential war material, was lost. As most of the people who braved patriot reprisals and stole themselves away fled to British lines, their labor then supported the movement and strength of the enemy. Moreover, as the British army offered freedom to those who enlisted, many of those who managed to escape posed a fearsome threat to white Americans: an armed Black force for whom defeat of the rebellion constituted their own liberation. Both the Americans who campaigned to free themselves from the English monarchy and the British strategists determined to keep them within the empire understood that the million or so enslaved Americans, one-fifth of the colonial population (not counting native peoples), constituted a potential fifth-column whose power could determine the outcome of the contest.

Once the Crown determined that it had to crush American opposition militarily, patriots feared the freedom of the masses they enslaved more than ever before. To patriot leaders of the Revolution, the prospect of a sudden, unregulated emancipation was the opposite of their understanding of liberty, as it led to anarchy, which was merely the rule of the strong over the weak. Ruminating on what would happen if there was a general release of slaves, the *Pennsylvania Journal* observed: "Most of the free states in the world have been formed by men just emerged from a state of slavery. No wonder, therefore, they have been liable to disorders, and a speedy dissolution. What sort of government would the negroes in the southern colonies form, if they were suddenly set at liberty?"[1]

As the Revolutionary War dragged on (a pace dictated in part by the choice to not recruit slaves with the promise of freedom), white patriots faced the prospect of an anarchic emancipation made possible by the conflict's disruption of the customary means of policing and repression. As the numbers of people who successfully fled their bondage mounted, the patriots were confronted with a stark choice that could not be deferred or diverted: either they had to redouble their efforts to contain enslaved people, even at the cost of losing the war, or they had to accept that the institution of slavery could abruptly end. Most chose to risk defeat rather than live in a society in which Black people were suddenly freed.

American patriots began capturing and reenslaving fugitives from slavery in great numbers with Cornwallis's surrender at Yorktown. Governor Thomas Nelson of Virginia wasted no time scrambling to recover escapees from slavery. The same day that Cornwallis surrendered his army, Nelson wrote to Cornwallis directing him to ensure that no Black people "endeavor to lie concealed" upon the ships that were then embarking for New York. According to William Gordon, one of the first patriot historians of the United States whom Washington allowed to examine his personal papers after the war, British officers were struck at the eagerness of their American counterparts to recapture escapees from slavery. Gordon recounted how, as General Cornwallis was negotiating the terms of his surrender, the British thought it improper that the Americans insisted that the Black people in their camp be handed over, yet were reluctant to put this demand in writing. Gordon writes the British thought there was "a manifest impropriety in the Americans stipulating for the return of the negroes, while they themselves were avowedly fighting for their own liberties."[2] In the end, "upwards of two thousand negroes" were seized by Continental forces when Cornwallis surrendered Yorktown, according to America's first secretary of foreign affairs, Robert R. Livingston.[3]

One month after the Battle of Yorktown, Benjamin Harrison assumed the duties of Virginia governor and pressed America's ally, the French commander, to order all Black people in their camps held until their ownership could be determined. As Harrison requested that "all the Negroes without distinction that are amongst your Troops" be confined, this included many Black soldiers who had fought for American independence. When the French commander refused and marched his army toward Philadelphia, Harrison informed Virginia's representatives in Congress so they could organize a formal response. Harrison also pressed George Washington for help in dragging those people of color in French camps back to their American masters.[4]

Orders were immediately issued from Washington's headquarters for all "negroes or mulattoes" serving any patriot or allied French units to be immediately seized and jailed. (Major Ross had suggested that only those "Negroes and Mulattoes who have joined the American or French Army since the Siege of York & Gloucester shall be sent to the Gaurds at the said Redoubts," but the general orders issued by Washington's command had no such limitation.) The reason for this drastic action was that "It having been represented that many Negroes and Mulattoes the property of Citizens of these States have concealed themselves on board the Ships in the harbor, that some still continue to attach themselves to British Officers and that others have attempted to impose themselves upon the officers of the French and American Armies as Freemen and to make their escapes in that manner. In order to prevent their succeeding in such practices."[5]

About that same time, James Madison, then serving in the Congress then meeting in Philadelphia, received a letter from his old friend Edmund Pendleton, his former colleague in Virginia's House of Delegates, former president of that state's Committee of Safety, and now president of Virginia's Supreme Court of Appeals. Pendleton asked Madison to help his nephew capture and reenslave Bob, a young man who had run off and joined French troops marching through Virginia. Pendleton described Bob as "about 22 yrs old, five feet eight inches high, rather thin made, is a little bow legged, and has a down look when spoke to." Bob also had "Marks" on both shoulders from a beating he suffered at the hands of American soldiers who accused him of stealing. His injuries were so serious that Bob "lay up for two Months." Currently, Pendleton was pretty sure Bob had joined up with the French army. "We have heard the slave was with the French Army at Baltimore. . . . Will you do me the favor . . . to endeavor to recover him . . . & in case you succeed, to have him confined to Gaol 'til my nephew can send for him"?[6]

Madison immediately agreed to "recover" Pendleton's nephew's fugitive property and also offered his legal counsel, writing, "it will be impossible to dispose of the Slave in this State, there being a legal prohibition agst. it. Even his coming into [it] will operate as a manumission, unless the case of runaways be provided for which I believe is the fact. I will enquire more exactly into [the] matter."[7] Nevertheless, Madison sought out the consul-general of France, François, Marquis de Barbé-Marbois, as to the best way to wrest Bob from the French army. The Marquis advised him to wait until the army encamped while marching. As they were now, they were divided into several divisions and the search would be more difficult. Madison noted that his even asking this of the marquis made him "unpleasant" and noted the French seem to object to the implication that they have a "defect of vigilan[c]e against an illicit resort of slaves to the army."[8]

Finding that the French were not eager to hunt down his friend's property for him, Madison then turned to the American army, contacting Lieutenant Colonel John Jameson, an officer in Washington's command, to make enquiries with the French.[9] At the same time, Pendleton's nephew dispatched his overseer to Baltimore, near where the French army was encamped, to capture Bob. He sneaked into the French army camp, concealing himself for two or three days, until he saw his chance and grabbed Bob in an officer's tent. The overseer was discovered and thrown in the guardhouse, where he probably would have spent much time but for the Pendleton family's power. Pendleton had a local federal officer, Colonel Darby Lux, intervene with the French and secure the surrender of both the overseer and Bob in return for a payment of $20.

As the overseer had to go in search of a horse he had lost in the affair, he chained Bob and left him with Colonel Lux. Bob, as determined as ever, somehow escaped again. Edmund Pendleton dashed off a letter to Madison, assuming that Bob would have headed to Philadelphia, and warned his friend to be on the lookout, and if he succeeds in capturing him, to evade Pennsylvania's laws by selling him to someone from out of state.[10]

In early September Pendleton sent the news that "my nephew's slave was recovered & confined in Baltimore Goal." Madison wrote back congratulating his friend, "I am very glad to find that the recovery of Mr. Pendleton's slave hath at length been accomplished."[11]

The extraordinary efforts that Madison, Pendleton's nephew, and his bounty hunters all undertook to capture Bob speaks to the high value placed on enslaved people at that moment in time—not only for their own market value, but for the invaluable effect upon others held in bondage to see one of their own dragged back into chains from such seeming safety.

Bob was not the only man who had volunteered to help the French army who was dragged back to slavery by the patriots. In March of 1782, Jean-Baptiste Donatien de Vimeur, Comte de Rochambeau, complained to Patrick Henry that Black soldiers in his legion had been "taken up indiscriminately." Rochambeau politely asked Henry to tell the commander of the "Charlotte courthouse" to return them.[12]

In the days following the battle of Yorktown, Major David Ross Jr., a planter from Maryland who later represented that state in the Continental Congress, wrote to George Washington warning him that slaves were escaping from their York and Gloucester masters and fleeing to the British lines and even hiding amid the allied armies.

While Ross opened his memo by claiming that the runaways he was concerned about were just those from the plantations surrounding the battlefield, he quickly forgot this pretense and revealed he was actually worried about a much larger Black population. Ross appealed to Washington's instinct to preserve slavery and wrote: "By a little trouble & exertion at present a valuable property may be recovered to the citizens of those States and more especially the unfortunate people of So. Carolina and Georgia."[13]

As the British retreated to a handful of coastal strongholds, American leaders scrambled to recapture the men and women who had claimed their liberty by escaping to British camps. As soon as American leaders realized that the British were prepared to evacuate rather than surrender the people claimed as American property, they threatened to seize British property and cancel British debts in retaliation. Months before the mass evacuation of Charlestown dramatized that the English were resolved to uphold wartime promises of liberation in exchange for service to freedmen and women, South Carolina governor John Mathews threatened the British commander of the southern district, General Alexander Leslie, with confiscations of loyalist property if slaves were not returned. Leslie and Mathews reached an agreement whereby each pledged to refrain from removing property, but when word of mass repatriation of Black people from Charlestown to British Florida spread, Mathews went along with his revengeful legislature that seized loyalist property and rendered American debts to British merchants uncollectable by prohibiting them from entering collection suits in state courts.[14]

Georgia's legislature was so alarmed by the number of African Americans the British were preparing to carry away from Savannah in July of 1782 that they voted to raise money through the sale of bonds with which they hoped to purchase African Americans from British officers. Their plan was to then turn around and sell them at public auction. Few British officers took up this offer, while some, like Colonel Clarke, expressed sympathy for the Black "refugees": "an attention to Justice, and good faith, must plead strongly in behalf of the negroes, many of whom have certificates of services performed." Over the following month a flotilla of transports carried 1,568 people of color to Jamaica. Over the ensuing six months, another 1,786 Black Americans were taken to St. Augustine, Florida. In total, it was reported that some 5,000 Black people left Georgia in the British evacuation, "who, according to some accounts, were at least three-fourths, and to others, seven-eighths of all the slaves in the province of Georgia."[15]

In spite of the tremendous cost of holding people in bondage in the midst of the chaos of war, the structures of government that had served to administer the war revealed themselves to be inadequate to the new task of recovering the many thousands who had successfully escaped slavery, whether into British camps or across the southern border into Spanish

Florida. The ferocity of British forays and campaigns up and down the breadth of the South had taught southern leaders the hard lesson of the need for a permanent and more centralized union for their own security, a security in which internal and external threats amounted to the same thing.

Very early on it was also recognized that the issue of enslaved people escaping to the sanctuary of British-held cities was one that tested the mettle of the American union. Pressured by powerful slaving interests, Virginia governor Benjamin Harrison tried to enlist his state's congressional representatives in his efforts to secure a flag of truce and permission to inspect British camps for Virginian runaways. The delegates as a group wrote back that diplomatic contacts between heads of individual states and the British were "disaccording with the Spirit of the confederacy." Such claims were to be left to federal diplomats and negotiators.[16]

Men, women, and children who escaped to British protection were not the only people patriot Americans endeavored to drag back into slavery. As the war for independence wound down, many African Americans who had struggled to claim some portion of self-ownership lived in a twilight between liberty and slavery. Some had fled loyalist owners who themselves had abandoned their properties in the face of patriot reprisals and confiscations. Some had been promised freedom in exchange for military service but remained within reach of their masters and depended on officials from their home state or from the national army to uphold these commitments. Without access to courts and without white allies to sue on their behalf, many were simply swept up by former owners or even other claimants.

Continental soldiers were known to keep or sell captured Black men, women, and children as prizes of war. General Edward Hand of Pennsylvania received a petition from a Black man named Charles who, with his wife and daughter, had escaped captivity in Long Island, likely from a loyalist enslaver. But upon making what he hoped would be sanctuary across the Continental lines, Charles said that his family had been "taken up by a Fellow who is a Serjeant in one of the Virginia Regiments and sold to one of the Inhabitants as Slaves, he therefore most humbly craves that your honor will take his unhappy case into consideration and if thro' your means he obtains his freedom with his wife and Daughter he will (as in Duty

bound) be ever ready under your honors command to fight against all En-
emys of the Honble. United States in defence of Liberty and the rights of
Mankind."[17] Military commanders were empowered to sell enslaved people
they captured from the British. South Carolina passed a law indemnifying
Brigadier General Thomas Sumter and his officers from any later civil suits
arising from such sales.[18]

After the war, many masters scrambled to reclaim their human property
that had gone off to fight for their independence. In December of 1784, a
Connecticut master captured a man who had fought with the Continental
army since 1777 and had "been discharged with badges of honor." Claiming
before a local court that the veteran had absconded from his service, the
judge ordered the veteran locked up in jail while the case proceeded. When
it was later learned that his master had received a bounty for the man's
enlistment, and, as Congress had decreed at that time that only free Black
men could serve in the Continental army, accepting the payment amounted
to willful manumission and the court set the veteran free.[19]

Free Black soldiers in the Continental army faced constant threat not
only from the enemy but from their fellow Americans. Lieutenant James
McFarlane of the 1st Pennsylvania Regiment reported that one of the men
he enlisted into his regiment, a man who explained his dark complexion by
saying he was from Spain, had been kidnapped and sold into slavery. His
commander, Brigadier General William Irvine, gave McFarlane leave to
bring this up with General Washington, but even though the name of the
kidnapper was known, a William Irwin, there is no record of Washington
taking any action in the matter.[20]

While still in camp and dealing with the myriad details of keeping his
army in fighting shape, the issue of a Black soldier claimed as another man's
property reached George Washington's desk in February of 1783. Jonathan
Hobby claimed a soldier in the 3rd Massachusetts Regiment and petitioned
that he be surrendered. Washington empaneled a court of enquiry to inves-
tigate the claim, and they returned their report two days later. "[T]he said
Negro was legally purchased as a slave by the said Mr Hobby in the year
1777—That in Jany 1781, said Hobby being absent without the state, the said
Negro was inlisted as a Soldier for three years, by a class in the Town of

Concord where he then lived, and that said Hobby was not knowing nor consenting to this inlistment. The court though they are of opinion that said Negro is the property of Mr Hobby."[21]

While the five officers agreed that the soldier claimed by Hobby was his legal property, they recommended not releasing him until his term of enlistment was up. Clearly, what happened to him then was none of their concern.

Unsatisfied with this outcome, Hobby appealed to the commander of the court of enquiry, and they agreed not to seal their decision but to refer the whole matter to Washington: "they are Sensible it will be Severe on Mr Hobby to put his interest as an Individual in a scale with that of the public and as a process in the State will be attended with delay and expence in pitty to Mr Hobby they Submit the matter to the General to do as he shall think proper." Hobby then seized his opening and wrote to the great general directly, saying, "I feel my self unhappy in Troubling your Excellency." But the stakes were too high for Hobby to desist, and he told Washington that the court "have given it as their Appinion, that my Remedy Lays in the State in which he was Inlisted In Answer to which, I wod say, that from the Circumstances Attending his Inlistment & Mustering I am precluded from Every Remedy . . . and a Total loss of him must Interely Ensue." Hobby asked for "one moment of yr Excellencys attention" to the matter.

It is not recorded what became of the soldier whom Hobby wished to reenslave, but given Washington's record of giving his soldiers back to their masters, it is likely Hobby got his man. About the same time as Hobby lodged his petition with the army, James McHenry, namesake of Baltimore's fort, sent a personal letter to Washington asking him to intervene on behalf of Mary Dulany, "one of the best old ladies in the world who has one of the cleverest young ladies for a daughter." Dulany had asked McHenry to help her recover a man she owned who had served since 1781 in the regiment commanded by Colonel Joseph Vose. Upon investigation, it appeared the soldier in question was not to be found, but Washington assured McHenry, "Had the Negro been in Camp I should have been happy in restoring him to Mrs Dulany."[22]

Samuel Sutphen was twenty-nine years old when he was sold by his owner to Caspar Berger, a German stonemason who wanted to wiggle out of his service in the New Jersey militia. Sutphen was sent to join his unit after finishing planting four acres of corn and was put to work building breastworks near Communipaw, what is today Jersey City. Sutphen could see New York City from where he was posted.

Sutphen's militia was called out sporadically, a few days, weeks, or as much as a month at a time, but they were always disbanded in time for planting or harvest seasons. Nevertheless, Sutphen participated in many fights. In that first year, Sutphen recollected, his unit was "in the heat of the battle of Long Island." After their defeat, he and two others of his company were taken to safety in the skiff of a Black pilot. Sutphen fought at Princeton, Brunswick, and numerous skirmishes over the next year.

When Sutphen's owner was conscripted back into service in 1779, he sent Sutphen in his place for a nine-month tour of duty. Sutphen remembered there being one other African American in his company, "a free mulatto man" named James Ray. They were sent north, to Fort Schuyler, Utica, and Buffalo, to "repel the Indians."

Dismissed at Buffalo a week after New Year's, Sutphen had to march home in the snow, but on his trudge back his company skirmished with a party of Hessians and Highlanders near West Point. Sutphen was shot, the bullet slicing a tendon in his heel and striking his gaiter button and driving it into the bone just above the ankle. It was not until the next morning that the surgeon attended him and cut out both the button and the bullet from his right leg. Two weeks and five days later Sutphen set out again, hobbling home to New Jersey.

That was Sutphen's last service, and when the war was over Sutphen attempted to claim the freedom he was promised by his owner. "[I] demanded my freedom from Berger" but instead "he sold me to Peter Ten Eyck for £110, a slave for life." Berger had paid £92.10 for Sutphen when the war started, so he made a tidy profit and successfully avoided shouldering a musket for the duration. Sutphen was sold numerous times in the coming years but managed to work and save money until, after twenty years more in bondage, he was able to purchase himself.[23]

On rare occasions, luck was on the escapee's side. Jack Arabas was enslaved by Thomas Ivers in New York and enlisted into the Continental army, probably as Ivers's substitute. Arabas fought through the war, believing that in return for his service he would be rewarded with his freedom. After Arabas was discharged, Ivers attempted to drag him back into bondage. Arabas attempted to escape, but was seized somewhere in New England. While transporting Arabas back to New York, Ivers availed himself of the usual public facilities for holding people in slavery, the local jail. Arabas was locked in the jail in New Haven, but while there some allies handed a petition for *habeas corpus* to a local judge, who allowed Arabas a hearing, resulting in his being released. The judge went further and declared Arabas a "free man, absolutely manumitted from his master by enlisting and serving in the army."[24]

Service in Rhode Island's famed black regiment did not lead to freedom for a number of the enslaved men who were sold to the state and mustered into its ranks by their owners. One man named Fisherman apparently mistrusted his owner's and his officers' promises of eventual freedom and deserted to join the British before he was mustered. A man named Prince was stripped of both his uniform and his freedom when his owners changed their minds about allowing him to enlist and petitioned the state assembly for Prince's return. John Burroughs fought in the regiment until the end of the war and was freed by his grateful state, but in 1791 he was kidnapped while sailing to New Orleans and enslaved. Burroughs was one of the two veterans of the regiment on whose behalf their white commander unsuccessfully appealed to the state legislature for help in securing their freedom.[25]

In Virginia, it became so common for white masters to seize and reenslave war veterans who had been promised their liberty that in 1783 the assembly passed a law declaring all Black substitutes who had been promised their freedom were to be manumitted. It is unclear from the historical record whether this measure actually freed any former soldiers, as the law only authorized the state's attorney general to prosecute double-crossing masters, but it is not clear whether he ever did so. The fact that Virginia's legislature had to subsequently pass special legislation to free three famous former Black war heroes (James Armistead, a spy who provided crucial intelligence on the distribution of Cornwallis's troops prior to the Battle of Yorktown; Saul Matthews, who also operated as a spy behind enemy lines;

and Caesar Tarrant, who piloted American warships) indicates that this law may not have been much more than a gesture. In contrast, the North Carolina legislature enacted a law that permitted the reenslavement of war veterans except those freed on the grounds of "meritorious service."[26]

Securing slavery in the wake of the war required not only recapturing those who had gained their freedom during those chaotic years but securing and reinforcing the borders of the nation to prevent others from attempting to flee. The young republic, though secured by an ocean to the east, also had vast expanses of frontier to the west and south that it did not control. Such territories invited not only dreams of self-liberation by escape, but the possibility of the concentration of fugitives into maroon communities with the numbers to defend themselves.

Many colonists understood the threat to slavery posed by an open western frontier long before the Continental Congress took steps to close it as a haven for runaways. Even the antislavery campaigner Anthony Benezet observed in 1763, "In Georgia & Carolina the Negroes are not hemmed in by the Sea, as they are in the Islands, but have back Country uninhabited for some hundreds of miles, where the Negroes might not only retire, but who expect to be supported & assisted by the Indians."[27]

Slavery's most troublesome border was the one stretching between Georgia and East Florida. With the coming of peace, British leaders elected to abandon East Florida, trading it back to Spain in exchange for the Bahamas in 1783. According to one London informant of Benjamin Franklin, English policymakers could not wait to unload it. "It was a prevailing opinion here, that Florida was a sand-bank; that with Spaniards & Americans for neighbors, it was never worth holding by itself; that its negroes would always be running away; that the Indians would probably be made troublesome; that the troops would die; and that after all, it would turn out at last Americas."[28]

Under Spanish rule, American enslavers had much to complain about. From the time the Spanish retook control of Florida, its governors stood on precedent from their previous occupation not to respond to "English" appeals for the return of fugitives. Governor Vicente Manuel de Zéspedes made this clear in responding to a request from Georgia's governor for the return of a man who had escaped slavery: "One of the provisions of the old rule is that no fugitive Negro from Georgia be returned, as the London court refused to reciprocate."[29]

Georgia's legislature formally complained of this treatment to Congress in 1788, and a congressional committee confirmed that "sundry negroe Slaves belonging to Citizens of Georgia had fled to East Florida, and were there protected and detained" and recommended that the chargé d'affaires of the United States at Madrid "represent to his Catholic Majesty the Inconveniences which the States bordering on his Dominions experience from the Asylum afforded to their fugitive Slaves" and to "solicit his Orders to his Governors to permit and facilitate their being apprehended and delivered to their Owners."[30] This issue burned at the top of the priorities of the United States in dealing with Spain for the next year.

News of Florida officials' protection of fugitives from slavery steadily reached American leaders. James Seagrove, the U.S. customs collector for Georgia, stationed in St. Marys, reported in the summer of 1790 that two men had fled by boat from their owner and made it to St. Augustine, where the governor told their owner "do not you know sir, that as soon as a Negro enters his Spanish Majesty's Dominions in Florida that he is free . . . do not let me see or hear that any more of your Country Men come on such errand—or they shall find difficulty in returning."[31] Georgia's governor, George Walton, sent John Jay an account of the escape of sixteen men who stole a boat but were overtaken by their pursuers on Cumberland Island. Three succeeded in crossing the river into Spanish territory. One of the enslavers confronted the Spanish commander of the fort at St. Marys, who informed him that the man he sought, "Harry," had been sent on to St. Augustine but that he could not go there without a permit. After formally applying as instructed, he was told that "no such Permit would be granted as the Deponent's Business was to obtain his Negro, and as no Negro would be given up to their Owners by the Spanish Governor or his Ministers." Governor Walton concluded, "There are but few inhabitants in this part of Georgia that have not had negroes, who have obtained their freedom by crossing the St. Mary's to Florida, and the people have been impatiently waiting for the arrival of the new Governor, expecting that he would have orders not to harbour them: but in case he countenances it and grants them protection, you may rely on the inhabitants making reprisals; for they will no longer consent to losing their property without any redress."[32]

When John Jay informed America's chargé d'affaires in Spain of his re-appointment, he had only one point to discuss with him: "we are solicitous to know whether you have done any thing, & what, & with what Success on the Subject of the asylum given in Pensacola—to fugitive Negroes from Georgia &c.—This gives much Uneasiness, & it is said occasions much Loss to our People in that Quarter. It is to be hoped that your Representations will induce the Court to order their Governors to deliver up these Fugitives." Thomas Jefferson later wrote to underscore the importance of this mission, stressing that "the Practice complained of in Mr. Jay's Letter . . . has not been discontinued, and is of such a Nature as to require pointed Attention." Jefferson would write several more letters urging action over the following months.[33]

Finally, in late 1790, the king of Spain issued orders "not to permit, under any pretext, persons held in slavery within the United States [to] introduce themselves as free persons into the province of Florida." While pleased with development, the general assembly of Georgia resolved to ask President Washington to "procure a restoration of the negroes who have taken refuge in the Spanish provinces" and to station a naval vessel in the St. Marys River, as it would be "one of the best expedients for the prevention of future grievances of this nature."[34] Also skeptical of the practical reach of the Spanish king's orders, Secretary of State Jefferson dispatched a special envoy to Florida governor Juan Nepomuceno de Quesada. The envoy was given a letter from President Washington with very specific instructions. "Your first care will be to arrest the farther reception of fugitive slaves, your next to obtain restitution of those slaves, who have fled to Florida . . . and to procure the Governor's order for a general relinquishment of all fugitive slaves, who were the property of citizens of the United States."[35]

Governor de Quesada met with America's envoy and sent him home with a formal response that specified the procedures for Americans to claim their fugitives (they had to pay for the costs of detaining their human property and present sufficient official documents proving their claim). But de Quesada evaded the Americans' demands for restitution or return of those who had earlier been granted sanctuary, it being "the opinion of Government, that they ought not to be restored."[36]

Diplomatic efforts with Spain seemed to have sealed at least part of the southern border against attempts of enslaved people to flee. But many thousands of miles of western frontier were controlled by various native nations, each of which had to be coerced to act as America's border guards. Every military campaign against native peoples from the era of the Revolution to the end of the century had as one of its goals the recapture of fugitives from slavery. American leaders ensured that every agreement and treaty reached with native nations in these years contained a clause requiring indigenous peoples to capture and return runaways from slavery.

Patriot leaders endeavored to secure America's borderlands from fugitives escaping slavery by forcing native peoples to return those who fled into their lands. Colonial governors of Georgia and South Carolina reached agreements with the powerful Creek nation to return fugitives in exchange for bounties paid in blankets and guns. Such agreements paid higher rewards for the return of escapees back to slavery, but offered payment for the heads of fugitives as well.[37]

On the eve of the Revolutionary War, Virginia's governor organized a military expedition to force similar agreements on the native peoples of the Ohio valley. The campaign was a "Great Sucksess" one of its commanders, Lieutenant William Crawford, gleefully reported his to his friend George Washington. Crawford recounted how his men had burned several villages and forced a group of Shawnee to agree to his terms. These terms were, in order of importance, that "they have to give up all the Prisoners taken ever by them in war both white People and Negro's," and to agree not to venture east of the Ohio River. In addition to terrorizing the Shawnee and the Mingoes, Crawford did Washington a favor by surveying lands he had claimed in the area. Crawford asked his friend one small favor in return: "One faviour I would ask you if it did sute, when those Negros of Mercers are Sold and they are Sold at Creadit (12 months) I would be Glad to Purchess a boy and Girle about 14 or 15 years old." In this one letter, Crawford exposed the deep ties between American determination to conquer native nations, patriot leaders' greed for western lands, their perceived need to strengthen slavery by forcing native peoples to serve as slave patrols, and the casual traffic in enslaved people.[38]

Later, as the war raged in the North, the revolutionary governments of Georgia and South Carolina seized the moment to prevent their western frontiers from becoming sanctuaries for those fleeing slavery. In the spring of 1777, commissioners from these states held a large peace meeting at De-witt's Corner at which leaders of the Cherokee nation were forced to cede all lands east of Unacaye Mountain and to agree to apprehend and deliver to Fort Rutledge "every runaway negro." As a further incentive for this service, they would be paid "100 pounds weight of leather."[39] The following year Congress approved a treaty that forced the Delaware to agree that they would not "entertain or give countenance . . . or protect in their respective states, criminal fugitives, servants or slaves, but the same to apprehend, and secure and deliver to the State or States."[40]

While bottling up the British in their last southern stronghold of Savannah in the last days of the war, General Anthony Wayne was attacked by England's Creek allies. Wayne's regiments successfully repelled the assault and forced the Creek leaders to sue for quarter. Wayne rounded up the Creek leaders and forced them to agree to his terms for peace, which Wayne described to Washington: "as a first stept towards it, they have already delivered up the Negroes, Cattle &ca which they had taken from the Inhabitants of Georgia!"[41]

Once the war was over, Congress's Indian agents ranged across the breadth of the young republic's western frontier and forced native nations to agree to what had become a pattern treaty. First was the Treaty with Six Nations, which bound the Senecas, Mohawks, Onondagas, Oneidas, Tuscaroras, and Cayugas to return all "prisoners, white and Black," then in their territories. American negotiators cared little that many of those they considered "prisoners" had become incorporated into their tribes, viewed their "captors" as their liberators, and were now being returned to slavery. To guarantee that the Six Nations upheld this agreement, the American negotiators took six native hostages into confinement.

Nearly identical language was incorporated into the treaties forced upon the Wyandot (1785), the Cherokee (1785), the Choctaw (1786), the Chickasaw (1786), and the Shawnee (1786). The importance of forcing the return of fugitives from slavery was evident in that this provision was listed as "Article One" in each of these so-called "agreements."[42] Subsequent treaties with these nations, such as the Treaty of Shoulder-Bone (1786) and the Treaty of New York (1790) with the Creeks, reiterated the requirement that "negroes" be returned. About this same time General Washington commanded all negotiators with Indian nations to conform to these treaties "In the general objects of the restoration of Prisoners, Negroes &ca."[43]

In spite of all these efforts, leading southern politicians remained unsatisfied with what these treaties had accomplished. South Carolina's Pierce Butler complained that it was "vague and Weakly worded." Butler instead said he "wanted the restoration of the Negroe Property an express condition of the future payment of the money that the Indians are to receive." In particular he thought General Henry Knox had treated them too kindly: "Genl. Knox had it in his power to [demand the?] restoration of the Negroes taken. I blame him for not doing so."[44]

Eventually, grumbling from politicians in Congress like Butler put additional pressure on the Creeks and other native peoples to surrender African Americans, which they apparently were reluctant to do. Henry Knox, the secretary of war, informed Washington that it was his "Agent's opinion, that it is a thing impossible for the Indians to comply with the Treaty of New York so far as respects giving up the Negro's, and other property taken from the Citizens of Georgia" and instead suggested that Congress pay their former owners instead. General Knox calculated that a campaign against the Creek would cost the treasury much more than a simple indemnity payment. He was sure that the "former owners of Negro's would be pleased with this mode of Settlement."[45]

Enlisting native peoples into being America's slave catchers was, by the time of the ratification of the Constitution, a policy observed at the highest levels of the young federal government. When Secretary of State Thomas Jefferson first sat down with his British counterpart in New York for a frank, one-on-one exchange of views, the British agent, George Hammond, asked Jefferson if it was his government's intention to "exterminate the Indians and take the lands." Jefferson replied that it was not, because they viewed them as having a valuable role for the foreseeable future. "We consider them as a Marechaussee, or police, for scouring the woods on our borders, and preventing their being a cover for rovers and robbers."[46]

The extraordinary spectacle of America's prophets of liberty insisting on recapturing thousands of people who had escaped literal bondage laid bare the damage the war had done to the naive prewar faith that the corrupting institution of slavery could be easily done away with. While the British never set out to be emancipators, their battlefield and peacetime strategies weakened the atmosphere of terror and hopelessness that the enslavement and control of African Americans depended upon. Despite patriot leaders' resolute belief that slavery was antithetical to the virtues and safety of a democratic republic, when forced with the choice between liberating enslaved people all at once or tightening their chains, they overwhelmingly chose the latter. Perhaps in their eyes the clear distinction between these two things blurred and they convinced themselves that strengthening their tyranny over people in bondage was itself an essential step toward abolition. Whatever their understanding of their actions, the white community's fear of men and women escaping their bondage contributed to their growing recognition of the need for a strengthened federal system to maintain the multitudes in their captivity at least until some imagined distant time when abolition might be possible.[47]

TWO

America's Broken First Treaty of Peace

Americans' anger at the British for providing sanctuary to runaways from slavery served as the background for the negotiation of the terms of peace. Perhaps no other negotiations in the history of the United States were as consequential in shaping the fundamental contours of the nation. Not only were its future social, economic, and political relationships to England, to other European nations, and to native peoples at stake, even the extent of its territory and the character of its own government were molded at the bargaining table in Paris.

None of the diplomats foresaw the dire consequences of tying the return of American citizens' human property to the payment of British debts and the American states' protection of loyalist property. Both sides miscalculated when they agreed to this bargain. Congress underestimated the determination of the state leaders to avoid paying British merchants what they were owed and to punish those they considered traitors by seizing their estates. Neither Parliament nor the Crown initially understood the complications of returning fugitives to American slavery. After all, many Americans who escaped slavery and fled to the safety of British camps in Charlestown had been returned to their Tory owners. Only when the British commanders conducting the evacuation of the last American strongholds refused to hand over the men and women they sheltered to patriot enslavers did it become apparent that what began as a simple quid pro quo had rapidly devolved into an intractable standoff.

Congress did not at first appreciate that its ability to negotiate trade agreements or to force the British surrender of western forts depended on restraining the states that had eagerly enacted laws sequestering debts and seizing Tory lands. Like Doctor Frankenstein, Congress only gradually came to realize that it had no power to reign in the monster it had created. When Congress finally became aware that the nation's future depended on reversing state laws over which it had no control, the nation's most influential leaders pushed for a fundamental restructuring of the division of powers between the states and the central government.

This process began to unfold in September of 1782, after British troops evacuated Savannah with thousands of Black refugees from American slavery, and Congress voted to "as speedily as possible" send "authentic returns of the slaves and other property which have been carried off" to its diplomats negotiating peace terms with the British in Paris. The vote on this measure did not break down along sectional lines, as only Maryland and one representative from New Hampshire, one from Rhode Island, and two of the three delegates from New Jersey voted no.[1]

Congressmen then hammered out instructions to their peace negotiators that clearly connected the return of escapees from slavery to respecting British creditors and loyalist property. Their first attempt calling upon their diplomats to "contend in the most earnest manner for a restitution to the citizens of the United States of such slaves and other property" was voted down in favor of a stronger demand that directly tied British return of fugitives from slavery to an American pledge not to confiscate loyalist property. Congress declared that the "many thousands of slaves" who had been "carried off" was such a "great loss of property" that the states will consider it "an insuperable bar to making restitution or indemnification to the former owners of property which has been or may be forfeited to or confiscated by any of the states."[2]

The first state to follow Congress's lead was Pennsylvania, which instructed all its county officials to make a record of "all losses of negro or mulatto slaves and servants, who have been deluded and carried away by the enemies of the United States." When news of his home state's action reached Paris, Benjamin Franklin told his British counterpart that "I have no doubt that similar acts will be made use of by all" the other states.[3]

The British viewed these developments anxiously because they understood the nature of America's decentralized confederation and were already suspicious that they were negotiating with a party who could not hold up their end of any bargain. British negotiator David Hartley told Franklin that some in England expressed "alarm" at the possibility that "the unity of government in America should be uncertain, and the States reject the authority of Congress." Hartley noted that a recent letter of Washington's had "given weight to these doubts."[4]

Franklin may have misstepped when he decided to highlight the weaknesses in the American federal structure as part of a negotiating strategy of demanding restitution from the Crown while denying that a similar reciprocity was possible on the American side. Franklin argued that nothing could be done about state confiscation laws because of America's federal structure: "the confiscation being made by virtue of laws of particular States, which the Congress had no power to contravene or dispense with." Franklin advised British negotiators that the best course would be for England to drop its objections to America's confiscations of loyalist properties and in turn he would "write to America" and stop the inventory of lost American property, presumably including people.

Ultimately, the peace negotiations in Paris stalled over a handful of issues, the question of compensation for escapees from slavery carried off by the English, the confiscation of loyalist estates and the legal barriers thrown up to repayment of American debts, and the scope of American fishing rights off the Grand Banks of Newfoundland. When the arguments grew heated, Franklin pulled a paper from his pocket and read a statement he had prepared for just this impasse. Franklin demanded that the king "make compensation . . . for the tobacco, rice, indigo, and negroes, &c., seized and carried off by his armies." He then fused together the issue of slavery's fugitives and American debts to British creditors, asking, "Will not the debtors in America cry out that if this compensation be not made they were betrayed by the pretended credit and are now doubly ruined, first by the enemy and then by the negociators at Paris, the goods and negroes sold them being taken from them, with all they had besides, and they are now to be obliged to pay for what they have been robbed of?"[5]

Meanwhile, Franklin's fellow negotiators, John Adams, John Jay, and Henry Laurens, were worried that simply refusing the principle of payment of restitution would destroy the possibility of reaching an agreement. Instead, they assured their English counterparts that while Congress could not override the states, they could "recommend it to the States, to open their courts of justice for the recovery of all just debts." This for the moment satisfied the British side, breaking the logjam by giving them a face-saving though hollow guarantee.[6]

Among the agreed upon articles of peace was Article 7, which specified that as Britain withdrew its troops from the territories of the American states, it would do so "without causing any destruction, or carrying away any Negroes or other property of the American inhabitants." At the time this provision was agreed upon, the English army was providing sanctuary to more than ten thousand escapees from American slavery in their last strongholds of Charlestown, South Carolina, and the New York islands. As the British had pledged to abandon these and their other remaining forts in the delineated U.S. territories, American leaders justly assumed that the British were obligated to hand over the fugitives to their former patriot masters.

The simple fact that Congress demanded and their negotiators in Paris delivered an agreement to recapture thousands of freedmen and women has largely been silenced in histories of the Revolution. One of the most persistent ways that historians have downplayed the importance of reenslaving the men and women who had escaped to British protection is the false claim that the provision demanding that Britain not "carrying away any Negroes" was a mere afterthought, added at the last moment and not, therefore, of much concern to the Americans. Like all powerful myths, this one has a grain of truth in that the one southern member of America's negotiating team, Henry Laurens, seems to have formulated the precise wording of this clause. Though credited with suggesting this language, it is clear from the historical record that restoration of the fugitives to their American masters had long been a demand of the American negotiators. Nevertheless, many historians have pinned the blame solely on Laurens, speculating or implying that his ties to human trafficking and his own extensive plantation holdings in South Carolina drove the negotiations.[7]

Henry Laurens has frequently been characterized as a South Carolina slave trader, which he was, but being so did not mean he was not an opponent of slavery. This misunderstanding springs from a simplistic framing of this period as being divided between the selfish forces protecting slavery and the enlightened reformers battling against it. In reality, white views of slavery were far more conflicted, contradictory, and nuanced than some Manichaean struggle between good and evil. Laurens was born into a wealthy slave-exploiting family in the portion of North America that most resembled the cruel societies of Barbados and the other sugar colonies of the British West Indies. While amassing thousands of acres of prime rice lands and hundreds of slaves, the Laurens family expressed great unease with their situation. Henry Laurens's father, John, predicted slavery's eventual demise. His brother James, a Charlestown merchant, refused to partner with him in the "Guinea trade" in 1767, which he said he disapproved of. Henry wrote sincerely to his son John about his dislike of slavery and its injustices and supported his son when he lobbied the South Carolina assembly to recruit slaves into a Black regiment on the promise of emancipation. As soon as Henry was released from the Tower of London in 1782, he was reported to have "associated intimately with a number of distinguished advocates of negro emancipation," including abolitionists Thomas Day and Richard Price.[8]

Laurens was in London in 1772 when Lord Mansfield read out his landmark decision in *Somerset v. Stuart*, effectively rendering the keeping of people enslaved impossible in England proper. He commented on the momentous decision to his friend Alexander Garden, a renowned physician in Charlestown, praising it as "suitable to the times."[9] Laurens would later write that England's self-congratulatory attitude toward abolition was akin to a pious man's "prohibiting fornication under his own roof and keeping a dozen Mistresses abroad."[10]

The key to understanding Laurens's attitude toward slavery, and thereby that of his entire generation of fellow patriots, is to appreciate that he hated slavery for the harm it did to white people, not principally out of benevolence to those held in chains. Slavery, Laurens and many other patriot leaders believed, corrupted the republic by enticing citizens with the "glare of precarious riches" and, worse, filled up the nation with those of black skin, the "stamp of providence." White abolition in the late eighteenth century was envisioned as being accomplished by what Laurens termed "working by gradual steps," beginning with ending the slave trade, as that was how the Black population was increased. All the while, the prime purpose of eradicating slavery was to benefit the white nation. "Nothing in my Opinion can recover the credit of this Country or save it from total ruin, but a prohibition of the importation of Negroes at least for a limited time. To recover and save the honor of the Country, an abolition of Slavery by wise and progressive measures is necessary."[11]

For white abolitionists like Laurens, importations of enslaved people doubly damaged the American republic. By increasing the number of Blacks and thereby cheapening labor, it deterred the immigration of virtuous white yeomen and their families. Rather than peopling the western lands with "negroes" and their masters, better to found a civilization consisting of "poor white adventurers," those "valuable citizens" who build up "the riches of the State." African Americans were a "difficulty" to the rise of the white republic and they ultimately had to be kept apart from white society. Laurens thought it best for descendants of Africa who had gone through several stages of "whitewash" and were of "fairer complexion" to "confine them to their original clothing" and set them apart. "They may and ought to continue a separate people . . . subjected by special laws, kept harmless, made useful and freed from the tyranny and arbitrary power of individuals."[12]

Accounts of Laurens joining the negotiations on the "last day" and inserting Article 7 rest on a perception that Laurens was anterior to the negotiations until then. But as soon as he was released from British captivity that spring, months earlier, he began meeting with high officials, including "frequent conversations" at the house of Prime Minister Lord Rockingham. Laurens was also known to have spent much time with the Duke of Richmond, one of Rockingham's key advisers, and with Lord Shelburne, secretary of state for the Home and Colonial Department, and met in the Netherlands with England's chief negotiator, Richard Oswald.

The idea that Henry Laurens swept into the negotiations at the last minute and intruded the clause demanding the return of fugitives from slavery simply does not stand up to the known facts. Laurens did not receive his commission as an official emissary of the United States until November 12, 1782, just a fortnight prior to the signing of the provisional articles of peace, and he actually arrived on the last days of negotiations. On November 17, two days before Laurens supposedly pushed the issue of "carried off negroes" into the negotiations, John Adams had conversations with members of the British legation, Benjamin Vaughn and Richard Oswald, in which he brought up the "the Burning of Cities, and The Thefts of Plate, Negroes and Tobacco" among American grievances.[13]

A week before Laurens arrived in Paris, according to the head of the British delegation, Richard Oswald, it was Adams and Jay who "complained of our mode of evacuating the Garrison of Savannah, as if we had carried off, in the way of booty, (they used that word) a number of Negroes to be Sold in the W. Indies." Oswald replied that they must have been "misinformed" and that the only enslaved people shipped out of the city were those who belonged to loyal Britons. Oswald thought the Americans' level of concern about the evacuation of African Americans was troubling enough to report it to his superior, Thomas Townshend, that "the People there are apprehensive about some part of this kind of Property, which happens to be in the hands of our Garrison."[14]

While in formal negotiations on November 29, according to Adams's notes, it was Franklin who first raised the issue of the "Compensation to the Sufferers in America" for "the carrying off of Goods from Boston, Philadelphia, and the Carolinas, Georgia, Virginia &c. and the burning of the Towns, &c." It was then that Franklin drew from his pocket the list of grievances he had prepared. The following day, when Laurens suggested an additional clause that "British Troops should carry off no Negroes or other American Property," this was merely a clarification of a negotiating position all the Americans had insisted on before he arrived.[15]

When Laurens brought up a further prohibition on carrying off any further escapees, his suggestion was met with unanimity among all the negoti-ators: Adams recalled in his journal that there was ready agreement among all the American diplomats that the British should not evacuate with Af-rican Americans. "Mr Laurens said, there ought to be a stipulation, that the British troops should carry off no negroes, or other American property. We all agreed. Mr Oswald consented." Clearly, Adams thought this was correcting an oversight rather than any novel addition to the agreement.[16]

Additionally, diplomatic correspondence from the earliest days of nego-tiations clearly indicates that the issue of compensation for "negroes carried off" was part of the instructions given to the patriot emissaries.[17] Franklin discussed the issue of the British harboring Americans' human property with his English counterpart, Richard Oswald, in the spring of 1782 and had enough time to send notes of these discussions and to request guidance from Philadelphia, and for the Continental Congress to deliberate and re-turn instructions well before Laurens arrived in Paris. Franklin received his copy of congressional instructions demanding that he insist on the return of escapees from slavery by September 13, 1782, at the latest. According to later accounts from Lord Shelburne, Franklin was so insistent on the return of escapees that he "threatened to sell the German prisoners [in America] unless the Negroes were restored or paid for."[18]

Repeatedly through that autumn, America's negotiators received orders from Congress to press on the issue of the fugitives from slavery. On Sep-tember 10, Congress voted to send to Paris a full accounting of "the slaves and other property which have been carried off or destroyed in the course of the war by the enemy." To ensure that this issue was attended to quickly, Congress immediately voted a second resolution instructing Secretary of Foreign Affairs Livingston to "in the meantime" tell Franklin and the other diplomats that "many thousands of slaves and other property to a very great amount have been carried off or destroyed by the enemy."[19] Livingston sent copies of both of these resolutions to Franklin three days later.

Franklin failed to send any letters to Livingston for several months, a stretch from March to August, when events moved quickly back in Amer-ica. During this time Livingston came to believe that of the three priorities he had laid out as the basis of negotiations back in November, only the issue of loyalist property would be a sticking point: "I see nothing that will obstruct your negotiations," he wrote to Franklin, "except the three points of disenssion . . . the restoration of confiscated property has become utterly impossible, and the attempt would throw the Country into the utmost confusion—the fisheries are too important an object for you to lose sight of, and as to the back lands, I do not concieve that England can seriously expect to derive any benefit from them that will be equivalent to the Jealousy that the possession of them would awaken and keep alive between her and this Country."[20]

America's diplomats began discussing the intertwining issues of fugitive slaves and English debts as early as October. Franklin wrote Livingston on October 14 that in their preliminary negotiations "Something has been mention'd about the Refugees and English Debts; but not insisted on, as we declar'd at once that whatever Confiscations had been made in America, being in Virtue of the Laws of particular States, the Congress had no Authority to repeal those Laws, and therefore could give us none to stipulate for such Repeal." Here the meaning of the word "Refugees" could refer to either loyalists who fled America or the fugitive Black Americans the British army took with them, or both. But the fact that Franklin used the term "refugee" rather than the term commonly used up to this time in his correspondence to refer to absconding loyalists, namely "Tories," points to his alluding to escapees from slavery.[21]

On November 9, 1782, John Adams met with the French foreign minister, Count Vergennes, at Versailles, and the allies strategized exactly what the Americans should demand of the British in their peace negotiations. Vergennes expressed his opinion that the Americans should of course restore the estates and property of the loyalists, as "all the Precedents were in their favor." In fact, the count could not think of single example in memory in which European states did not restore the estates of their defeated adversaries. Adams did not agree, and countered: "And when you come to the Question of Compensation, there is every argument of national honor, dignity of the State, public & private Justice & Humanity, for us to insist upon a Compensation for all the Plate, Negroes, Rice, Tobacco stole, and Houses & Substance consumed, as there is for them to demand Compensation to the Tories; and this was so much the stronger in our favor, as our Sufferers were innocent people, and theirs guilty ones."[22] Clearly, weeks before Laurens joined their delegation, the issue of "Compensation for all the . . . Negroes" was not only pressing on Adams's thoughts, but was already joined as a counterweight to English insistence that its loyal citizens be made whole.

Depicting Henry Laurens as being responsible for the clause requiring the return of slavery's fugitives to the Americans erases the fact that Congress had been growing ever more deeply concerned and vocal about British harboring of escapees for at least a year prior to his appearance in Paris. In the end, America's peace negotiators did little more than dutifully follow their government's instructions.

Article 7 was never an "afterthought" or a minor note to the negotiations, as the theory that Laurens "snuck" it in at the last moment would imply, but was from the beginning an element entangled with other, more vexing issues dear to both sides. While royal commissioners could abandon forts and relinquish territories without provoking strong political opposition in the House of Commons (in an empire the size of Britain's, such things came and went like the seasons), Parliament could not as easily agree to abandon its loyal subjects who remained in America or the debts English merchants were owed. On the other side of the table, American negotiators were keenly aware of the blood and loss that fueled the hatred between patriots and Tories. How could the patriot leaders agree to restore loyalist estates and force newly established state courts to respect debts to those they had sacrificed to defeat?

While Franklin drew rhetorical connections between debts and enslaved people, Henry Laurens and Richard Oswald lived this dilemma. These two men who faced off across the negotiating table were not only well acquainted, but tangled up by business ties, debts, and obligations. Henry Laurens's close friend and business partner John Lewis Gervais (who named his first son Henry Laurens and, after he died at the age of two, then named his second son Henry Laurens as well) had purchased a large plantation and a number of enslaved workers from Oswald in 1769 and failed to make all the payments on their note. Laurens brokered an agreement between the two men in 1774, but Gervais stopped payment once war erupted. Gervais would later claim that he could not pay his debts because the British had stolen all of his human property. As Oswald and Laurens discussed the issues of American debts to English creditors, they could not but help see each other embodying the opposite interests at stake.[23] Laurens later told Gervais that he raised his situation in the heat of their negotiations, writing him, "I spoke forcibly alluding to your particular circumstances at the time of discussing the 4th & part of the 7th Articles of the Provisional Treaty."[24]

Almost as soon as he and Oswald shook hands and completed the provisional treaty, Laurens sent a letter to Gervais in South Carolina in which he urged him to make good on his debt to the British negotiator: "the Basis of a definitive Treaty of Peace between Great Britain and the United States [is] agreed Debts on each side are to be paid, let me entreat you to think seriously of our Dear Friend Mr Oswald."[25]

This advice was not well taken, as Gervais harbored personal grievances against the British military for raiding his plantation and manor home and transporting all of the people he claimed as his personal property to Charlestown. The first letter Gervais wrote to Laurens after his release from the Tower of London seethed at the loss of his enslaved workers: "they have carried off all my negroes They have had a great spleen against me particularly, I believe I am the only one in the State, whose whole property they have removed . . . in a Word they have left me nothing but my Land, which thank God they could not carry away."[26] By the time Laurens had arrived in Paris to finalize the treaty, Gervais, formerly the president of the South Carolina Senate, had been elected to Congress and voted with the rest of delegation on September 10, 1782, to have the secretary of foreign affairs compile a full list of slave property being withheld by the British in violation of the treaty and to inform America's negotiators in Paris that "many thousands of slaves and other property to a very great amount have been carried off" and that "in the opinion of Congress the great loss of property . . . will be considered by the several states as an insuperable bar to their making restitution or indemnification to the former owners of property which has been . . . confiscated by any of the states."[27]

Throughout his two years in Congress, Gervais was a consistent advocate of tying the return of fugitives from slavery to the payment of English debts. Gervais wrote Laurens his belief that putting roadblocks in the way of British creditors was warranted so that debtors would not be driven to "Distress," a circumstance that would be "ruinous, & would do as much mischief, & be felt nearly as Severely as the Invasion of the State has been." British merchants were suing American debtors to claim the "very Negroes the British have plundered from them" and complained "I have not heard any body expecting remissions of their debt on that Account."[28]

Henry Laurens had no doubt that when the British army evacuated New York with thousands of fugitives from American slavery in tow, or the governor of East Florida refused to return escapees to South Carolina enslavers, the Crown was violating the terms of the treaty he had helped write. In the spring of 1784, he wrote Gervais with his assessment of the situation: "That the seventh Article of the Treaty of Peace so far as respects the carrying away any Negroes or other Property of the 'Inhabitants of the United States' has been violated on the part of Great Britain is certainly true."[29]

Historical theories that saddle Henry Laurens with responsibility for pushing Article 7 into the Treaty of Paris overlook the obvious fact that the agreement reached in November of 1782 was provisional and that six more months of negotiations followed to polish the treaty into its final form. During this time both sides presented modifications and alterations to the original document, and during these talks there were many opportunities to clarify, expand, or discard the demand for the return and reenslavement of African American fugitives.

There was during this time a distinct opening to rethink the American position on reenslavement. Britain's chief negotiator, Richard Oswald, was recalled after the resignation of the Earl of Shelbourne's government in early 1783 and its replacement by the more liberal North-Fox coalition. Amid this turmoil, a sympathetic supporter of American independence, David Hartley, was appointed to take Oswald's place.

While Oswald and Laurens, just like their countries, were enmeshed in roles of creditor and debtor, Hartley and Franklin were warm friends. The two had met at the home of Joseph Priestly while Franklin lived in London in early 1774.[30] Like Franklin, Hartley was an inventor and philosopher, and the two had similar interests in the problem of fire protection. While Franklin worked on protecting buildings from lightning, Hartley came up with a method of fireproofing them that he boasted would have prevented the Great London Fire and for which Parliament granted him a patent for thirty-one years.[31]

Like Jay, Adams, Laurens, and Franklin, Hartley opposed slavery in principle, certainly more than his predecessor did (Oswald seized his opportunity and purchased a Florida plantation worked by 170 enslaved people in the waning years of the war). While serving in the House of Commons, Hartley proposed a plan that would address many of the Americans' complaints about oppressive British tax and trade policies while also taking the first steps toward ameliorating, or even eventually abolishing, slavery in the North American colonies. Hartley's plans are worth examining in some detail as they—for a moment, like a flash in the dark—brilliantly illuminated the limits of what later historians like Bernard Bailyn, Gordon Wood, and Sean Wilentz would interpret as patriot abolitionism.[32]

In the aftermath of the British disaster at Bunker Hill, several members of Parliament drafted plans of reconciliation with the Americans. On December 7, 1775, the House of Commons considered a series of motions from David Hartley, member from Kingston upon Hull, to end the rebellion through conciliation. Hartley's plan involved allowing Massachusetts to restore its assembly and council; pardoning and indemnifying the rebels; the king relying on a system of requisitions rather than specific taxes for the colonies; and establishing "a permanent Reconciliation between Great Britain and its Dependencies in North America, and [restoring] His Majesty's Subjects in North America to that happy and free Condition, and to that Peace and Prosperity, which they enjoyed in their constitutional Dependance on Great Britain before the present unhappy Troubles."[33]

During debate, Hartley suggested that while peace and unity within the empire could be achieved, it had to come at a cost. It would not be wise to simply hand the Americans all that they asked for without asking for something in return. Hartley then suggested that the price of the king's concessions would be steps toward curtailing the absolute power of enslavers. During his long and highly regarded speech that was subsequently reprinted on both sides of the Atlantic, Hartley joined American independence and the abolition of slavery.

Realizing he could not realistically call upon Parliament to offer the Americans peace in exchange for freeing their enslaved populations, Hartley proposed a modest first step, a symbolic act that would indicate that the Americans were acting in good faith. To this end, Hartley submitted a motion to extend civil rights to the enslaved: "That Leave be given to bring in a Bill to establish the Right of Trial by Jury in all Criminal Cases to all Slaves in North America, and to annul all Laws of any Province repugnant thereto, and to require the registering of the same by the respective Assemblies of each Colony in North America." Hartley's motion as put to the Commons was seconded by George Savile. Lord North spoke against the motion because of its "unseasonableness." Edmund Burke supported it in his usual elliptical manner, "the very reason assigned why the present motion should not be agreed to, was the best reason for agreeing to it." Lord John Cavendish supported it, but "despaired of success." In the end, none of Hartley's motions for reconciliation passed and Americans condemned them as more parliamentary meddling with their internal affairs. Hartley later lost his seat because of his pro-American views, though he returned to the Commons in 1782.[34]

Before he arrived in Paris, David Hartley was handed explicit instructions to "open your business fairly and ingenuously to the Commissioners of the United States." Hartley's boss, Charles Fox, predicted that the negotiations were straightforward and uncontentious, and so instructed Hartley that he need not even treat them as a struggle: "The points which make the objects of the present negotiation are so evidently advantageous to both parties, and it is so impossible (if fairly considered) that any opposition of interests can occur in the discussion of them, that there does not seem here any occasion for that reserve such in negotiation of another sort is often highly prudent."

England's policy makers were eager to roll back those parliamentary laws that were passed during the war and prohibited trade with the rebellious American provinces. Hartley was told that by the time he sat down with his American counterparts, a bill for this purpose should have already passed as a gesture of goodwill. In return, Hartley was to request similar actions on the part of the Americans, at least a pledge that they would undertake "a similar removal of prohibitory acts on the part of their Constituents."[35]

Americans could hardly have dreamed of more favorable tailwinds to propel their bargaining to a happy conclusion. Henry Laurens met with the new foreign secretary, Charles Fox, and reported happily to Franklin that he had "a disposition to proceed to business with us with liberality and effect."[36] It was at this moment that John Adams drafted a set of supplemental articles to the standing agreement that he shared with his fellow diplomats, who must have approved of them, and then with David Hartley, who also agreed to them in principle. The first of these additions was apparently Franklin's brainchild and essentially gave each country's citizens equal standing in the other's territories, "excepting such Individuals of either Nation as the Legislature of the other shall judge fit to except." A second article radically proposed a common open market across the British Atlantic, free of all "Charges and Duties." A third banned all future confiscations or prosecutions pursuant to the war without exception. In the end, none of these provisions made it into the final treaty.

Revealingly, Adams left untouched the old language of the provisional treaty when it came to the fugitives from American slavery. Though his proposed amendments revised Article 7 to include a strict deadline for the withdrawal of the English army, Adams made no changes or stipulations in the language requiring Britain to withdraw without "carrying away any Negroes or other Property of the American inhabitants."[37] Clearly, none of the members of America's all-star diplomatic team had any difficulty with the prospect of dragging thousands of men, women, and children back into their chains.

Adams may have retained the exact phrasing of the original agreement regarding "carrying away" because of the continuous pressure he felt from Congress to do so. All through the previous year a steady stream of directives from Philadelphia demanded that they push the English to return the fugitives.

Not surprisingly, Hartley was particularly receptive to a proposition from John Jay to provide one important exception to the principle of free trade between the two nations: Britain would respect any prohibitions the United States placed on the importation of enslaved humans. As Hartley explained to Foreign Secretary Charles Fox, "The American States have for many years been discontented with the system of slavery prevalent among them, but not having hitherto had the command even of exclusion from their own ports, any attempt towards the gradual abolition of slavery has been suppressed in the beginning."[38]

Fox readily agreed to this point in principle: "With respect to the Article of Slaves, if it be the Policy of the United States to prohibit the Importation of them, it never can be competent to us to dispute with them their own Regulations, either upon this, or any other less invidious Branch of Commerce: But then the Prohibition ought to be general, and they ought not to suffer the importation by any other European Nation."[39] Nevertheless, for reasons that remain clouded by lack of documentation, no such trafficking exemptions ever made it into the actual draft commercial treaties considered by the two sides. Whether the Americans got cold feet, or whether there was pushback from London, remains to be uncovered by future investigations. What is clear is that by the time Jay got another chance to negotiate such issues with the Crown in 1794, America had adopted a new constitution that prohibited such treaty language until the year 1808.

❈ ❈ ❈

While the vastly different terrains of American and British politics go far in explaining why the two sides' interpretations of Article 7 diverged so diametrically, they are not the complete answer. Underlying the factions and self-interested motivations were some irreconcilable principles of law, right, and property. British leaders' conception of governmental order and their philosophical understanding of the law was more bound by precedent than was that of the upstart American rebels, who had given themselves license to remake the world.

British negotiators grounded their arguments on the early treatises of international law compiled by Grotius, Rutherford, and Vattel. By these authorities, it was inarguable that the enslaved people they came to possess in wartime had passed into their possession, become in effect their property to do with as they wished. If it was legal, right, and moral to enslave one's enemy and seize their property in war, then it must be equally legal, right, and moral to choose to liberate them.[40]

From the very beginning of the negotiations the British construed Article 7 differently from the Americans. In their view, any promises they had made about not "carrying off," returning, or compensating for those claimed as American slave property applied only to those who somehow snuck into their camps after a peace treaty had been agreed upon and the war was legally over. All others had been legally freed under the rules of war and now possessed their freedom, which under British law could not be stripped from them.

Americans never wavered from their opposite view that enslaved people could be seized, they could be taken, but they could not be freed without an act of government. Just as patriots refused to accept that the Spanish or native nations could liberate the men and women who sought sanctuary among them, neither were they willing to concede this principle to the Brits. A clear example of this assumption is found in the draft of treaty language that Benjamin Franklin prepared in case the British side balked at American demands for access to the Grand Banks fisheries. It demanded compensation for the property stolen or destroyed during the war, including people: "It is agreed that his Britannic majesty will earnestly recommend it to his Parliament to provide for and make a compensation . . . for the tobacco, rice, indigo, and negroes, & c ., seized and carried off by his armies under Generals Arnold, Cornwallis, and others from the States of Virginia, North and South Carolina, and Georgia." Franklin's provision did not recognize that men and women freed during wartime were legitimately emancipated, or distinguish such people as being in different legal categories depending on when they arrived in British camps. Rather, it reveals that no special status was afforded the freeing of people during wartime compared to those liberated during the peace.[41]

Congress too consistently treated runaways from slavery as property that could change hands but not as property that could somehow lose its status as property. Early in the war Congress had to establish policies about what to do with runaways seized by patriot privateers on the high seas. Congress charged a committee to consider "what is to be done with negroes taken by vessels of war, in the service of the United States" in October of 1776. The exegesis of the war delayed further development of a full policy until the summer of 1781, when a different committee proposed that "Upon the recapture of a slave, belonging to a citizen of the United States, the same rules shall be observed, as in the recapture of vessels." In other words, the fugitive shall be returned to his or her owner upon payment of a fee of one-third of his or her value. Anyone not claimed within a year and a day (a time during which they would presumably be jailed) would be emancipated. Over several more readings and amendments, this language, which began as applying only to ocean-going vessels taken by American naval vessels and quickly expanded to cover the captures of freebooters, finally expanded to cover any enslaved persons recovered on either sea or land "without regard to the time of possession by the enemy" and passed in that form as American law on December 4, 1781.[42]

Note that there was no provision made for any process to determine if a person claimed as property was in fact liberated by their British captures or not. No quarter to the possibility of such emancipation was given. Essentially, any Black person unfortunate enough to be seized on water or land and claimed as a patriot's property was to be sent back into chains. Had there been even an inkling that British claims to have freed the men and women they rallied to their standard was legitimate, this language would not have been so absolute.

Likewise, in December of 1782 a congressional committee charged with establishing a policy for the general return of recaptured property also considered the status of slave property. Their recommendation was to treat recaptured people differently from other forms of property by returning them without demanding the usual recapture fee from the previous owner. Clearly, Congress's only concern at the time was how to facilitate the return of runaways most efficiently.[43]

Patriot insistence that the people who had fled bondage and enjoyed the protection of British forces be returned, rather than resting satisfied with the much simpler solution of obtaining monetary compensation for their owners, begs explanation. No other issue arising from the disentanglement of British and American interests after the war aroused a similar degree of passion and intensity as did that of the "carried off negroes." Why did American revolutionaries risk a rupture of trade with their largest trading partner and, even, a resurgence of war, to recapture slavery's fugitives?

All the reasons that were in play are dark and sinister. Perhaps the basest was the fact that the value of a recaptured person was far greater than their value as a commodity. A recaptured person, dragged back to their community of origin and punished, served as an invaluable object lesson for anyone else contemplating flight or resistance. As the point of dragging a person back from great distances was to emphasize that escape was futile, the instructive value of such a person was greater the further the escapee ran and the more liberty they had enjoyed. By subjecting a recaptured person to spectacular and horrifying punishments, the hope-crushing effect was accentuated and the terrorizing of a subject people made complete.

These are not hypothetical statements. Colonial and early American court records brim with evidence of the use of horrific punishments to instruct others in the futility of escape. Just to take one example from around the time these events occurred, Thomas Lucas petitioned North Carolina's assembly for compensation for murdering his property, Peter. Peter, Lucas complained, "not liking the man your Petitioner placed him to work with, ran away." Peter was later apprehended after "having robbed an Hen house" and was "precipitately tried & executed, more your Petitioner believes from a supposed necessity of striking terror into a Gang of Runaways who infested the said Town & neighbourhood than from any particular act of villainy in the said Slave." Lucas, being a relatively poor white man, asked the legislators to "indemnify him for the Execution of the said Negro" because his act was one in which "his private Expence have been made a Sacrifice to publick Policy."[44] When President George Washington sent an agent to recapture Ona Judge, a young woman who seized her opportunity to flee his grasp and had been found living in New Hampshire, Washington instructed his bounty hunter not to punish her if she accepted her fate and did not resist: "if she put[s me] to no unnecessary trouble and expence;

[and] conduct[s] herself well for the time [illegible] she will escape punishment for the [illegible], & be treated according to her merit[s illegible]. To promise more, would be [an im]politic & dangerous precedent."⁴⁵

Washington's last phrase was telling: it would be "[im]politic" and set a "dangerous precedent" not to punish her if she did resist. This reveals that he too saw such punishment as a needed public act to reinforce the system of terror that bound the enslaved to their masters.

Likewise, in a 1770 article in which he imagined a debate between an Englishman and an American over the nature of slavery, Benjamin Franklin had the American define for his counterpart what a slave was. Part of his definition was someone "who is subject to severe Punishments for small Offences, to enormous Whippings, and even Death, for absconding from his Service."⁴⁶

News of such atrocities traveled quickly along arteries of communication whose wide-ranging agents were the Black pilots, ferrymen, and wagon-drivers who carried much of America's commerce from place to place. One of the agents attempting to recover human property on commission in New York City reported back to his employer that the Black folks in the city were well aware of the fate that awaited them if they were taken back because they had heard that those dragged back had "been treated with very great severity by their former masters."⁴⁷

The likelihood that escapees from patriot bondage would be subject to extreme abuse was well known to British commanders, whose own profession required a thorough knowledge of the leverage of terror. One of General Carleton's officers wrote home to Edinburgh in 1783, praising his commander's policy toward the Black people under their protection. "It is true, we have sent above 800 to Nova Scotia, with 10,000 refugees; but Sir Guy Carleton very properly and humanely observes, that, as the faith of Government was pledged to the negroes, he will not give them up . . . for it would be the height of cruelty to deliver them up, as at least one half of them would be tortured to death."⁴⁸ Here, then, is another possibility as to why the Americans were so eager to reclaim the escapees even at the risk of a hard-negotiated treaty, a hard-won war, and a fragile peace. Torturing and killing a number of these men and women would further secure the existence of slavery by demonstrating that no one could escape and the consequences for trying were horrific.[49]

England's most senior diplomats likewise assumed that returning fugitives from slavery to the patriots would result in extraordinary punishments and even their murder. Foreign Secretary Charles J. Fox, who would later that year succeed in pushing Parliament to go on record as opposed to the human trade, shared such concerns with his diplomat, David Hartley: "To have restored Negroes, whom we had invited, *seduced* if you will, under a Promise of Liberty, to the tyranny and possibly to the Vengeance of their former masters would have been such an Act as scarcely any Orders from his Employers (and no such Orders exist) could have induced a Man of Honour to execute."[50]

Secretary of Foreign Affairs John Jay in his 1786 report to Congress detailing his interpretation of the Treaty of Paris observed that were the British to return the people to whom it had afforded refuge to their American masters, they would be severely punished: Jay noted sympathetically that "it would have been cruelly perfidious to have afterwards delivered them up to their former bondage, and to the severities to which such Slaves are usually subjected."[51]

British commanders in the South were also well aware of the demonstrative punishments patriots were eager to inflict upon the fugitives they recaptured. General Leslie confided to Carleton that he was hesitant to return the people he harbored in Charlestown to their owners for they could not "in justice be abandoned to the merciless resentment of their former masters."[52]

Accordingly, General Leslie demanded in the draft agreement hammered out with South Carolina's Governor Mathews "That no slaves, restored to their former owners by virtue of this agreement, shall be punished by the authority of the state for having left their masters and attached themselves to the British troops and it will be particularly recommended to their respective owners to forgive them for the same."[53] This pact soon fell apart, as Leslie raided outlying plantations for supplies and South Carolina militia made sporadic forays against British sentinels, ultimately capturing three Redcoats who Leslie demanded be returned before he would consider surrendering his fugitives from slavery. In the end, neither side relented, and Leslie sailed off with 5,327 people of color, most of whom ended up in Jamaica, though others were scattered throughout the Atlantic from St. Lucia to Halifax. Some eventually turned up in New York, and some made it all the way to England.[54]

In addition to desiring the social control benefits of recapturing actual escapees, some more far-sighted patriot leaders realized that reenslaving people had wider geopolitical implications. The ever strategic-minded Benjamin Franklin shared with his fellow peace negotiator Henry Laurens his theory that the British insisted upon providing sanctuary to American runaways because they were preparing for a future conflict with America. Only by keeping their word to the escaped men and women who sought refuge in their camps could Britain hope to one day be more successful in provoking an even more powerful slave insurrection. "But General Carleton, in violation of those articles, has sent away a great number of negroes, alleging, that freedom having been promised them by a proclamation, the honor of the nation was concerned, &c. Probably another reason may be, that if they had been restored to their masters, Britain could not have hoped anything from such another proclamation hereafter."[55]

Franklin repeated these suspicions again in a piece he wrote on the eve of the Constitutional Convention in Philadelphia but did not publish until a year later: England "chose to keep faith rather with its old black, than its new white friends; a circumstance demonstrating clear as daylight, that, in making a present peace, they meditated a future war, and hoped, that, though the promised manumission of slaves had not been effectual in the last, in the next it might be more successful; and that, had the negroes been forsaken, no aid could be hereafter expected from those of the colour in a future invasion."[56]

Franklin seemed to never fail to see the broader strategic implications of events and policies, and here he advocated the physical recapture of fugitive men, women, and children then under the Crown's protection as a means of weakening British power in North America. The vast numbers of enslaved people were a force that Americans had feared for generations, a fear that had fueled a smoldering rejection of slavery itself. Patriots like Franklin saw only their young nation's doom in any sort of sudden smashing of the chains and calculated that his cherished republic's future depended on policies that both limited slavery and retarded the growth of the Black population. In the meantime, the customary instruments of torture and terror were required to secure the nation's borders from foreign meddling.

During the final round of negotiations Adams, Franklin, and Jay wrote a detailed defense of their reasons and purposes in the agreements they made and forwarded to Congress. It is clear from their explanations that America's diplomats assumed that Congress had clear and complete authority to override state laws that might conflict with their treaty, even though they had told their British counterparts the opposite so as to gain leverage in the negotiations. "We had been informed that some of the States had confiscated British Debts," they observed, "but although each State has a Right to bind its own Citizens, yet in our Opinion, it appertains solely to Congress, in whom exclusively are vested the Rights of making War and Peace, to pass Acts against the Subjects of a Power with which the Confederacy may be at War." Nevertheless, the issue of upholding the integrity of foreign property and debts they saw as paramount because the standing of the United States in the eyes of the other European powers was of greatest importance to the future of the nation. "In our Opinion no Acts of Government could dissolve the Obligations of Good Faith, resulting from lawfull Contracts between Individuals of the two Countries, prior to the War . . . the Purity of our Reputation in this Respect in all foreign Commercial Countries, is of infinitely more Importance to us, than all the Sums in question."[57]

Franklin well understood that what had been gained at the bargaining table could be easily lost back home if the agreement he signed widened sectional discord and led to a breakdown of the fragile federal system. Perhaps, too, he glimpsed how the unresolved and hopelessly tangled issues of British debt and runaways might become the catalysts for such a reaction.

THREE

The "Carried Off" and American Protest

During the years leading up to the Philadelphia convention that rewrote the nation's foundations in 1787, the Continental Congress devoted much of its time and attention to reenslaving the thousands of people who had seized their opportunity during the late war and escaped.

The year 1783 began with news of the evacuation of Charlestown. General Nathaniel Green included in his report to Congress on the evacuation of Charlestown a complaint about the British reneging on their promises to surrender fugitives from slavery. "They took with them a great deal of property, and between 5 and 6000 Negroes, the greater part of which they had once promised to deliver up."[1] When word spread that many of these men and women had sailed to New York, South Carolina's congressional delegation wrote a strongly worded letter to General Carleton, that city's English commander, demanding that he restore to South Carolinians "all their negroes and other property, of considerable value, which were carried off by the British Troops and Royalists, when they left Charlestown."[2]

On March 12, 1783, the fast packet ship *Washington* docked in Philadelphia with the first copy of the provisional peace treaty that American diplomats had agreed upon in Paris. When Congress took up discussion of the treaty, the only article discussed was Article 7, the clause that patriots believed compelled the British to return their fugitives from slavery. So concerned were the congressmen that this particular clause be observed that they passed a specific resolution instructing the commander in chief "to make proper arrangements with the Commander in Chief of the British forces, for receiving possession of the posts in the United States occupied by the troops of his Britannic Majesty; and for obtaining the delivery of all negroes and other property of the inhabitants of the United States in the possession of the British forces."[3] Congress also appointed commissioners to go to New York and demand that General Carleton relinquish the Black fugitives to whom he had given sanctuary. Orders were also debated and drafted and sent to Franklin, Jay, and Adams in Paris instructing them to include the return of slavery's fugitives in any final terms of peace.

Several states followed suit. South Carolina's governor appointed two commissioners, George Readhead and John Johnston, to travel to New York and a third, William Livingston, to Florida and "demand & receive all the publick & private Property which has been carried off." South Carolina's congressional delegation sent Washington a letter requesting that he and his appointed commissioners afford them "any Aid which may facilitate the Object of their Mission." Readhead and Johnston were turned away as soon as they arrived in New York, while Livingston was arrested in Spanish territory and sent home on "parole."[4]

Virginia's governor, Benjamin Harrison, gave his permission and a letter of introduction to Captain John Willoughby Jr. to hunt the ninety or so people who had fled Willoughby's Norfolk County plantation. While Harrison had turned down other similar requests for an official pass and letter of introduction to Sir Guy Carleton, he granted one to Willoughby, whose loss was so great that he had been "ruin'd" and word had spread that "on the prospects of peace the privateers Men were kidnaping them and sending them to the West indies, and that in a little Time there would be very few left in N. York."[5]

Willoughby, who also happened to be the Norfolk County sheriff, was later joined by Thomas Walke, a Princess Anne County justice of the peace and a member of the Virginia House of Delegates. Walke came from a long-established wealthy family of Princess Anne County. His great-grandfather, also named Thomas, as all the first sons in the family were, emigrated from Barbados in 1662. His grandfather was a merchant who, when he died in 1722, owned extensive lands along the Lynhaven River and along the Back Bay, as well as houses in Norfolk and New Town, and at least eighteen enslaved people. Walke's father expanded the family's holdings, adding a mill, a dry good store, grazing land on Cedar Island, all of Doe Island, and an 800-acre plantation on the Bowrons River. When he died, his land holdings were so extensive that he donated 221 acres to the county "for the use of the poor orphans and disabled people of the parish." He hoped the county would build an orphanage but also thought it might be a good plan to "sell said land and apply the proceeds for breeding negroes for the use of said orphans." The family's holdings of other humans had grown to at least forty by 1760. The fourth Thomas Walke, and the one who concerns us here, was his father's principal heir and took possession of the family manor, Upper Wolfsnare, in what is today Virginia Beach. (It is worth noting here that Walke later served in the Virginia convention that ratified the U.S. Constitution and he voted for adopting it.)[6]

Sir Carleton refused to meet with Walke and the others, and instead sent a message with his aide-de-camp that no people claimed as property would be surrendered who had fled to British protection during the war and that "he thought it unnecessary for us to wait longer on business of that nature." Walke recounted his experiences in a letter to the Virginia delegates to the U.S. Congress, one of whom was James Madison, and offered his opinion on what course they should take: "This appears to me to be such a glareing piece of injustice, and open violation of the above mentioned article of the treaty . . . if there is not an immediate check put to the proceedings of the British General in this matter, the injury will be inconcieveable, as I am well assured several hundreds of the above mentioned slaves sailed during the last week to Nova Scotia."

Walke and his fellow state-appointed fugitive hunters were just one portion of a larger group of bounty hunters and enslavers in pursuit of runaways that crowded into New York City in search of Black people they could kidnap. Boston King, a man who had fled his captivity in South Carolina, joined the British, and scouted American positions, eventually made his way to the Manhattan island. King recounted the constant menace of patriot fugitive catchers: "we saw our old masters coming from Virginia,

North-Carolina and other parts and seizing upon slaves in the streets . . . even dragging them out of their beds."[7]

Carleton complained to New York's Governor Clinton about the "multitudes" of impatient "Claimants" who "crowded in" through his lines and directed their "Menaces & insults" toward "those whom I not only esteem for their personal worth, but whom I found myself obliged to protect." Their behavior had forced Carleton to take a firmer stance and "rendered it absolutely necessary to interpose some check, and to convince those of illiberal disposition, that menaces might draw after them some what more than disregard." Carleton then appealed to the governor to not make an international issue of the "Negroes": "confiscations, as well of personal as real property, have, by each party been made, and will, I trust, by each, be finally renounced."[8]

Clinton responded that any such "confiscations" that Carleton made would justify the Americans' breaking the treaty on their part and threatened such action if he persisted. "Negroes and other Property that have been carried off are to be considered as composing the Confiscations alluded to by your Excellency, I would beg Leave to observe, that in this case they are Confiscations made subsequent to the Treaty and may afford a Precedent for Measures which I should have considered as repugnant to the Spirit of it."[9]

Carleton justified his protection of the African Americans within his lines to other American leaders as well. Ezra l'Hommedieu, who was both one of New York's congressmen and a member of the state's assembly, complained to Governor Clinton that Carleton "endeavours to justify his Conduct in carrying off the Negroes."[10]

It should be noted that Carleton's protection of the fugitive African Americans in his camps was not motivated by a philosophical opposition to slavery itself. Through this period of time the general made it clear to his subordinates that his Black servant, Pomp, was his "property" in spite of the fact that Pomp had obtained one of the certificates of freedom handed out around the city.[11]

It was not until early April of 1783 that word of Parliament's ratification of the preliminary treaty arrived in New York. As soon as General Carleton learned that the treaty was official, he wrote to Robert Livingston pledging to order all his forces to stand down and to release the Americans he held prisoner. Carleton reminded Livingston of Congress's obligations under the agreement: "In like manner, no doubt can be entertained but that Congress in conformity to the 5th Article of the Provisional Treaty, will lose no time in earnestly recommending to the Legislatures of the respective States, to provide for the restitution of confiscated Estates, & to reconsider & revise all Laws of confiscation."[12]

Livingston responded in kind, urging Carleton to be sure and abide by what the patriots understood to be his obligations. Tellingly, Livingston tied the return of loyalist property to Carleton's sending the refugees from slavery that he protected back into the possession of their former masters:

> it must be obvious to your Excellency, that a recommendation to restore to the Loyalists the Estates they have forfeited, will come with less weight before Legislatures composed of men whose property is still withheld from them by the Continuance of his Britannic Majesty's fleets & Armies in this Country, than it will do, when peace & the full enjoyment of their Rights shall have worn down those Asperities which have grown out of Eight years War. This reflection will I doubt not induce you to give every facility in your power to the execution of the 7th Article of the Provisional Treaty, and to fix as early a day for the evacuation of New York and its dependencies as may consist with your Orders.[13]

Carleton's reply to this was curt but appeared to American leaders to accept their interpretation of Article 7 and to initiate a process for returning these men, women, and children back to their chains. "As I observe in the 7th Article of the Provisional Treaty it is agreed, after stipulating that 'all prisoners on both sides shall be set at liberty,' that 'His Britannic Majesty shall, with all convenient speed, and without causing any destruction, or carrying away any Negroes on other property of the American Inhabitants, withdraw all his Armies, Garrisons, and Fleets from the United States, and from every Port, Place and Harbour within the same, &c.'"[14]

While he waited for Congress to send official envoys to oversee his embarkation, Carleton asked two American officials at hand, Daniel Parker and Major David Hopkins, to temporarily serve in this capacity and "represent to me every infraction of the letter or spirit of the treaty." Both Americans were invited to inspect the very first transport fleet to leave the city and judged that Carleton was being sincere in his claims of upholding the letter of the international law. Parker told Washington that Carleton's intentions were "perfectly Consonant to your Excellencys."[15]

Things began to fall apart almost immediately after this. In spite of Parker's high hopes for a smooth and uncontentious embarkation, that first day's inspection soon ran into a startling difference of opinion. When Parker and Hopkins found Black passengers on board one of the transports and "ordered" them off the boats, Carleton refused to sanction their removal.[16]

At the same time, New York's governor, George Clinton, asked his attorney general, Egbert Benson, to arrange a personal meeting with General Carleton and to report back on what conditions and protocols the general might insist upon in relinquishing the city back to patriot control. Benson met with Carleton over the course of two days and was surprised to find the British commander evasive and unwilling to commit to any plan or schedule. "I do not recollect that a single instance I obtained from Sir Guy Carleton a determinate answer to any Question I proposed to him on the business you was pleased to honor me with, but on the contrary there was Evasion, and a Desire to turn the Conversation to other Subjects."[17]

Greatly worrying to Benson was Carleton's criticisms of the laws passed relating to British return of patriot property. Carleton "observed that the Law was in its spirit and Design rather hostile and immediattory, and that every such Measure on the part of these States had a Tendency to embarrass and to impede the great Work of Peace; that he could wish Matters might not be precipitated but rather that they might be left to mature of themselves." At the time this sounded to Benson like Carleton was justifying delay or obstruction and asked the general if this meant that he was revoking his cooperation, and Carleton denied any such implication.

While in Manhattan, Benson noted that there were approximately two hundred transports and other British ships in the harbor and that the usual numbers of soldiers and sailors were stationed along the fortifications. His conclusions were pessimistic. "I have the fullest Persuasion that Sir Guy Carleton is not seriously disposed to enter into a Convention, and that he only intends to save appearances to negotiate and by that means to effect a Delay, but I will not hazard a Conjecture for what purpose."[18]

Governor Clinton, upon reading Benson's report, was alarmed to the point of dispatching his attorney general to Philadelphia, where he could make this report in person to New York's congressional delegation, as the "Communications he is to make are too extensive to be the subject of a Letter & it might be improper to intrust them to Paper."[19]

On his way to Philadelphia, Benson met with John Morin Scott, New York's former brigadier general, secretary of state, and delegate to Congress, and regaled him with stories of his meetings with Carleton. Scott immediately dispatched a note to Clinton expressing his alarm at what Benson had told him; "from [his] . . . Accounts it is obvious that Sir Guy aims at procrastination; and that no preparayions are making for speedy departure of the British."[20]

Perhaps fearing that he may have overplayed his hand by his noncommittal attitude toward Benson, Carleton wrote directly to Congress with a much more conciliatory posture. Carleton's reassurances and seeming willingness to allow federal officials a role in the embarkations of the escapees Americans sought apparently did not convince New York's congressmen, Alexander Hamilton and William Floyd, who wrote Clinton in "confidence" about their additional, if not even deeper, concerns over Carleton's behavior. First, they conceded that Carleton's noncommittal posture to Benson may have been because he viewed him as New York's official rather than the confederation's diplomat: "it is possible Sir Guy's Reserve may have arisen from an unwillingness to enter into Stipulations with a particular State." Carleton's subsequent message to Congress appeared to express a more cooperative policy, but this too Hamilton and Floyd suspected was a ruse to hold onto as many cards as he could: "this present Letter has the air of Candour and good faith; but it is also possible there may be an intention of Delaying the Evacuation of the posts in hopes of influencing our measures with Respect to the British Adherents."

While everyone understood that holding onto Manhattan and the other

New York islands was Britain's greatest bargaining chip, Hamilton and Floyd also alluded to the issue of the fugitives from patriot slavery: "We also Communicate to your Excellency in Confidence, that there is a Doubt as to the true construction of the Preliminary Articles to wit: Whether the evacuation of the posts & the other matters mentioned in the 7th Article are to take place on the ratification of the preliminary; or Definitive treaty . . . perhaps the Ambiguity of Sir Guy's Conduct may be attributed to the same doubt."[21]

Hamilton and Floyd's understanding of the technical minutia of the controversy over the status of the escapees reveals something of the place of this issue among the priorities of America's leaders. Disagreements over the meaning of Article 7, such as whether it applied to those Black refugees who were brought to New York after November of 1782 or only those who arrived in the past month, had only just begun to emerge among those charged with negotiating the treaty's implementation in Paris and London.

When Congress ratified the Treaty of Paris that same month, it also ordered General Washington to "make the proper Arrangements with the Commander in Chief of the British forces" to take over the western forts and for "obtaining the delivery of all Negroes and other property of the Inhabitants of the United States."[22] Washington duly followed his orders and sent a letter to Carleton inviting him to meet personally so as to resolve those subjects that required "more precision and despatch." Carleton readily agreed and set the location somewhere around Tappan that he could reach easily with his frigate.[23]

Washington was aware of Carleton's sudden refusal to disembark Black Americans when the two men met at Washington's headquarters near Orangetown, New York, a few weeks later. Elias Boudinot, president of the Congress, had sent him a copy of Thomas Walke's letter detailing the "Numberless difficulties" thrown in the way of those attempting to "reclaim our Slaves that were wrested from us by the British Enemy" and how after complaining to General Carleton of these problems was told that "no Slaves were to be given up who claimed the benefit of their former proclamations for liberating such Slaves as threw themselves under the protection of the British Government." Walke had sent this letter to Congress with his opinion that Carlton's conduct was a "glareing piece of injustice" and an "open Violation" of Article 7. Walke's tone grew shrill: "If there is not an immediate check put to the proceedings of the British General in this matter, the injury will be inconceivable, as I am well assured several hundreds of the abovementioned Slaves sailed during the last week to Nova Scotia."[24]

When the two generals met at Orangetown, New York, on May 6, Washington brought with him Governor Clinton and his attorney general (who was also the commissioner charged with guarding against the unlawful removal of enslaved Americans), Egbert Benson. Serving them wine and food was Samuel Fraunces, whose Queen's Head Tavern, at the corner of Pearl and Broad in Manhattan, would later be the weekly meeting place where American commissioners attempting to interdict the embarkation of African Americans met with Carleton's lieutenants.[25]

Carleton lawyerly explained to Washington that those fugitives who had fled to British protection during the war were entitled to the full benefit of whatever promises had been made to them and insisted that the only "negroes" encompassed by the treaty were those who arrived in British lines after the armistice. Over Washington's loud protests, Carleton also made clear that, according to his reading of the treaty, he was not obligated to turn over any of the people under his protection, only to ascertain their identities for purposes of future compensation.[26]

Two days later, George Washington delegated three officials to go to New York and record the names and descriptions of Black Americans embarking onto various ships sailing for all points of the British Atlantic. Formally referred to as the "Commissioners for Superintending the Embarkations at New York," two of the three, Egbert Benson and William Smith, were prominent New York lawyers (Smith would soon also be John Adams's son-in-law), and the third, Daniel Parker of Parker & Co., was a merchant with far-flung interests who had enjoyed lucrative provisioning contracts with the army while General Washington's aide-de-camp.

When the commissioners appointed by Washington arrived in Manhattan, they sent a note to Carleton's headquarters requesting a meeting at which they could present their official credentials. The general replied that he was "indisposed" due to sickness, and it took another five days for the meeting to be arranged. It was in this time that Carleton wrote Washington and laid out his interpretation of the treaty: that the "negroes in question, I have already said, I found free when I arrived at New York, I had therefore no right, as I thought, to prevent their going to any part of the world they thought proper."

Carleton's moral clarity in drawing the rule he was prepared to follow in all cases must have startled America's great military leader and one of its largest enslavers. Carleton wrote Washington that he did not imagine that "the King's Minister could deliberately stipulate in a treaty, an engagement to be guilty of a notorious breach of the public faith towards people of any complection." He further urged Washington to be reasonable and recognize that there was no chance of recovering fugitives who had been granted their freedom. "Restoration, where inseparable from a breach of public faith, is, as all the world I think must allow, utterly impracticable."[27]

Washington forwarded this letter to Congress, further stoking outrage.[28] Virginia's three delegates to Congress, one of whom was James Madison, sent a strong protest to Virginia governor Benjamin Harrison, complaining that they had not heard any details "touching the evacuation of that port, or the execution of the other articles of the provisional Treaty." Though mentioning the existence of "other articles" they were concerned were being violated, Madison and his colleagues only raised the one having to do with the emigration of people fleeing bondage at the hands of the patriots. Madison and the others demanded that the "breach of that which stipulated a restoration of the Negroes, will be made the subject of a pointed remonstrance from our Ministers in Europe to the British Court; with a demand of reparation; and in the mean time General Washington is to insist on a more faithful observance of that stipulation at N. York."[29] Harrison did just as his congressional delegation asked, forwarding to General Washington a "list and description of negroes" believed to be given sanctuary by the British in New York.

Now suspicious of Carleton's willingness to abide by their understanding of the treaty, the American commissioners, Egbert Benson, William S. Smith, and Daniel Parker, had their first meeting with the general on May 15, where it was agreed that the Americans and their English counterparts would meet every Wednesday at 10 in the morning at Fraunces's tavern to record the claims of anyone alleging that their "property" was preparing to sail away. Benson, Parker, and Smith kept up their meetings at Fraunces's tavern and made a total of twenty-nine shipboard inspections, continuing their activities right up until Carleton withdrew all his forces to Staten Island on November 25, 1783, a day memorialized as "Evacuation Day." The last British ship lifted sails and left the harbor on November 30.

Egbert, Parker, and Smith chose a small, unrelated case that could in principle test the British understanding of who could be considered one of the "negroes carried off." As the commissioners explained to George Washington, they first made a claim for the horse of a Mr. Vanderburgh. Vanderburgh's horse had been stolen three years earlier in Dutchess County and wound up in a British post in West Chester. Recently, Vanderburgh somehow discovered that his horse was in the possession of Colonel James DeLancey, and made demands of the officer, but was rebuffed.

America's commissioners viewed the Vanderburgh case as one that would most clearly test Carleton's willingness to abide by the treaty because the horse was not claimed as a prize of war. As the commissioners explained to their commander, this was a "clear unequivocal Case" where the "Proofs were at hand and not embarrassed with the Circumstances of a Capture in War or other Pretences under which Property is with-held here."[30]

Carleton's staff reviewed the complaint but denied the claim on the grounds that the commissioners had not shown that the horse was actually in danger of being transported out of the country. The commissioners decided to press on this point, and they found another case to test this principle. As they later explained, the English denial "left room for an idea that, possibly, property about to be sent away would be restored, and we [took] . . . the first fair occasion which should present itself, to remove all doubt on this point."

For this purpose they raised a complaint about "a negro, named Thomas Francis, now on board a vessel called the Fair American, in this harbour, and about to be carried off to the island of Jamaica." Francis was claimed by an American citizen named Philip Lott as his personal property, a fact that Lott proved by a bill of sale from a New Jersey enslaver. In November of

1782, Thomas Francis made his way across American lines and into a British camp and volunteered his services. The commander of the city of New York promptly enlisted Francis into a corps known as the Jamaica Rangers.

Francis's actions exposed the gulf dividing American and English interpretations of the peace treaty. According to Carleton's interpretation of the treaty, Francis was free, as his service in a Crown army liberated him. Patriots, however, simply saw him as both a negro and Lott's property and therefore barred from being "carried off" by the British. Benson, Parker, and Smith could now only conclude that "We conceive it is now reduced to a certainty that all applications for the Delivery of Property will be fruitless."[31]

Instead of wasting time submitting their complaints, the trio of commissioners switched tactics to attempting to document British infractions as best they could. For the next month they boarded ships at harbor and counted "negroes who appeared to be the property of the Citizens of the United States." On June 13, they climbed across gangplanks and up and down ladders into fourteen ships bound for Canada. They counted at least two thousand people awaiting their transport northward, and among them more than one hundred Black men, women, and children.[32]

Over the course of their mission, the embarkation commissioners succeeded in forcing the British to hand over three people to their former American masters. But they were far less successful in cajoling the canny men and women awaiting their ships to sail to reveal the names of their former masters. The commissioners resorted to filling their ledgers with as much information as they could glean of fugitives' former residences, when they may have escaped, and other information that might one day be useful to a patriot who claimed them as their personal property. Generally, commissioners were given access when the ships were contracted by the government, but they were refused by private merchants.[33]

After fourteen ships sailed for Nova Scotia with what Benson, Smith, and Parker counted to be "One hundred Negroes—Seventy three of which appeared to be the property of American subjects," the three congressional commissioners felt compelled to send to General Carlton their formal complaint that "the Permission from your Excellency to any Negroes belonging

to the Citizens of these States, to leave this City, [was] an Infraction of the
. . . Treaty of Peace."[34]

George Washington thought the evacuation of these African Americans
"indiscriminately and without examination in private Vessels" was "if not
publickly allowed" by General Carleton, "at least connived at." Washington
viewed it as such a flagrant breach of the treaty that the commissioners
should be recalled as they had been shown to be "without the power of restraining the Property of the Inhabitants of the United States from being
carried away."

Washington's letter to Secretary of Foreign Affairs Livingston reveals
three important points of his thinking about the fugitives. First, at one
point Washington concedes that the people he wished to reclaim were not
being "carried off" at all but were fleeing of their own volition. In an aside,
he referred to "the *departure* of all Negroes (who choose to go away)." Such
wording was contrary to the official rhetoric describing the runaways, which
disguised the true nature of patriot concerns by claiming that slaves were
just one among a variety of looted property, such as silver plate and horses,
that Article 7 was intended to reclaim. Washington at one point exposed
this lie when he noted that Black people were "the only species of property
that can at present require attention."

Lastly and most importantly, Washington revealed that he believed the
issue of the runaways was not one that mostly involved the private fortunes
of a few patriot enslavers, but one of much larger scope, or as he put it, one
of "considerable national concern." While contemporary scholars have long
read these events through the lens of their modern values and relegated the
demand for the return of fugitives from slavery to a trivial footnote in the
history of Anglo-American diplomatic relations, the man actually in charge
of executing the withdrawal of the British, a leader who understood the
terrain of the young republic's politics and attitudes as well as anyone of his
day, thought it a matter of "considerable national concern."[35]

With less than a month left before the official return of the city to patriot control, what had been a growing anxiety among New York's loyalists
boiled over. A group of "British tars" offended at a ship that anchored in the

harbor "with an affected display of thirteen stripes" stormed aboard, tore the American flag from the mast, and trampled it. Apparently taking nothing but this symbolic prize, the "canaille" then paraded the ripped and insulted colors through the streets, gathering a mob that was described at the time as a "chosen banditti of negroes, sailors, and loyal leather apron'd statesmen." The city's English governor, General Guy Carleton, issued orders that the offenders be identified and "punished with severity" because their "mischievous" and "disorderly manner" would only "prolong the Animosities, which it is the design of the Provisional Articles to assuage and extinguish."[36]

Carleton here referred to the terms of the peace agreed upon in Paris the year before that recognized American independence and granted the young republic all the land and native peoples between it and the Mississippi and fishing rights to the Great Banks of Newfoundland. In exchange, Americans pledged to respect the property and persons who had been loyal to the Crown and not to pass laws impeding the payment of debts to British merchants.

That Black New Yorkers were noted as being prominent participants in the American Flag Riot of October 23, 1783, was likely due to the ongoing efforts of American officials to recapture and reenslave the thousands of men, women, and children who had escaped their captivity and found refuge with the British on Manhattan, Staten, and Long islands. While other loyalists faced the choice of evacuating or staying and trusting that the terms of the treaty would protect them from retaliation, Black Tories were left with the bitter choice of flight to unknown lands or return to their former masters.

On November 12, 1783, General Carleton sent his counterpart, General Washington, a list detailing when he planned to abandon each of his outposts around the city and announcing that he planned to vacate all his forces by the end of the month. That same day, Carleton's quartermaster placed an advertisement in newspapers offering to hire any seaworthy ship. A mail bag was hung at Berry & Roger's tavern on Wall Street into which any person could deposit their letters to be taken by the last ship. On November 25, Carleton surrendered the city to Washington with great pomp, salutes, toasts, and fireworks. Five days later, the remaining British fleet, consisting of Carleton's frigate and twenty transports, sailed to sea.

In the end it was the British who surrendered to the American commissioners a copy of their "Book of Negroes" containing the names of 1,388 men, 955 women, and 652 children, including two men, Daniel and Harry, and a woman, Deborah Squash, who had stolen themselves away from the ownership of George Washington.[37]

On January 18, 1784, the three commissioners stationed in New York issued their final report to General Washington, saying that their business was concluded. They reported that, with one or two exceptions, they did not receive responses to their complaints from Carleton. Worse, from their point of view, was the "abuse" of the treaty by the British, who printed "certificates with blanks" that Black persons in their camp "filled up as their convenience might require." These printed forms certified that the bearer had "resorted to the British lines, in consequence of the proclamations of sir William Howe and sir Henry Clinton," and therefore had permission to go to Nova Scotia "or wherever else [blank] may think proper." Commissioners complained that "whenever the negroes, at an inspection of embarkation, were examined, they always, except in a very few instances, produced a printed certificate from the commandant of the city," Brigadier General Birch.[38]

Washington, in turn, complained to the new secretary of foreign affairs, John Jay, that British cooperation with the American commissioners was "little more than a farce as they inspected no more property than the British chose they should be witness to the embarkation of."[39]

Britain's unabashed protection of runaways from American slavery enraged patriots across the land. A mass meeting was held at the county courthouse in Newark, New Jersey, where resolutions condemning Britain and the treaty were cheered. Among them was one that demanded that since the treaty had been "evaded in the seventh article, which respects the restoration of negroes and other property . . . we think it politick, and, at the same time, consistent with the strictest principles of justice, to withhold our compliance with the fourth and other articles of said treaty, which militate in favor of Great-Britain, until she shall have complied with the said seventh article, or made us restitution for that part of our property which may not be restored." Besides recommending that America refuse its own obligations under the treaty until the fugitives were reenslaved, the Newark meeting aired its belief that Congress under the current charter of government was powerless to act: "We know not on what principles it can be expected that the recommendations made, or to be made, by Congress, in conformity with the fifth article of said treaty, will be complied with by a single state in the union . . . altho' Congress must earnestly recommend, the Legislatures are not obliged to comply."[40]

Anonymous letter writers in the great American tradition of pen-named editorialists weighed in with similar sentiments. "Americanus," writing in Philadelphia's *Pennsylvania Packet*, denounced the "very extraordinary conduct" of General Carleton who was engaged in a "wanton detention" of Americans' "property," by which he mainly meant enslaved people: "By some new, and to Americans unknown construction of the English language, the British commander in chief has discovered that the said seventh article, means directly contrary to what it expresses . . . instead of preventing negroes or other property of the Americans being carried away, all negroes and other American property must and shall be carried away."[41]

Patriots had found "every obstacle . . . thrown in the way" when they attempted to claim and retrieve their human chattel. Now the British have "invented" a story that "America is violating the preliminary articles of peace" by "associating to prevent the return of the loyalists, to the enjoyment of what they have so justly forfeited." Like the Newark protestors, Americanus thought Congress weak to the point of being justly ignored. "The very end they propose to themselves by this delay and detention of property, will clearly be frustrated by the measure; for can any set of men be so stupid as to believe, that the legislature of the state of New York will . . . be now dragooned into any recommendation of Congress in favour of the loyalists?"[42]

"Brutus" addressed his open letter to the loyalists of Poughkeepsie: "You have the effrontery to accuse us with a breach of the provisional treaty at the very moment when you are committing the most open and dishonest violations of it yourselves. We ask, how many thousand negroes, the property of citizens of these States, have already been carried off in your fleets? Can an instance be produced where any of you have had the honor or honesty to pay a debt to one who resided without your lines?"

Reading further into Brutus's rhetoric, another wrinkle to this controversy can be seen. Brutus offered a justification for ignoring those parts of the treaty that the community of patriots found to be unjust. Recalling a decade earlier when patriots penned elaborate manifestos that provided moral footing for defying the king and the laws of Parliament, Brutus grounded his refusal to pay English debts or recognize Tories as equal citizens on the firmament of democratic rights. "It is sufficient that we have fought for the country, and therefore have an undoubted right, in common with our fellow citizens, to say who SHALL possess it."[43]

Word quickly spread across the colonies that General Carleton had freely allowed Black Americans passage out of the port of New York. The future leader of the U.S. Senate, Ralph Izard, wrote to Arthur Middleton, his predecessor representing South Carolina in Congress and a signer of the Declaration of Independence, with urgent news about the British protections of runaways. "I am sorry to learn that so many of your Negroes are still missing; and the more so, as I fear that it will not be an easy matter to recover them [as] . . . S'r Guy Carleton has very explicitly given it as his opinion that the Negroes within the British Lines can not be claimed by virtue of the Preliminary Treaty, as property belonging to the Citizens of the United States, because they have been declared free by proclamations."

Izard observed that the representatives of those states most affected by the absconding of their human property "have attempted everything in their power to obtain redress" but with no success. Then this influential patriot revealed that he considered reenslaving the runaways important enough that some were willing to risk plunging back into war:

> A majority of Congress were afraid to make an express declaration that the British had violated it [the treaty]. It was said that a renewal of hostilities might be the consequence of such declaration. . . . It is most certain that without money, and without credit we are by no means in a condition to continue the War; but bad as the British Ministry are, I can hardly think

it possible that they should have the effrontery to support Carleton in the measure I have mentioned. Besides it is very well known that though we are not at our ease, they can not be said to be on a bed of Roses: Peace was almost as desirable an event to them, as to us. We therefore urged the necessity that Congress should signify their disapprobation of Carleton's conduct, and would not consent that the Army should be furloughed, till our proposition (which I now inclose) was complied with.

Congressman Izard thought that America's failure to force the Crown to drag these few thousand people back into chains had, more than any other issue, highlighted the flaws in the current blueprint of government: "This is a most impudent evasion of the Treaty; and yet we are not in a condition to help ourselves. The conduct of the States respecting Revenue, has so totally annihilated all Continental Strength, and credit, that no Enemy need be afraid of insulting us."[44]

Patriots on both sides of other controversies over slavery were equally shrill in denouncing British "deceit" and "depredations" in their harboring of escapees from slavery. John Dickinson, a champion of abolition while president of Pennsylvania, wrote to Congress in 1783 complaining that "a considerable number of negroes belonging to Citizens of this State are now in New York," and he requested "that the most effectual Measures may be immediately taken by Congress . . . for securing such property."[45] Virginia congressman Hugh Mercer similarly "descanted on the insidiousness" of the British and "warmly opposed the idea of laying ourselves at the mercy" of Great Britain even though "Congress knew that they were violating the Treaty as to Negroes."[46]

Congressman Bland proposed not releasing British prisoners as had been agreed to "until an answer be given as to the delivery of slaves."[47] Madison seemed to have agreed with Bland, as a week later he told Jefferson that he thought the "discharge of the prisoners" that had already occurred ruined the possibility of enforcing "fair dealing on the other side" regarding the "Negroes leaving N.Y." Madison called Carleton's reasons for not returning the men and women Americans demanded, that the Crown was bound to "the necessity of adhering to the proclamations under the faith of which the Negroes eloped into their service," as a "palpable & scandalous miscon-struction of the Treaty."[48]

Though there were a number of issues unresolved between the United States and Britain (western forts that had not been handed over as agreed, damage assessments not paid, etc.), congressmen mentioned only their out-rage at the British commander in New York providing sanctuary to their former slaves. That this entire discussion was tied to the question of the restitution of "slave property" was made clear when Congressman Hugh Williamson proposed that British prisoners be released "pari passu, with the British Commander (at New York)," meaning one at a time, in turn. Though this was creating a potential flashpoint for new hostilities, the rest of the body agreed and issued an order to General Washington to make such arrangements until the "delivery of the posts, negroes, &c."[49]

Worried that keeping Tories and Redcoats in their stockades was possi-bly insufficient to push the British to return their fugitives from slavery, it was suggested that the scheduled disbanding the Army of the United States be postponed. Again, the extant *Journal of the Congress*'s proceedings make it clear that the leading concern was the British harboring of escapees. One representative said that keeping the army intact was necessary because the British commander of New York, Sir Guy Carleton, "has suffered many negroes the property of the citizens of these United States to be carried off, contrary to the 7th article of the Preliminary Treaty." The congressmen then voted to issue a formal protest to the Crown over Carleton's "permit-ting negroes belonging to the citizens of these states to leave New York and to insist on the discontinuance of that measure." Putting teeth behind this protest, they also moved that the discharge of officers and soldiers in the ten thousand-man army be delayed until "the definitive treaty of peace is concluded." This was a major undertaking, as it was admitted that Congress had a "want of means to support them."

This prompted some debate, with Daniel Carroll of Maryland and Hugh Williamson of North Carolina suggesting a middle course of furloughing the troops rather than discharging them. This would allow them to return to their homes in the interim. When faced with the choice of discharging the army as planned or giving the soldiers a furlough but retaining them in the army, Congress unanimously chose to keep the standing army until the British handed back the people the American government claimed as its citizens' property.[50]

Joseph Jones of Virginia shared news of this development with General Washington, saying that "from appearances the period of disbanding [of the army] will be more distant" because it by necessity "goes hand in hand with the evacuation of our Country by the British forces." Jones, too, tied the furlough policy to the issue of British harboring of fugitives from slavery. According to Jones, British evacuation hinged on the "views and designs" of General Carleton "or those who direct his movement," and in this he seemed to depart from the usual English "fairness and liberality." Jones said his constituents were writing to him asking what was being done to recover their runaways, and they warned that if the British were "practicing their old game of deception," especially "respecting the Negros in their possession claimed by our citizens," then "it will prove an effectual bar to the restoration of confiscated Estates."[51]

As he was instructed to do by Congress on May 26, Secretary of Foreign Affairs Robert Livingston forwarded a sheaf of letters between Washington and Carleton to Adams, Franklin, Jay, and Laurens in Paris proving that the British commander had chosen to violate Article 7 of the peace treaty. Livingston offered his own outraged commentary on the general's intention to harbor the refugees. It laid bare the deeper beliefs and values underlying at least some of the furious responses to what amounted to Britain's defense of a wartime policy of abolition. "Nothing can be a more direct violation of the 7th: Article of the Provisional Treaty, than sending off the Slaves, under pretence that their Proclamation had set them free, as if a British General had, either by their laws, or those of nations, a right by Proclamation to deprive any man whatever of property."

Livingston wrote openly what most others simply presumed and never said aloud, that any justification for protecting escapees on the grounds that they had been freed by wartime proclamations was invalid because the enslaved could not be emancipated by military order. Livingston and many others who had no direct financial interest in recapturing these particular men, women, and children, nevertheless had a stake in protecting slavery itself, mostly because they viewed it as a bulwark of public safety and international peace.

On behalf of the confederation government, Livingston instructed the four diplomats to "remonstrate on this Subject, and inform Congress of the Effect of your Representations."[52] Elias Boudinot, the president of the Congress, also sent Franklin a stack of newspapers and told him, "It has been exceedingly ill judged in the British to retain New York so long, and to persist in sending away the negroes, as it has irritated the citizens of America to an alarming degree."[53]

As congressional leaders pressed America's diplomats to do more to recover fugitives from slavery, Adams, Franklin, and Jay could only weakly promise to "apply to Mr. Hartley" on the subject of "the transportation of negroes from New York, contrary to the words and intention of the provisional articles."[54] The three diplomats then duly notified their British negotiating partner, David Hartley, that Congress had ratified the Provisional Articles but raised a few outstanding issues. At the top of the list was "intelligence lately received from America . . . that a considerable number of negroes, belonging to the citizens of the United States, have been carried off from New York, contrary to the express stipulation contained in the said Article." Much further down in their letter, in fact the last point mentioned, was the slowness of the abandonment of frontier forts.[55]

In the end, Congress could do little more to sate its anger at English violations of Article 7 than instructing all of its ambassadors posted throughout Europe to press Britain to return the claimed human property.[56] To facilitate their claims, America's Foreign Affairs Office was ordered to compile a full list of all the "Negroes carried away . . . which were the Property of the Citizens of such States."[57] This task was so large that the secretary, John Jay, requested funds to "employ a large additional Number" of clerks.

❀ ❀ ❀

In response to the British evacuation of escapees from slavery, several states enacted further punitive laws against British creditors and property claimants in direct violation of the provisional peace treaty between the two nations. Most states had begun confiscating loyalist property and shielding American debtors long before the terms of the provisional peace treaty were known. Virginia's patriots, for example, began shielding American debtors from recovery suits even before independence was declared by closing the colony's courts. By the time economic protest turned into war, Virginians owed British creditors £2 million, half of all the private debt to English interests of all of the thirteen states combined. One angry Tory remarked, "the more a man is in debit, the greater patriot he is."[58] Soon after Crown armies began their sweep through the southern states, the Virginia assembly passed the Sequestration Act of 1778, allowing repayment of debts in depreciated paper currency. At the time diplomats were drafting the terms of the provisional peace treaty, Virginia canceled all British debts incurred after the spring of 1777, a largely symbolic move given the paltry volume of trade during the war.[59]

Virginia assemblyman Joseph Jones told James Madison that "Sir Guy Carleton's conduct respecting the negro property . . . will be made use of to justify a delay in paying the British debts" and that Carleton's seizure of the enslaved "confirms in their opinions, if it does not increase the number opposed to the payment of British debts." Likewise, Virginia politician Edmund Pendleton wrote to Madison that "some Gentn have received wth. great pleasure the Account of Sr. Guy Carleton's . . . conduct respecting the restitution of Our slaves, considering it as a proper excuse for not paying British debts."[60] Whether opportunistic or emotional, those factions who had long campaigned to cancel their foreign debts were joined by allies upset at this gesture of British abolitionism.[61]

Once it became clear that London had no intention to return those claimed as patriot's human property, especially those carried off from New York by General Carleton, state legislatures passed a raft of new and harsher laws penalizing loyalists and British creditors. Some states then explicitly tied their earlier laws to a demand that the Crown allow them to reenslave those whom they sheltered. North Carolina assemblyman Archibold Maclaine learned in mid-January of 1784 that "the Virginians are so exasperated [at the 'carrying our negroes to Nova Scotia'] that they have passed a law not to pay any British debts."[62]

Alarmed at this brewing disunion of efforts by individual states, George Washington sent a "Circular to the State Governments" in the summer of 1783 that expressed the paramount importance of upholding foreign treaties: "it is only in our united character as an empire, that our independence is acknowledged, that our power can be regarded, or our credit supported. . . . The treaties of the European powers will have no validity on a dissolution of the union; we shall be left nearly in a state of nature."[63]

Washington's letter had little effect. South Carolina responded to Congress's ratifying the definitive peace treaty in the spring of 1784 by limiting suits for recovery of past debts owed to British subjects to interest only and providing for fractions of principle to be paid on a schedule stretching five years into the future. Debtors were legally permitted to pay old sterling debts in either depreciated paper currency or even with land whose value was determined by their friends and neighbors. Additionally, the state's legislators were most inventive in fashioning a number of procedural barriers to filing recovery suits that effectively made it impossible for distant merchant houses to access state courts. Georgia's assembly largely copied South Carolina's laws. British merchants reported that Georgia's judges freely proclaimed from the bench that their courts were closed to them. Maryland, too, allowed old hard money debts to be paid in state paper currency. British diplomats shared with Adams their estimate that the 273,554 worth of Virginia currency paid under state law to satisfy British debts was only worth £15,044.[64]

At the vanguard of these protests was Virginia. So upset were Virginians at the carrying off of their human property that the only member of Congress to vote against the preliminary treaty was Hugh Mercer, a delegate from Virginia.[65] The issue of the "carried off" was foremost on the mind of leading Virginians when that state began consideration of an additional law blocking English creditors from collecting their debts.

Virginia's governor, Benjamin Harrison, thought it obvious that the debts to English merchants and Britain's return of the fugitives from slavery were a "reciprocal obligation." Why should "the virtuous whigs of this country" be forced to have "the remainder of their property taken to pay these very debts if they are not reimbursed for this part of their losses"? Harrison urged his delegate in Congress, James Monroe, to continue to work to push Congress to "take the proper steps either [to recover] the negroes or full compensation for them." He then warned, "If they do not I cannot think this country will ever come into the proposed measures at least till they have made full compensation out of the british debt to those who have been thus deprived of their Slaves. . . . If they do not succeed it will shew to the southern States that they are not inattentive to their interests."[66]

In the spring of 1784, Monroe replied to Harrison with the exciting news that the Congress had finally made its quorum and was about to "engage in the business of the utmost consequence both foreign & domestic." First on Monroe's list was "what can be done with respect to the negroes who were carried from N. York." Monroe wondered if it may be appropriate for Harrison to appoint "some gentn. of character" to go to New York and ascertain the exact number of "negroes" who were "carried off" as grounds for claims of compensation. He then immediately pivoted to the issue of "Our debt to the B. merchants," implicitly linking these questions together.

Monroe then estimated the debt of Virginians to be nearly three times the sterling then in circulation in the state, a sum that "puts it out of our power to comply with that article" of the treaty. "What then is the remedy?" Monroe pondered, but he really had his answer at hand: "We just obtain delay at least in the payment till by continued frugality & a succession of crops we can pay it. And to obtain this delay . . . we must have something to offer as compensation for the delay." Though Monroe never explicitly said that the issue of the "carried off" would serve well as "something to offer as compensation," the obvious structure of his letter made this point for him.[67]

Elsewhere Monroe expressly connected the issue of "the infringement of the article of the treaty with G. Brittain respecting the negroes in their removal from N. York" to the states' reluctance to comply with the terms of the peace treaty. Again, writing to Harrison, Monroe shared his hope that the Crown would concede the American position on the issue and thereby "remove all cause of umbrage from these States."[68]

But Monroe's deep interest in the British evacuation of Black refugees was more than just a bargaining chip with which to leverage a swap of debts. Monroe clearly saw it as an issue that brought to the fore the "great questions" of the relationship between the states and the national government. Monroe wrote again about the "subject of the Negroes" and the importance of obtaining an accurate count of their numbers and told Harrison that this issue was "of consequence to the federal interest & must therefore have the preference to any wh. relate only to particular states." Speaking as one of Virginia's congressmen, Monroe promised his governor that "I shall . . . most certainly pay great attention to this business & seize in conjunction with my colleagues the favorable moment to bring it on."[69]

Virginia's governor, for his part, understood clearly that the issue of the fugitives "carried off" and British debts would be tangled together. Harrison shrewdly predicted that the British "will endeavor to avoid the delivery of the negroes or payment of their value by a [strange] construction of the treaty," a potential calamity to which "the Interests of the Southern States are alone concerned." He worried that the northern states "may be willing to pass it over in silence or perhaps to give it up" and predicted that were they to follow this road, "those States whose interests have been given up" will "retaliate on the property of their enemies."

Harrison thought the root of this predicament lay with the northern composition of the diplomatic team that bargained on behalf of all the American states. "I have ever looked on it as a misfortune to the Southern States that our Commissioners in Europe were all from another quarter, for tho' I most readily agree they are men of Sense and honor, I am yet of Opinion that those qualifications cannot give them a sufficient knowledge of our situation & trade, as they have never lived amongst us."

Though he had the unique vantage point of sitting in the state's highest office, Harrison did not have a guess as to how this would all play out: "I am not able to say what will be the determination of the Assembly on our British Debts tho' I expect & hope they will comply with the treaty as far as our circumstances will permit of."[70]

In the end, Virginia's assembly did formally link their longstanding debt and loyalist confiscations to British protections of American runaways. Some legislators proposed retaining British prisoners of war "until an answer be given as to the delivery of slaves." A pending bill to halt the further sale of confiscated loyalist property was laid aside, according to Madison, because "the British military officers in the United States showed no inclination to enforce the terms of the preliminary peace treaty by returning slaves and other property."[71]

In the summer of 1784, Virginia's assembly moved to begin a formal inquiry "concerning an infraction on the part of Great Britain, of the seventh article of the definitive treaty of peace between the United States of America and Great Britain, so far as the same respects the detention of slaves and other property, belonging to the citizens of this Commonwealth." James Madison attempted to head off this movement, but a substitute resolution calling for the repeal of all laws that "prevents a due compliance with the stipulations contained in the definitive treaty entered into between Great Britain and America" failed by a vote of 57–37.[72]

This "inquiry" was but a formality, as a fortnight later the delegates resolved that Britain's "detaining the slaves" constituted an infraction of Article 7 and formally instructed its representatives in Congress to urge that body to remonstrate against this violation. More importantly, the assembly voted to "withhold their co-operation in the complete fulfillment of the said treaty, until the success of the aforesaid remonstrance is known, or Congress shall signify their sentiments touching the premises."[73] Specifically, the Virginia legislature stated that it would not repeal its confiscatory acts until such time as "reparation is made . . . or Congress shall adjudge it indispensable necessary."[74]

Seven senators (Nathaniel Harrison, Henry Lee, John Brown, William Lee, William Fitzhugh, and Burwell Bassett) voted against these articles and signed their names to a statement of "Dissention." They reminded their colleagues that refusing to execute Congress's will and the letter of the law threatened to tear apart "that federal bond, by which their existence as an independent people is bound up together, and is known and acknowledged by the nations of the world." They noted that Congress acted to ratify the treaty with the full knowledge that Sir Carleton had allowed Black people to evacuate and refused George Washington's demands for their return. Moreover, they reminded their fellow lawmakers that not only had Carleton's actions not been endorsed by the Crown, but that America's chief diplomat in Europe, Doctor Franklin, had communicated that "in his opinion a full and ample reparation would be made by Great Britain, when applied to, for the detention of the said negroes." Even worse, the dissidents warned, undermining the treaty in this way threatened to reignite the war they had just celebrated winning. "Because continuing legal impediments to the recovery of British debts, in direct violation of the treaty, will subject the property of the citizens of this state to be seized by the British government, and is therefore a proceeding full of temerity, violence and damage."[75]

Arthur Lee, the scion of one of Virginia's largest enslaving families who drafted one of the earliest plans for gradual emancipation, noted in a letter that Virginia and other states' laws restricting British creditors and claims were passed in direct response to Carleton's evacuation of escapees. "The first violation of the treaty was on the part of the commander in chief in New-York, allowing the negroes to be carried off . . . this [is] a not undesired reason for those of our citizens who were indebted to British subjects, to exclaim against the payment of British debts."[76]

These developments also troubled James Monroe, who wrote to Jefferson in Paris, begging his advice on the "great objects" of how to improve the operations of the federal government. Monroe was sure "a variety of points may arise to you when you look back on our country, in wh. our policy may [no] doubt be much improv'd." Monroe then offered the points that came to his mind, namely, "The laws prohibiting the executions for recovery. of Brith. debts are still in force. An address or something of that nature is made to Congress upon that subject, desiring their sense of the propriety of keeping them in force until satisfaction is made for the removal of the negroes from N. York."[77]

It was against this background that Virginia rushed to be in the vanguard of states pressuring London to return the "carried off." Virginia legislators redoubled their efforts to cancel British debt and formalize their loyalist confiscations as soon as the issue of "carried off" arose. This probably explains why, but it does not mean this demand was insincere or cynical. Rather, those factions who had long campaigned to cancel their foreign debts now were joined by allies furious at this gesture of British abolitionism.[78]

By the spring of 1785, North Carolina's delegates to Congress reported back to their governor that relations with Britain had reached a critical impasse. Congress had delegated John Adams to go to the British court to "insist on the delivery of the Western posts and a compensation for the negroes that were carried away in open violation of the Definitive Treaty of Peace, and to prevent matters from getting to that pass which might again involve us in a War with that Nation."[79]

It was not just southern states that reacted to Britain's evacuation of American fugitives from slavery with punitive laws. Massachusetts passed a law in November of 1784 suspending all debts and interest owed to British creditors for most of the preceding year. New York canceled all British debts incurred during the war, seized loyalist estates, and permitted Americans forced from their homes and farms during the war to bring suit in state courts for back rent from those who occupied them under British license. Immediately after the definitive peace treaty was approved, Pennsylvania moved to render it virtually impossible for British creditors to recover debts incurred prior to that date in state court.

Alexander Hamilton viewed the growing movement to obstruct English creditors and seize loyalist property in his state as an impediment to normalizing trade with the old empire. "I observe with great regret the intemperate proceedings among the people in different parts of the state in violation of a treaty the faithful observance of which so deeply interests the United States," Hamilton wrote New York's Governor Clinton. Hamilton reminded the governor that the treaty "exceeded the hopes of the most sanguine" and established American borders and rights to Atlantic fisheries "even better than we asked," and he then pointed out that New York's lucrative fur trade will be lost if the Americans "furnish a pretext . . . for delaying" the British evacuation of its frontier forts. He then lectured Clinton that "no part of the 6th [article] can be departed from . . . without a direct breach of faith" and that the "power of making treaties is exclusively lodged in Congress." In doing so, Hamilton expressly connected the anti-Tory movement and the issue of British harboring of fugitives from slavery. Hamilton acknowledged that the British excuses for "the negroes, who have been carried away" were based on a "doub[t]ful construction of the treaty."

Americans would be in their rights to "justly accuse them with breaking faith" but have refrained from doing so for fear of a complete breach and a "renewal of war."

While Hamilton fretted over the fate of the peace treaty, it was not just its immediate benefits that concerned him. Rather, he understood that America's place in a world of competing empires would inevitably come to depend on its ability to fulfill its promises. "Will foreign nations be willing to undertake any thing with us or for us, when they find that the nature of our governments will allow no dependence to be placed upon our engagements?"[80]

With his broad understanding of American institutions, of America's relative place in the world, and of the nation's possibilities, Hamilton came to view the harassment of loyalists and English creditors as being unavoidably linked to the fugitives from slavery and ultimately to the international trade and the western frontier that would build its economy. Consequently, Hamilton risked his reputation and took a public stand against the debt-shielding and loyalist confiscation laws.

Years before Alexander Hamilton dipped his quill to argue for the ratification of the new constitution in newspaper columns that would later be collected as part of the famed *Federalist Papers*, he wrote a similar series of articles calling on the New York legislature to comply with the treaty by repealing laws that confiscated loyalist property and revoked loyalist citizenship. Writing as "Phocion," Hamilton observed that "a breach of the treaty on the part of the British, in sending away a great number of negroes, has upon my principles long since annihilated the treaty, and left us at perfect liberty to desert the stipulations, on our part." Hamilton praised Congress for its wisdom and restraint in not declaring the treaty voided by these infractions, though he admitted they were perfectly within their rights to do so.[81]

Phocion in another letter connected the issue of confiscations to the peace treaty and stridently argued that Congress possessed the sole power to negotiate treaties, and states were then bound to their terms: "Have they not the sole power of making treaties with foreign nations? Are not these among the first rights of sovereignty, and does not the delegation of them to the general confederacy, so far abridge the sovereignty of each particular state? Would not a different doctrine involve the contradiction of *imperium in imperio?* . . . it follows from this, that these states are bound by it, and ought religiously to observe it."[82]

Hamilton probably knew his argument was hollow—that Congress enjoyed a grant of power it could not exercise—as it was the opposite of what he would write a couple years later in *Federalist* number eleven. Here, the very fact that Hamilton was pleading with a state legislature to comply with a duly ratified treaty proved that the Confederation Congress lacked the powers he attributed to it. Unable to simply declare states incompetent to violate the treaty, Hamilton was reduced to pleading, "Do not equity and prudence strongly urge the several states to comply with it?"

Despite Hamilton's best efforts, New York's assembly proved just as intransigent as Virginia's. Governor Clinton formally informed his state government of the ratification of the peace treaty and urged them to a "due observance thereof" at the end of January 1784. Clinton included in his official message a copy of Congress's resolution of January 14 urging the states to comply. Two months later, both chambers of the legislature voted on a resolution disavowing the treaty and declaring its refusal to comply with Article 5. New York's legislature nursed their wartime grievances, recalling in their preamble that "adherents of the King of Great Britain . . . cruelly massacred, without regard to age or sex, many of our citizens, and wantonly desolated and laid waste a very great part of this State . . . in enterprises which had nothing but vengeance for their object." They then declared that they would not restore those banished to citizenship, they would not restore confiscated property because "no compensation is offered on the part of the said King . . . for the damages sustained by this State and its citizens." Though claiming that "this Legislature entertain the highest sense of national honor, of the sanction of treaties, and the deference which is due to the advice of the United States in Congress assembled, they find it inconsistent with their duty to comply with the recommendation of the said United States on the subject matter of the fifth article."[83] Then, on May 12, 1784, New York passed "An Act for the speedy Sale of the Confiscated and forfeited Estates within this State, and for other Purposes therein mentioned" that Hamilton labeled baldly as "equivalent to new confiscations."[84]

News of American legislatures' attempts to extort the return of liberated African Americans by embargoing debts to British merchants reached London as fast as the swiftest packet ships could traverse the sea. The *Westminster Magazine* mentioned the Virginia law "to prevent the recovery of British debts, till full retribution is made them for the negroes taken from that State, who were in New York when the Preliminaries were signed," on the first day of August 1784. It noted that "their charge for them is 500,000 £ sterling."[85]

When the House of Lords debated the provisional peace treaty on February 17, 1783, the treaty's opponents presented a detailed and comprehensive inventory of the many ways the American states violated its articles. Lord Shelburne attempted to undercut these criticisms by proclaiming that he and the other negotiators had always known that Congress's powers over the states were limited. Shelburne almost pleaded when he began, "If better terms could be had, think you, my lords, that I would not have embraced them?" Shelburne noted that his options were to accept the states' weak guarantees for the loyalists or to continue the war: "[W]ho would plunge this country again knee deep in blood and saddle it with the expense of twenty millions" just to make the loyalists whole, he asked.

Lord Hawke supported Shelburne by noting that Congress did what it could to fulfill the treaty, but the Congress, they knew at the time, had no power. "In America . . . congress had engaged to recommend their [the loyalists] cause to the legislatures of the country: what other terms could they adopt?" The Congress, Hawke pointed out, was quite like the king's own. "Can the crown undertake for the two houses of parliament? It can only recommend." Lord Walsingham agreed, "We had only the recommendation of congress to trust to, and how often had their recommendations been fruitless?" Walsingham noted that just recently Rhode Island had refused to comply with a congressional duty of 5 percent.

Lord Sackville went on the attack: "The king's ministers had weakly imagined that the recommendation of congress was a sufficient security for these unhappy men." Sackville pulled from his pocket a copy of a resolution of the Virginia assembly from December 17 refusing to abide by "demands or requests of the British court, for the restitution of property confiscated by this state."[86]

News of American states' violations of the treaty of peace circulated widely in England. As early as 1786, a volume reprinting thirty-two New York state laws confiscating loyalist property, interfering with the collection of English debts, and restricting trade with England, *Laws of the Legislature of the State of New York, in Force Against the Loyalists and Affecting the Trade of Great Britain and British Merchants and Others Having Property in that State*, was printed in London.[87] Perhaps intuiting that Americans and their supporters would not be much swayed by accounts of how these laws had ruined the fortunes of those loyal to the Crown, the editor in his preface struck at the Americans' own hopes and dreams for the future by pointing out that such actions would only retard the tide of immigration American leaders pined for. "Were the Laws of all the States in the Union, passed before and since the Treaty of Peace submitted to public Consideration, it may be presumed, that the Spirit of Emigration, which has for some time past prevailed, would be at an end; as those who think themselves oppressed in their native Country, would find Misery and Distress in an extreme Degree in that Land of Freedom and Independence so highly recommended by the Advocates for America on this Side the Water."[88]

By the end of 1784, two and a half years before the convening of the Constitutional Convention, leaders of Congress and their trio of all-star diplomats, Jefferson, Adams, and Franklin, had come to understand that their government was unable to uphold their end of the favorable peace treaty they had wrung from the British. They feared the consequences not only for their political and economic relations with Britain but their ability to make any agreements with other European powers. Jefferson, Adams, and Franklin were compelled to beg the Crown for concessions to their agreement because of their own failure to enforce it over their states. The American diplomats admitted to the Duke of Dorset, Britain's "Ambassador Extraordinary and Plenipotentiary" in Paris, that "there are Some unusual circumstances attending the English debts in America contracted prior to the war, that Seem to merit consideration, and to Show the reasonableness & utility of explaining & modifying that article."

So deep was America's institutional impasse that the trio also urged that "provision Should be speedily made for the Satisfaction of the masters whose negroes were Carried away with other property." In other words, since the federal government could not force its own states to comply, the English government would have to fulfill all of its obligations and excuse American violations to keep their treaty from crumbling.[89]

In early 1785, two prominent members of the team that had successfully negotiated the peace treaty with Britain were given more authority over the nation's foreign policy. John Jay became secretary of foreign affairs and John Adams was appointed ambassador to Britain. However, even though both men were dedicated to weakening slavery in the new nation, the drive to obtain the recapture of (or payment for) fugitives from American slavery did not slacken. In one of Jay's first instructions to Adams, the issue of fugitive return and British debts was not only linked but stressed as an urgent matter: "I herewith enclose Copies of a Number of Papers respecting the Transportation from hence of Negroes by the british Army contrary to the Treaty of Peace, and also Copies of some Papers on the Subject of the Debts due from american to british Merchants—on these two Subjects your Instructions partly turn."[90] These issues were urgent because as long as they went unresolved and American states continued to disrespect the standing treaty, any hope for future commercial arrangements with the British empire were dim.

In London, John Adams also worried that his countrymen's refusal to uphold the terms of the existing peace treaty because of British refusal to return the fugitives from slavery who had been "carried off" would compromise all his efforts toward obtaining commercial and maritime concessions. Adams's worries only deepened when he learned from congressional leader Elbridge Gerry that he was only narrowly approved by Congress as ambassador to England, and this after "many attempts have been made to determine the Choice" and "States were tenacious of their Vote, for several days." In the end, Adams received five votes, Livingston four, and Rutledge two, meaning a majority of the states voted against him. Gerry told Adams that his opponents thought him unreliable on the issue of the repatriated escapees. "[I]t appeared that the Southern States were impressed with the

Idea, that You being totally averse to the Slave Trade, would not exert Yourself at the Court of London to obtain Restitution of the Negroes taken and detained from them in Violation of the Treaty."[91]

Adams immediately set about lobbying key congressional leaders, claiming that he was sincerely dedicated to obtaining payment for American fugitives freed by England. Adams assured Richard Henry Lee, one of the leading Virginian politicians, that he viewed the "Negroes . . . carried off" as a top priority: "When Astronomers are calculating the Motions of the heavenly Bodies, they are often obliged to neglect les infiniment petites, that their Results may be the more certain.—I do not reckon however, the 'Debts' and the 'slaves,' among those infiniment petites. They are great and important Quantities, and Shall have a proportional Attention paid to them."[92]

At the same time, Adams told Elbridge Gerry, the politician as influential in Massachusetts as Lee was in Virginia, that his personal opposition to the international trade in people would not diminish his determination to squeeze payment for the lost fugitives given sanctuary by the British: "It is very true that I have little Admiration of the Philosophical Philanthropy or Equity of the Slave Trade. This Defect however has never prevented, nor will ever prevent me from doing all in my Power to obtain Restitution of the Negroes taken from the Southern States and detained from them in violation of the Treaty. I am not conscious that any Philosophical Speculations Upon this Subject, have ever influenced my Conduct in this Respect, nor do I See that they ought to enter into this Business."[93]

While his opponents were unable to derail his appointment as minister to England, powerful enslavers were able to engineer a key appointment to his staff, one that provided Adams with personal insights into British violations of Article 7 in New York. Jacob Read, a leader of South Carolina's congressional delegation, wrote to Washington in March of 1785 asking him "as early as possible" to forward his copy of the "Roll of Negroes &ca taken by the Commissioners for superintending the Embarkations at New York" so as "to enable our Ministers in Europe to proceed to execute the Instructions of Congress of 1785 on the Subject of Negroes Carried Off in Contravention of the Treaty of peace."

Read then bragged that "I had the happiness to succeed in my endeavors to send Col Wm Smith as Secretary to the Legation," meaning the diplomatic mission to London headed by John Adams, just appointed as ambassador to England. Read's intervention to engineer Smith's appointment was likely related to his previous work as one of the three commissioners superintending the New York evacuation. Smith quickly ingratiated himself with Adams and soon became not only his trusted advisor but his son-in-law.

Tellingly, after relating these bits of news, Read ruminated on the state of the nation: "From the want of a full Congress, the great National Questions still remain untouched & will not be Attempted till late in the Spring when tis hoped we may Assemble the whole force of the Union & try if we can act as a Nation, Which by the bye I very much doubt now the Common tye of danger is removed." Clearly, Read was less than optimistic about the ability of the confederation structure to address the most pressing "National Questions," a disfunction most evident in the broken peace treaty and the inability of the Congress to obtain the return of patriots' human property.[94]

When Adams was finally officially appointed as the "Minister Plenipotentiary to represent the United States at the Court of Great Britain," Congress gave him a detailed set of instructions. If the order of the items on this list of concerns was reflective of congressional priorities, recovery of the lost American fugitives "carried off" was second only to regaining possession of the frontier forts and more important even than weakening British trade restrictions. The second instruction was: "You will remonstrate against the infraction of the treaty of Peace by the exportation of Negroes." This was then followed by "You will represent to the British Ministry the strong and necessary Tendency of their Restrictions on our Trade to incapacitate our Merchants in a certain degree to make remittances to theirs." Adams embraced these directives enthusiastically, telling John Jay that their "Right, &. Power and Equity are too clear, to leave any plausible Pretences for delay."[95] Adams's commitment to this agenda never wavered, even when he could feel the winds shifting under Lord Carmarthen and he told Jay that they must be "cautious" and not draw too many inferences from casual conversations: "[For] it by no means follows, that they are determined to do, what their Honour and their Publick Faith, obliges them to do according to our Ideas of their Obligations. it by no means follows that they will

Surrender the Posts, restore the Negroes, relieve the Debters, or make an equitable Treaty of Commerce."[96]

It is significant that in the summer of 1785, a full two and a half years past the British evacuation, America's top negotiator was still working to "restore" the fugitives, rather than seeking compensation for them. It would be another nine months before Adams's rhetoric shifted to demanding "payment for the negroes." For Adams, like other patriot leaders, the issues of the British debts and British evacuation of runaways were interwoven. Adams met with a representative of an influential group of Glasgow merchants who had been lobbying Parliament to press the Americans harder to pay their debts and told them they should support America's efforts to reclaim their fugitives from slavery. Adams told the Scottish traders that "there were, two Things, which fell very hard upon the Debtors in the State of Virginia and New York": Britain's holding of the western forts curtailed the lucrative fur trade and "the great Number of Negroes, which had been carried away." Appealing to their bottom line, Adams observed, "if these Negroes had been restored according to the Treaty, they would have been at Work to earn Money to pay their Masters Debts, but the carrying them off was a double Loss to the owner."[97]

Adams suggested that in the absence of an international agreement, the states could collect these debts themselves and use the proceeds to compensate masters for their lost human property. Adams's suggestion eventually found traction in Congress, which voted in August to send to the governor of each state a full accounting of the "numbers, Names, and owners of the Negroes belonging to the Citizens of each State and carried away by the British in Contravention of the late Treaty of peace."[98]

While Adams was lobbying to keep his job from across the ocean, John Jay tried to convince members of Congress that demanding compensation for war damages or the return of stolen "property" was a fool's errand. Jay forwarded to Congress Adams's dim assessment of the possibility of negotiating any restitution. Jay reported secretly to Congress that a "judgment of the temper of the nation in general, and of their parliament in particular, may be formed from Mr. Adams' letters; and they, in the opinion of your secretary, represent it in a point of view so unfavourable as to promise no success." Jay unsuccessfully urged Congress to instruct Adams "not to bring on any *formal* demand" respecting lost American property.[99]

Congress met Jay's recommendation halfway and stopped short of issuing demands on the Crown, but also directed Adams to admit the United States was in violation of Articles Four and Six of the treaty dealing with loyalist property and British debts, and that they considered Britain in violation of Article 7, requiring the return of slavery's fugitives. Adams was to tell his British counterparts that the United States was working to bring the states into compliance, and he was instructed to share with them copies of Congress's two resolutions to the states on the matter. As for the African Americans carried away on British ships, Adams was to propose a conference of commissioners charged with estimating "the value of the Slaves or other American Property carried away contrary to the 7th Article," and this payment was to be made after the states repealed their obnoxious laws. Almost as an afterthought, the British were to evacuate their frontier forts at the same time.[100]

Congress made it clear what their priority was between the question of the compensation for the "carried off" and the abandonment of the western forts later in July when Jay quietly dropped from the wording of the former resolution any specific reference to the western forts. New York's Melancton Smith and Virginia's William Grayson tried to put a pledge to surrender the forts "within the limits of the United States" back into the resolution, but Massachusetts's Nathan Dane and Virginia's Edward Carrington moved to strike reference to the "posts and places now held by his Majesty." Their narrowing of the diplomatic demand to just compensation for slavery's "carried off" passed eighteen to three (or eight states to one).[101]

Grayson was one of the most astute observers of the goings on in Congress, and he noted that John Adams thought the issue of the forts and posts the British refused to vacate was entirely secondary to that of the Americans' debts to British and the "negroes carried off." Grayson recorded Adams's opinion: "with reguard to the Posts it was so connected with other matters as not to be decided on singly."[102]

Given Congress's insistence on pressuring Britain to return the fugitives from slavery, all Adams could do was ask Jay to send him "the whole

Amount & Evidence of the Claim" that concerned "the Negroes carried off contrary to the Treaty" as well as "explicit Instructions of Congress to demand Payment for the Negroes in Money, and especially at what Prices they Should be Stated."[103] Jay never forwarded detailed information about the exact values of escaped slaves. However, he laboriously catalogued all the state laws and actions that were in violation of the provisional peace treaty and bemoaned to Adams, "there has not been a single Day since it took Effect on which it has not been violated in America by one or other of the States."[104]

There was indeed a bright line connecting the actions of Virginia and New York, the evacuated Black fugitives, the unpaid debts, and the British refusal to evacuate their western forts. Adams thought he would make ground by connecting all these issues to the need for a general commercial treaty to regularize trade with Great Britain. He confided to Jay in the spring of 1785 that he hoped to "convince the British Ministry, of the necessary Tendency of their restrictions on our Trade to incapacitate our Merchants in a certain degree to make Remittances to theirs," and that this would be the loose pebble that could release a landslide of agreements on the other issues, "the Surrender of the Forts, the Restitution of the Negroes, the Explanation respecting the Debts, and those other matters pointed out in his Instructions, in which the Right & Power and Equity are too clear, to leave any plausible Pretences for delay."[105]

Such expectations were dashed when Adams met with Prime Minister William Pitt on August 24, 1785, and again when Adams met Foreign Secretary Carmarthen later that fall. According to the British notes of this meeting, "Mr. Adams began the conversation by recapitulating the complaints of the United States on the subject of the posts not being yet evacuated, and no satisfaction having been given for the negroes who were carried away." By this time the American side had given up on trying to cajole the Brits to make concessions, and Adams now took the shaky stance that Americans were not in violation, as all that the treaty's wording technically required was that no prohibitions be put in the way of the collection of old debts, not that they necessarily had to be paid. (At the same time Adams described Massachusetts's stay laws as a "direct Breach of the Treaty" and American behavior toward England as "dishonest" to confidants back home.)[106]

Adams's bluster accomplished little but pushing the royal negotiators to dig in their heels. He dutifully drafted a "Memorial" to the Royal Ministry, and later that summer Adams was granted an audience with King George III that was cordial but again led nowhere. In response, the British government formally presented Adams with a list of the eight states and their obstructionist laws that would have to be removed for the English army to quit their posts.

In the end, Adams completely failed to move his British counterparts even an inch toward the American position. Adams's failed mission was partly the product of British knowledge that his support back in Philadelphia was weak and partly the product of his own uncompromising character. These qualities were highlighted by a British agent in America who had dinner with Jay and pried from him news on the doings of Congress that he quickly relayed to Lord Carmarthen, especially the news that Adams's appointment would not be renewed. The informer noted that Adams had "lost ground in every respect, with Congress as well in the particular state he belongs to" because of his "Mulish disposition." His report concluded that most Americans "pretty generally thought that had a Man of a Modest conciliating disposition been sent to London a much better understanding would have long before this have subsisted between His Majesty & these States."[107] Judging Adams by this yardstick, London concluded there was nothing to be gained in conceding ground to such a man.

It took the better part of a year, but through the course of his failed mission to London Adams came to realize that English leaders had come to the conclusion that the American Congress was so weak and the states so fractured that it was not worth negotiating. At one point, English negotiators told Adams that they were uninterested in reaching agreement unless a treaty had the separate consent of all thirteen states. Adams reported to Jay that "the British Cabinet have conceived doubts, whether Congress have Power to treat of commercial Matters, and whether our States should not Seperately grant their Full Powers to a Minister." How could this possibly work, Adams wondered. "The Idea of thirteen Plenipotentiaries meeting together in a Congress at every Court in Europe, each with a Full Power and distinct Instructions from his State, presents to view such a Picture of Confusion, Altercation, Expence and endless delay, as must convince every Man of its Impracticability."[108]

Adams's frustration poured over in a letter to John Jay: "We cannot unite, in Laws and Measures which would make one.—By the best Judgment I can form, the Posts upon the Frontiers will never be evacuated, nor the Maryland stock recovered, nor the Rhode Island demand satisfied, nor the Negroes paid for while there remains in force a Vote of any Assembly suspending Proscess for the Recovery of British Debts."[109]

Near the end of his term in London, Adams concluded that Congress would never have the power it needed to override the stubborn legislatures whose laws blocking payment of English debts had derailed all his attempts at compromise on the issues of forts, fugitives, and trade. "It is my Duty to be explicit with my Country, and therefore I hope it will not be taken amiss, by any of my fellow Citizens, when they are told, that it is in vain to expect the Evacuation of Posts, or Payment for the Negroes, a Treaty of Commerce, or Restoration of Prizes, Payment of the Maryland or Rhode Island Demand, Compensation to the Boston Merchants, or any other relief of any kind, untill these Laws are all repealed." Adams desperately proposed that each state collect British debts and pay compensation to enslavers directly.[110]

Here in Adams's reports to Jay can be seen the wheels already in motion driving toward a fundamental reorganization of the federal system. Adams, like most other leading American policymakers, had become convinced that a more powerful centralized federal government was necessary to reign in the ease with which popularly controlled state legislatures could break apart the nation's vital international agreements. More than a year before the Philadelphia convention to consider "amendments" to the Articles of Confederation was announced, Adams had arrived at this same remedy to America's ills based on his experiences attempting to extol payment for fugitives from American slavery and the abandonment of British occupied forts. He wrote Jay in the spring of 1786: "It is very possible that the Cabinet of St James's may decline, even entering into any conferences at all, upon the Subject of a Treaty of Commerce, untill the Powers of Congress are enlarged. if they should the People of America cannot be too soon informed of it, and turn the deliberations in their Assemblies to this Object."[111] This is just what the two of them did.

As negotiations with England had clearly reached an impasse, Jay grew even more determined to spur Congress to use what power it had to apply pressure to the states to clear up the nation's violations of Articles IV and V. In October, Jay took to the floor of Congress and read a lengthy report detailing each state's violations of the standing peace treaty and presenting his frank views of what Americans owed the British and what the British government owed them.

Jay faced an uphill battle to convince Congress that it needed to apply more pressure on the states to rescind their laws violating the British treaty. Earlier that year he had shocked southern representatives when he presented a proposed treaty with Spain that would have closed the Mississippi River to American shipping for a period of twenty-five to thirty years. All members of Congress, especially those who had purchased vast tracts of western land for resale to homesteaders and plantation builders, understood that closing the main artery of commerce would depress land values and stifle settlement. Only New Englanders were willing to swap western expansion for the commercial opportunities the Spaniards dangled to Jay, including opening the port of Havana to American shipping. In a series of nakedly sectional votes, Congress voted to reject Jay's proposed terms but failed to muster the required supermajority to replace them. Southerners were so alarmed that they even attempted to repeal Jay's authority to negotiate treaties altogether and to replace him with a pair of commissioners of their own choosing.[112]

Given Jay's earlier clash with the southerners in Congress, who had good reason to suspect that the New Yorker favored the sectional interests of the maritime North over the staple-growing South, it is surprising how little ground he conceded to southern interests. While noting that both sides had violated their treaty, Jay factually pointed out that Americans were the first offenders: "In whatever light, therefore, deviations from the Treaty prior to its final conclusion and ratification may be viewed, it is certain that deviations on our part preceded any on the part of Britain; and therefore instead of being justified by them, afford excuse to them."[113]

Not only did Jay stress American violations as the bigger issue in obtaining the normalized relations with England they all sought, but he also downplayed the scope of British infringement of Article 7. Jay distinguished between different classes of the enslaved who had been expatriated by the British, some who were legally recoverable and some who were not. The enslaved seized as British armies swept inland were, by the laws of war, unrecoverable. Here Jay took enslavers' own longstanding legal bulwark of declaring people to be property and not human beings and turned it against them: if the enslaved were simply property and not people, then by the laws of war they constituted booty and "become the property of the Captors." Jay perhaps unnecessarily belabored his point when he then wondered aloud "Whether men can be so degraded as under any circumstances to be with propriety denominated Goods and Chattels," and noted that this was a question upon "which opinions are unfortunately various, even in Countries professing Christianity and respect for the rights of mankind. Certain it is that our Laws assert, and Britain by this Article as well as by her practice admits, that Man may have property in Man."[114]

Importantly, it is clear from Jay's remarks that one of his goals in his report to Congress was to convince the American leadership to step back from its insistence that the "carried off" be physically returned to them. While Jay excluded from Article 7 the enslaved that had been captured as "booty," he conceded that any person who fled their masters for freedom with the British remained enslaved and were recoverable because no law recognized the ability of an army to liberate people and thereby negate the property of Americans by simple proclamation. This had been the longstanding American position, and its reach encompassed most of the thousands evacuated from New York.

Even John Jay, who expressed the most sincere sympathy with the plight of the "carried off," in his explosive report to Congress in the fall of 1786 never challenged the prevailing American view that all the people who fled their masters and served under the Union Jack were not and could not be emancipated by British law, and thus "still remained as much as ever the property of their Masters." Jay expounded further, "They could not by merely flying or eloping extinguish the right or title of their Masters—nor was that title destroyed by their coming into the enemy's possession, for they were received, not taken, by the enemy—they were received not as Slaves but as friends and freemen, by no Act therefore either of their own or of their friends was the right of their Masters taken away." Jay thought this state of affairs was unjust and immoral, and he was courageous enough to say so, but ethics did not guide his hand as an officer of the nation, the law did.[115]

Jay then appealed to his fellow patriots' morality and gave an impassioned speech as to why they should allow these people their freedom in exchange for British monetary compensation. Calling this question "a painful dilemma," Jay observed that England "had invited, tempted and assisted these Slaves to escape from their Masters, and on escaping had received and protected them," and so "it would have been cruelly perfidious to have afterwards delivered them up to their former bondage." The only solution, both practical and moral, "was to keep faith with the Slaves" by recognizing their freedom "and to do substantial justice to their Masters by paying them the value of those Slaves." Jay concluded to a skeptical audience, "In the opinion therefore of your Secretary, Great Britain ought to stand excused for having carried away these Slaves, provided she pays the full value of them; and on this he thinks the United States may with great propriety and justice insist."

In other words, Jay's speech is clear evidence that well into the autumn of 1786, many patriot's insistence on the enforcement of Article 7 was not figurative or symbolic, but an actual movement for the bodily return of the men, women, and children who had escaped their bondage. Jay offered his opinion that Congress should drop its demand for return and with "great propriety and justice insist" upon payment of the "full value" instead. Indeed, Jay reported that "there is an intimation" that the British minister did not object to this arrangement.

As for the issue of the British-occupied posts and forts, Jay concluded this was entirely justified by American actions, as Britain had no obligation to surrender any of them until the treaty was ratified by Congress on January 14, 1784, and by Parliament on April 9. "From that time to this, the 4th and 6th Articles of the treaty have been constantly violated on our part by legislative Acts then and still existing and operating." Therefore, Jay argued, "Under such circumstances, it is not a matter of surprize to your Secretary that the posts are detained; nor in his opinion would Britain be to blame in continuing to hold them until America shall cease to impede her enjoying every essential right secured to her, and her people and Adherents, by the treaty."[116]

Having conceded precious little to the southerners in the room, Jay may have been impolitic to also chose this moment to state plainly his view of an exclusive federal jurisdiction in foreign policy. He may have been spurred to do so by earlier attempts of some southern politicians to claim that treaties could not infringe on a state's sovereignty. It was only a few months before, during the tussle over Jay's proposed Spanish treaty that would have effectively choked off the western half of the nation, that southern congressmen had retreated to a spread-eagled states' rights position to thwart him. While the Articles of Confederation had clearly and unequivocally declared treaties to be the supreme law and Congress to have exclusive authority to negotiate and approve them, southern representatives issued a declaration that rested on a theory of co-equal sovereignty that would bedevil the nation for the next eighty years: "By the second article of the confederation of these United States, each state retains its sovereignty, freedom and independence, and every power, jurisdiction and right which is not therein expressly delegated to the United States in Congress assembled. This is a fundamental law of the nation, and the powers granted in the ninth article to make treaties must be construed in subordination to it."[117]

The Articles of Confederation had no means to resolve this fundamental conflict of ideas about the nature of the treaty power because it had no federal judiciary, supreme court, or executive to enforce Congress's orders. Here then was laid bare a far more fundamental conflict of constitutional powers than any other. No other issue, not taxation, interstate commerce, international trade, nor even angry indebted farmers, required a wholesale structural revision. General Carleton's act of noblesse oblige toward the African Americans in New York City had uncovered a contradiction at the heart of the American confederation that could not be resolved without replacing it.

FOUR

The Rope of Sand

When historians describe the reasons why Americans changed their form of government in 1787, they generally focus on Congress's difficulty raising taxes, trade disputes among states, the insurmountable barrier of unanimity to amend the Confederation articles, the British refusal to abandon their western forts, British imposition of crippling trade restrictions, and the specter of armed veterans in Massachusetts demanding a moratorium on debts. These were certainly troubling problems, but few of them required for their solution a sweeping new apportionment of powers between the states and the federal government. Repeatedly in this period, knowledgeable American politicians expressed confidence and optimism that the issues of taxes, of interstate trade squabbles, of amendment, and even of domestic insurrection could be settled within the terms of the Articles of Confederation. Only two of these looming issues were widely recognized as being beyond the scope of that charter and the existing powers of the Congress to solve. Both involved enforcement of an international treaty over intransigent state governments. Because treaties were defined in the Articles as supreme law but Congress possessed few coercive powers over the states, the two questions of British trade and of European powers' control of western territories exposed an impasse that could not be resolved without granting the federal government radically new powers.[1]

Given that there are nearly a dozen pressing issues that the Constitution of 1787 addressed, how should historians determine which were most urgent and central in propelling this sweeping revision of the American state? Most historians have taken the word of James Madison, who, more than any other founding father, consciously crafted how the Constitutional Convention would be remembered. Madison intentionally downplayed the importance of protecting slavery in the thinking of the founders, as he, like Jefferson, Hamilton, Washington, and Jay, had come to be embarrassed by their involvement in enslaving people.[2]

It was well known to constitutional historians a century ago that the federal government under the Articles failed not because it was difficult to pass legislation (as every act required a supermajority), but for lack of power to enforce the will of Congress once a policy was determined. Max Ferrand, the early aggregator of the records of the state ratification debates, saw this back in 1913: "To the congress thus constituted quite extensive powers were granted . . . [but] when a decision had been reached there was nothing to compel the states to obedience." Congress under the Articles had neither executive nor judicial authority. "Under such conditions the decisions of congress were little more than recommendations." In other words, the existing blueprint of government did not lack enumerated powers, it lacked *power.*[3]

This observation might have answered why the Articles were ultimately superseded by the Constitution but did not explain when. At what point was the weakness of congressional power sufficiently demonstrated to compel most states to move to revise their basic structure of government? After all, history shows that even very dysfunctional states have a momentum that is hard to overcome and that even obviously inadequate structures of government can persist for long stretches of time.

When a key event is preceded by a myriad of forces, any one of which could be said to be its "cause," how does one decide which was most formative? America emerged from the chaos of war only to be beset by the chaos of peace. Congress was bankrupt and did not even have the funds to pay its victorious troops. Its former enemy banned all American shipping from their Caribbean ports, which was America's most lucrative trading destination. Most of the states set their own customs regulations, and several were feuding over import tariffs. Poor farmers crowded onto the poorer uplands in the western districts of their states and saddled with heavy taxes were whispering rebellion. Foreign rivals—Spanish, English, French, and native—maneuvered to box Americans out of their coveted Ohio, Kentucky, and Tennessee territories. And several states, pointing to the British "carrying away" of people they had agreed to surrender, flouted their disregard of the treaty that held the peace by seizing loyalists' properties and passing laws shielding their citizens from English debt collectors.

It is tempting to simply sidestep the question by noting that all these problems plagued the "Critical Period" leading to the nation's constitutional reorganization and saying each contributed to the feeling of crisis that impelled leaders to agree to such a colossal change. But this would disregard intriguing bits of evidence that threaten to thrust some of these causes to the front or diminish their relevance. Without making any claims to present a definitive judgment of the relative weight of all these factors, I want to thumb the scales in a few cases.

First, there is the question of federal finances. Money, after all, has long been a motivator for all sorts of historic intrigues, ploys, coups, and rebellions. There can be no doubt that when the guns fell silent and the federal government's French and Dutch financiers lost interest in bankrolling it, the new nation found itself bereft of the means to conduct its most basic functions. Many histories of the "Critical Period" have leaned heavily on an accountant's explanation for the happy resolution of the constitutional crisis. The outline of this argument is rather straightforward: Congress had no independent taxing authority or power to collect import or export duties and could only raise money in one of three ways. It could sell federal land, of which it had plenty, but much of which was neither surveyed nor yet cleared of those who called it home and were willing to resist its transfer to American speculators and settlers. It could borrow money, though as previously mentioned those taps had run dry. Finally, it could "requisition" funds from the states, which during wartime netted in total about one-third of all the sums requested. (There is a fourth possibility—printing money—but without the authority to tax this paper back into the treasury, any money it emitted would quickly devalue to worthlessness.)

On balance, then, Congress's debt crisis seems a good candidate for driving the constitutional juggernaut, except for one consideration: timing. Congress was financially comatose throughout this period, and the illness seemed worse in the earliest years, not in the years immediately preceding the calling of a convention in Philadelphia.

America's most vocal leaders began complaining of the national government's lack of ability to raise revenues from the thirteen states almost immediately after the Articles were ratified. In 1780 Alexander Hamilton detailed at length "the defects of our present system," and he pointed most to the issue of states failing to honor the requisitions Congress approved. He hoped then that Congress could be directly given the "power of the purse." As a military officer, Hamilton knew firsthand the consequences of the chaotic provisioning system the Articles had created. His solution was augmenting Congress with a true executive department and giving it "certain perpetual revenues, productive and easy of collection," such as a "land tax, poll tax or the like, which together with the duties on trade and the unlocated lands would give Congress a substantial existence, and a stable foundation for their schemes of finance."[4]

While frequently accused of lethargy both by contemporaries and modern historians, Congress acted relatively swiftly to address its funding issues. In February of 1781, Congress approved a plan to establish its own independent tax base, a 5 percent import duty on all goods arriving from foreign ports and a similar charge against all naval "prizes," the booty of authorized pirates.[5] While passed by Congress, under the Articles this amendment to Congress's powers also had to be approved by all the states. Most state legislatures quickly did so, but Rhode Island held out and then rejected the measure a year and a half later. Hearing of Rhode Island's disapproval, Virginia, the lynchpin of the nation, rescinded its vote and the whole scheme fell apart in the winter of 1782–1783.[6]

By the spring of 1783, Robert Morris, the federal treasurer, resigned. In his last report to Congress, Morris described the wreckage that were his accounts: "all the money now at our command, and which we may expect from the States for this two months will not do more than satisfy the various engagements which will by that time have fallen due." To those policymakers who kept faith that France would bail them out, Morris said bluntly: "there is no hope of any further pecuniary aid from Europe." To others who thought domestic loans might be secured or more promissory notes could be circulated, Morris had an even starker message: "we can have no right to hope, much less to expect the aid of others, while we show so much unwillingness to help ourselves . . . our public credit is gone." Morris urged a sweeping reform of the federal system; unless such deep fundamental changes were made, "until some plain and rational system should be adopted and acceded to, the business of this office would be a business of expedient and chicane." He concluded by admitting that he did not have "the disposition to engage in such business, and therefore I pray to be dismissed."[7]

Around the same time Congressman Gouverneur Morris (no relation to Robert) had grown so disgusted with the fecklessness of the states and the impotence of the common government that when disgruntled units of the army petitioned Congress for back pay, he wrote in code to his good friend John Jay his secret hope that they mutiny. "The army have swords in their hands. . . . I think it probable that much of convulsion will ensue, yet it must terminate in giving to government that power without which government is but a name." Six months later, when several hundred Continental army soldiers surrounded Independence Hall demanding action, Morris may have regretted his earlier wishes. Even in the face of an armed mutiny that drove Congress to flee to Princeton, then peripatetically to Annapolis, Trenton, and New York, no serious efforts at the sort of fundamental reform that Hamilton had envisioned years earlier was undertaken.[8]

Instead, Congress again passed an amendment to the Articles that would give it the power to collect lower import duties on a specified list of liquors, wines, tea, pepper, sugars, cocoa, and coffee (presumably goods mostly imported into Rhode Island) and the higher old proposed duty of 5 percent on everything else. Within a year, eight states had approved the new customs authority, including the influential states of Virginia and Massachusetts. By 1786, all but New York, the state that collected the largest share of customs duties on its own, had signed on to the new import taxes, and hope remained for the Empire State's approval until it finally buried it in February of 1787, well after the plans for the Philadelphia convention had been laid.[9]

This record of attempts to reform Congress's balance sheet indicates that America's national leaders believed throughout this period that *if* the federal government were given its own income stream through the custom houses, this issue *could* be solved. Simply put, the federal treasury did not require a wholesale restructuring of the relationship between the national government and the states. Such attempts at piecemeal reform did not ultimately fail and were not abandoned until delegates were already making their arrangements to attend the convention in Philadelphia.

Other economic issues besides the question of federal debts and funding certainly loomed large in the years leading up to 1787. Madison famously raged against those states that profligately issued paper currency. As revenues from trade declined, states raised taxes, often upon the backs of those with the least influence in their state capitals, which in many cases were also the least able to pay. Stirrings of dissent along the western fringes of several states failed to sufficiently alarm policymakers until popular militias formed and threatened government officials. This carousel of crises blurred together issues of currency, taxation, international trade, and popular rebellion as it wheeled around through time.

Arguably, the speed of this machine was set by the briskness of international trade, which was a greater share of the national economy than domestic exchange. In a fit of revived mercantilism and nationalist spite, in the summer of 1783 Great Britain barred American ships from carrying the goods that American citizens bought or sold with its Caribbean colonies altogether. This was a crippling blow to most seaboard cities and towns, and to the state treasuries that drew heavily on tariffs.

All understood that no single state could negotiate successfully with the British empire and that ultimately the solution to this international problem had to come from the nation's continental government. Recognizing that it lacked the usual coercive powers of other empires, Congress passed a provision that frankly admitted its incompetence and proposed a remedy that was simple but coarse: the power to bar the importation of any nation's goods. Warning that "[u]nless the United States in Congress assembled shall be vested with powers competent to the protection of commerce, they can never command reciprocal advantages in trade; and without these, our foreign commerce must decline and eventually be annihilated," it then sent this proposal to the states for approval in early 1784.[10]

Unlike Congress's proposals to reform its finances, this proposed power to bar imports was widely seen as an inadequate half-measure because, as a member of the Massachusetts legislature, Tristram Dalton, told John Adams, there remained the problem of "the propriety of individual States interposing." In other words, states would still have the power to institute their own trade regulations apart from Congress. Dalton worried that if even this inadequate plan did not pass the states, "the Court of G Britain may look on the Confederation as a rope of Sand."[11]

George Washington had used the same language a few months earlier when he confided to a friend that "the embarrassments of Congress—and the conseqt delays, and disappointments on all sides, encompass me with difficulties; and produce—every day—some fresh source for uneasiness." The great general did not heap all these embarrassments at the feet of the legislators in Philadelphia but could see that the whole edifice needed to be redesigned. The "Constitution of Congress must be competent to the general purposes of Government; and of such a nature as to bind us together, otherwise, we may well be compared to a Rope of Sand, and shall as easily be broken—and in a short time become the sport of European politics."[12]

Clearly, of all the problems facing the nation, many of the most influential leaders thought those associated with Congress's power to negotiate and uphold international agreements loomed particularly large. These flaws in the pillars of government were exposed by three interrelated grievances with Great Britain: the trade disagreement, a standoff over the promised evacuation of western forts and the territories they controlled, and the British refusal to surrender back into American slavery the thousands of people to whom they had promised liberty. All three were supremely tangled— even intractable—issues within the confines of a weak national government lacking effective powers over the states. But one of these did more to highlight the deficiencies of the Articles than the others: the issue of the fugitives from slavery.[13] Before detailing why this last issue was separate and deeper than the others, another leading candidate for the key issue must be examined.

Many histories of the "Critical Period" emphasize that the British failed to hold up their end of the treaty by failing to surrender the western forts to American forces. While there is some substance to this charge, much of the English failure to do so was a consequence of the logistical difficulties of coordinating a military evacuation over a great distance and disentangling their alliances with native peoples throughout the region.

Another little-commented-upon fact was that the American side was unprepared to accept the surrender of these posts due to the disarray of its peacetime army and Congress's general paralysis. Washington's most trusted general, Henry Knox, visited Congress in Philadelphia several months after the British evacuation of New York, and after a week of lobbying he was chagrined to find the national government unprepared to even begin planning for assuming control of the western forts.

The problem as Knox saw it was that the "eastern states" were unwilling to pass a resolution requiring them to contribute troops for the posts. Southern states were eager to commit troops but would not consent to merely *recommending* each state do so.[14] Washington agreed with Knox's analysis of the political situation and fretted, "It is a real misfortune, that in great national concerns, the Sovereign has not sufficient power to act—or that there should be a contrariety of sentiment among themselves respecting this power. While these matters are in litigation, the public interest is suspended—& important advantages are lost. This will be the case respecting the Western Posts."[15]

It was not until May 24 that Congress approved the appointment of a military liaison to venture into Canada and determine when the British commanders planned to abandon their forts. The following week, against General Knox's counsel, Congress authorized the recruitment of seven hundred men from militia units of Connecticut, New Jersey, New York, and Pennsylvania on only a twelve-month basis. Experience had shown that such short-term enlistments led to unreliable and disordered units, a problem that would be amplified by the difficulty of moving a force and all its supplies a great distance across difficult terrain. Knox fumed that the "measures taken by Congress respecting the western posts must defeat themselves by their own imbecillity." Knox told Washington that even if the British should "immediately deliver up the posts on our frontiers . . . we should be ridicuously embarrassed not having a man" to occupy them.[16]

Embarrassed they were when Lieutenant Colonel William Hull finally landed in Canada in July of 1784 and was easily rebuffed by Governor-General Frederick Haldimand. General Haldimand confided to Hull his opinion that he had not yet received proper orders to abandon the forts because the Americans were violating the treaty. Haldimand probably did not reveal that some months earlier he had written Lord North and requested that his orders to evacuate be delayed by at least a year so that British loyalists in America would have more time to recover their estates.[17]

Congress reconsidered their initial flawed plan to draw one-year militia to the frontier, but it was nearly another year before they extended those recruitments to three-year terms.[18] This frontier corps was placed under the control of Knox, who in the meantime had been elevated to the new office of secretary of war.[19] By the winter of 1785, only six of the projected ten companies had been raised, and they had only just begun to march westward, half of them to Forts Pitt and McIntosh, which were to be their winter quarters, and the rest only as far as southern Ohio.[20]

Washington had just returned from an expedition to Fort Pitt "to see the condition of the property I had in that Country, & the quality of my Lands," which he had purchased before the war began. He was chagrined to find much of it occupied by squatters, who he said "set me at defiance, under the claim of pre-occupancy." Disgruntled with the lack of legal authority on the fringes of the nation and the impotence of the continental government, Washington vented to his fellow general, "in my opinion, that there is a kind of fatality attending all our public measures—inconceivable delays—particular States counteracting the plans of the United States when submitted to them. . . . Would to God our own Countrymen, who are entrusted with the management of the political machine, could view things by that large & extensive scale upon which it is measured by foreigners, & by the State[s]men of Europe, who see what we might be, & predict what we shall come to." Washington then observed the sad fact that "our federal Government is a name without substance: No State is longer bound by its edicts, than it suits present purposes, without looking to the consequences."

He concluded, tellingly, by tying all these troubles to the great rivalries of European empires. "How then can we fail in a little time, becoming the sport of European politics, & the victims of our own folly"?[21]

Knox heartily agreed and indicated that the disorganization of the country's foreign affairs have laid bare the most vexing problems in its system: "Your remarks on the present situation of our Country, are indeed too just. . . . A Neglect, in every State, of those principles which lead to Union and National greatness—An adoption of local, in preference to general measures, appear to actuate the greater part of the State politicians—We are entirely destitute of those traits which should Stamp us one Nation."[22]

There can be little doubt that certain mercantile interests in London and Canada pushed the king's councils to slow-walk their obligations to abandon the seven heavily armed outposts that commanded the lucrative fur trade from the mouth of the St. Lawrence to the far reaches of the "Upper" provinces. But the Americans handed them easy excuses to do so when they loudly violated the standing treaty by seizing loyalist estates and throwing up roadblocks to English debt collectors. None of these actions were louder than Virginia's refusal to rescind its laws violating the treaty until the English handed over the thousands of fugitives claimed by its citizens as their property.

In addition to these factors, a local uprising in Massachusetts has long drawn attention as a proximate cause of the constitutional gathering because it played out in the year leading up to it. Shays' Rebellion, the brushfire rebellion of disgruntled western farmers who for a time threatened to topple the government of the Bay State, may have been dramatic, but it was not seen nearly as alarming or extraordinary by American leaders themselves as it has been by their chroniclers.

In October of 1786, after several months of armed protests by poor farmers in western Massachusetts, Abigail Adams wrote to her friend Elizabeth Shaw from London. Abigail thought "the only News which I can write you from this quarter of the World" relating to America was the important business of the treaty with England. "With regard to America, she has got her answer from this court, that when the Treaty shall be fully complied with on our part, then the post shall be evacuated the Negroes payd for &c."

Abigail had heard of the troubles in her own state and initially thought to offer her opinion on it, writing on her draft copy: "our Liberty is become licentiousness." Abigail was referring to the rebellion of western farmers. "There must be some crafty leader, some sly insinuating Serpent difusing his venom upon a deceived multitude for common Sense and plain Reason could not pervert and mislead my countrymeen thus."[23] But before posting her letter she thought better of her commentary and crossed it out. Clearly, in her mind the question of complying with the treaty and getting the "Negroes payd for" was a more pressing and important matter.

Soon after Abigail sent her letter, James Warren wrote to her husband breathlessly, "We are now in a State of anarchy & Confusion bordering on a Civil War," but then described the actual situation with much less hyperbole. Warren noted that the state legislature "at their last Session could not or would not see the general Uneasiness that threatneded this Event" and instead took a long adjournment. Warren then conceded that the problem was not intractable: "I do not say that they [the legislature] are Incompetent to the Business before them, or that the State of things is Incapable of redress, but it is possible, (at least) that they should set, till next Election without deviseing the Mode of doing it." In ending his letter, Warren revealed that he thought the larger issue was the problem of the government's finances. "I wish every thing may be so Conducted as to restore order, & submission to Government, but I fear it will be some time first. The Scarcity of Money is a great Obstacle, and the folly and Extravagance that Made it scarce, in a great degree remains."

So, like Abigail, James Warren did not think the marching about of farmers in western Massachusetts as important as other pressing national matters, either the problem of getting Black people returned in chains or properly paid for or establishing a sound national currency.[24]

At the same moment, Secretary of War Henry Knox bemoaned the state of national affairs to George Washington, specifically mentioning "the commotions in Massachusetts." Rather than simply condemn the "insurgents," Knox provided a thoughtful analysis of what the root of their grievances were. Knox observed that the rebellion was said to be caused by high taxes, but he noted that the "people who are the insurgents have never paid any, or but very little taxes." Rather, what aggrieved these poor country folk was seeing the government serve only the elites. "They feel at once their own poverty, compared with the opulent," and when government is weak, they feel "their own force, and they are determined to make use of the latter, in order to remedy the former." Knox then observed what Secretary of Foreign Affairs Jay would say in a speech to Congress a few months later, that states were undermining federal powers by claiming the right to interpret federal laws and international treaties according to their whims. "The powers of Congress are utterly inadequate to preserve the balance between the respective States, and oblige them to do those things which are essential to their own welfare, and for the general good." Knox warned that the federal government must be given more powers to head off such rebellions in the future. "Our government must be braced, changed, or altered to secure our lives and property."[25]

Even when elite Bostonians took up a private subscription to form a regiment to subdue the rebels, observers did not view this with the alarm a true revolution should arouse. John Quincy Adams, then a student at Harvard, returned to his dorm to find "my chamber full of Ladies, who had a view of part of the troops from the windows." John Quincy and his lady friends watched as more than a thousand troops trundled down the road from Charlestown out to meet the Shaysites. Over the next few weeks rumors flew thickly of an imminent attack on the local courthouse. Adams noted that "in the course of the day fifty different reports flying about, and not a true one among them." The threats did not keep him from his happy social life: "No appearance of rioters as yet, tho' it is this evening reported that there are 1500, within four miles of Cambridge. We dansed this evening."[26]

Though Congress had voted funds to assemble the army and deploy it to the Bay State, in the end only Virginia ponied up its requisition and the Continentals were never mustered. Massachusetts governor James Sullivan told John Adams about the insurgents interrupting the local courts, but he then offered a different assessment of the deep problem facing the nation, which was substantially the same as what Secretary of War Knox thought: "The Federal Government is Still weaker and we dare not try to compel a compliance with the requisitions of Congress in any of the States. our old

Whigs are all now talking very Seriously of a change of System. they consider these seperate sovereignties as insupportable and quite incompatible with a general Government."[27]

Luckily, the insurrection was quieted by Massachusetts on its own. It took General Lincoln with several thousand militia to finally scatter Shays' army in January. Lincoln reported happily to Washington, "The spirit of Rebellion is now nearly crushed in this State. . . . without the shedding of blood but in an instance or two where the Insurgents rushed on their own destruction."[28]

There can be little doubt that the challenges of workers and poor farmers from Massachusetts to North Carolina worried patriot leaders, especially when these years were punctuated by brush fire rebellions of poor farmers and frontier settlers. But the direct influence of Shays' Rebellion upon the crafting of the Constitution remains debated. In the end, Woody Holton's assessment seems most balanced, that it was "likely that many at the federal convention who swapped dire warnings about Shays' Rebellion would have traveled to Philadelphia and created a powerful national government even if the danger of revolt had remained hypothetical."[29] That being the case, then what were the other underlying or overarching factors impelling this legal revolution?

At the time of the Constitutional Convention, most policymakers agreed that the powers of government were not sufficient to repress those who needed repressing and to maintain the customary rights of property. But they also were not so sanguine about the consequences of their own rivalries—the competition for control of the western territories and, more importantly in the short term, control of foreign trade. Several states had longstanding commercial rivalries that constantly threatened to escalate into violence.

While commercial skirmishes among the states were worrisome to national leaders, even the most committed federalists did not view them as threats to the confederation. Just a year and a half before the Constitutional Convention convened, John Jay expressed confidence that the vexing issues of trade regulation could be solved within the framework of the Articles of Confederation. Jay sent Adams news of a Rhode Island measure regulating its foreign trade and observed that however "discordant the various Acts of the States on these Subjects may be, they nevertheless manifest Sentiments and Opinions which daily gain ground, and which will probably produce a proper and general System for regulating the Trade and Navigation of the United States both foreign and domestic." Jay expressed his belief that the "federal Government alone is equal to the Task of forming such a System" and hoped that "local Politics would cease to oppose vesting Congress with Powers adequate to that great and important Object."[30]

Nevertheless, trade issues provided a forum for discussing national issues outside of the sclerotic Congress. Historians have long traced the genealogy of the Philadelphia Constitutional Convention to a trade meeting that occurred the year before in Annapolis, Maryland. Generally, an antiquarian footnote in larger histories of the Constitution, the Annapolis meeting is not viewed as particularly important in shaping the issues that would drive the rethinking of federalism, but as merely a signpost of the deeper troubles that motivated it. However, a closer look at the resumes of some of the delegates who played important roles at Annapolis reveals surprising connections to the unresolved issue of the British evacuation of fugitives from slavery.

Sharing thousands of miles of sheltered coastline and estuaries, Virginia and Maryland naturally faced each other as shipping rivals. By the mid-1780s, the two states had attempted to monopolize the Chesapeake and the Potomac by charging tolls for moving goods across these waters and at times even attempted to embargo shipments to the other. Leaders of both states eventually agreed to send commissioners to a meeting at Washington's mansion at Mount Vernon to hammer out their differences.

The Mount Vernon meeting succeeded in restoring free movement among the states, though it expressly contradicted the prohibition in the Articles of Confederation of states negotiating commercial compacts or agreements apart from Congress. General Washington, who was hardly a disinterested party given his land portfolio that contained tens of thousands of acres along the Ohio River whose future development depended on the cooperation of the Chesapeake states, suggested that further progress could be made by including Pennsylvania and Delaware in a subsequent meeting. James Madison engineered a change of wording in a resolution of Virginia's House of Delegates that sent invitations to every state instead of just neighboring ones.

Ironically, the host state of the Annapolis meeting, Maryland, failed to send any delegates to the conference. Only Virginia, Delaware, Pennsylvania, New Jersey, and New York were represented. Of the twelve patriot leaders who gathered in September of 1786, the most famous were Madison, Hamilton, Randolph, and Dickinson. Of the lesser-knowns, only one later in life viewed his participation in this meeting as being particularly significant.[31]

Thirty years later Egbert Benson had retired to his quiet country home on Long Island, where he took in boarders, when he set down some thoughts about his role in the building of the nation. He chose not to recount his role in Revolutionary politics, his being a member of the first independent legislature of New York in 1777, or his role as attorney general of that state in the crucial decade that followed, or his serving in the first U.S. Congress under the Constitution. Rather, among the few details of his own life that he recounted was how he came to be one of the delegates to the Annapolis conference.

Benson was appointed by the New York legislature to represent the state at Annapolis. Four others were tapped for this duty, but three of them quickly made excuses and bowed out, leaving only himself and Alexander Hamilton. Benson, too, planned to excuse himself, as he had the state's business to conduct in Albany as attorney general, but he was persuaded against this by his friend and state supreme court justice John Hobart (upon Hobart's death Benson donated a marble memorial tablet for the wall of the supreme courtroom in New York's City Hall that described Hobart "as a man, firm—as a citizen, zealous.")

Benson remembered their conversation as "casual" but "terminated in a *conclusion* that the present opportunity for obtaining a Convention to revise the whole of our mode of system of GENERAL government, by *confederation* or *league*, ought not to be suffered to pass." Hobart urged Benson to pawn off his Albany work to an associate and "proceed to New York, and communicate to Mr. Hamilton what had passed between us." According to Benson, Hamilton "instantly" concurred that this was an opportunity to rechart the structure of government generally, and together they spread this idea among the other delegates once they arrived in Maryland. Benson stated unequivocally that the Annapolis declaration was actually drafted by Hamilton, leaving Benson to wonder, "Is this entitled to be viewed as the *origin* of the present Constitution?"[32]

Tracing the germ of the idea of turning this gathering to the purpose of revising "the whole of our mode of system of GENERAL government" to Benson is not simply an exercise in antiquarianism. Its significance rises above the level of detail-picking because Benson was perhaps the patriot leader most intimately involved in the details of the attempted recapturing of the thousands of men, women, and children given sanctuary by the British.

Benson was attorney general of the state of New York when Governor Clinton selected him to organize the British surrender of the city. He was then chosen by Congress to the commission charged with arranging for the surrender of the fugitives from slavery in New York. While it is hard to say specifically how these experiences shaped Benson's thinking, it is not a stretch to speculate that they would have impressed upon his mind the importance of having a strong federal government to uphold international agreements. Likewise, according to Benson's recollections, it was Alexander Hamilton who shared his enthusiasm for turning the gathering at Annapolis into a call for a wholesale rethinking of the "GENERAL" government. Hamilton, as was evident from his pamphlet war as "Phocion" against loyalist confiscations and debt embargoes, had come to similar conclusions.[33]

While Benson and Hamilton were important links in the chain that connected patriot leaders' attempts to recapture escapees from slavery in New York and the eventual redrafting of the U.S. Constitution, Benson's late-in-life claim that he and Hamilton came up with the idea of turning a meeting held to discuss trade issues into one brainstorming ways of reorganizing the federal government may not have been an exaggeration. Alexander Hamilton first began formulating an alternative charter to the Articles of Confederation in 1783, just a few months after he had complained of British violations of the Treaty of Paris by evacuating the human property of American patriots. The order of Hamilton's concerns reveals his assessment of the relative importance of each defect in the federal government and in this way presents something of a roadmap to which problems contributed the greatest momentum for constitutional change.

Hamilton's first complaint was the most general: the Articles confined "the power of the federal government within too narrow limits" and caused confusion as to the "proper bounds of the authority of the United States." Compounding this problem was the "confounding legislative and executive powers in a single body" that prevented the Congress from executing its own powers contrary to the most "well founded maxims of free government, which require that the legislative, executive, and judicial authorities should be deposited in distinct and separate hands." These first two ordered items on Hamilton's list were structural weaknesses, present and obvious without reference to the current events, social or economic circumstances, or immediate crises the nation faced. It is only his third item that seems ripped from the headlines of that moment: the "want of a federal judicature having cognizance of all matters of general concern in the last resort, especially those in which foreign nations and their subjects are interested," a clear reference to the roiling controversy over the status of Black fugitives, white loyalists, and British creditors.

Hamilton numbered the importance of creating a federal judiciary with supreme powers to implement treaties over the states above "vesting the United States in Congress assembled with the power of general taxation," which he listed next, or "making proper or competent provision for interior or exterior defense," which was seventh, or "vesting in the United States a general superintendence of trade," which was eighth.[34]

Perhaps events did unfold exactly as Benson recounted them, but these ideas were hardly unique to this pair of founders. Circumstances and events that had unfolded since the beginning of the peace negotiations had starkly illustrated the need for such reform, and many people who occupied high vantage points in society readily saw the need for fundamental change in the distribution of the powers of the states and the "general government."

More than a year before the call went out for the Annapolis meeting, various clusters of influential merchants and political leaders in the principal trading cities had begun corresponding about the problems the nation faced and how the government could be remade to fix them. The scattered letters that have survived from these private exchanges reveal much about the thinking of some of the richest and most powerful men in America at the time.

The dozen men who humbly called themselves the "Philadelphia Committee of Merchants" were hardly just a group of businessmen. Among them were owners of some of the richest shipping companies in the nation. Samuel Howell's trading company was the first to import goods directly from China to the United States. John Nixon owned warehouses, a wharf, and a trading company extending along Front Street. They also included a sitting member of Congress, Charles Pettit, as well as two of his predecessors, George Clymer and Thomas Fitzsimmons. Other political leaders included future member of Congress Tench Coxe and the then vice president of Pennsylvania, Charles Biddle, who was both a banker and father of Nicholas Biddle, who famously feuded with Andrew Jackson over a different bank.[35] The letters of this "committee of merchants" should be given much weight in understanding the factors that led to the Constitutional Convention. The fact that of these twelve "merchants," one, Coxe, would attend the Annapolis meeting and two others, Fitzsimmons and Clymer, signed their name to the nations' new constitution after four months of hard deliberations is telling.

This elite group of Philadelphians drafted a response to a query they had received from a similarly powerful group of Bostonians in April of 1785. The Boston Brahmins had sent letters to business partners and others in various cities soliciting "sentiments respecting the general commerce of the United States" and an "harmony of measures" to be taken. In their reply, Philadelphia's "merchants committee" attributed the nation's commercial doldrums to Congress's lack of power over the states, a deficiency all the more destructive because of the importance of finding a place in the international puzzle of treaties. The committee warned that England and France "are in the capacity, [and] will reap all the benefits of our open trade without imparting any advantages in return, untill we shall be able to meet their restrictions and exclusions with some effectual system adapted to our new situation." Continuing, they observed that "however necessary or desirable this might be a great difficulty lies in the way: the defect in the constitutional power of Congress made the harder to supply from the jealousy of some of the States of the authority of that body."³⁶

Such elite activism carried great weight with the sorts of men who gathered in Annapolis. The delegates who gathered at Annapolis mirrored the concerns of those bankers and merchants in determining to "take into consideration the trade and Commerce of the United States, to consider how far an uniform system in their commercial intercourse and regulations might be necessary to their common interest and permanent harmony." They quickly determined that the subject of interstate trade could not be settled apart from the greater questions of federal power. Such questions of power had been thrust into relief by the weakness of the Congress in the face of state violations of the Treaty of Paris. While not spelling out all the connections between British harboring of fugitives from slavery, state laws seizing loyalist property and blocking English creditors from recovering their debts, English refusal to abandon their western forts, and the ongoing impasse in negotiations for an Anglo-American trade agreement, the delegates in Annapolis spelled out clearly that they could not address the trade issue alone because the issue was systemic. "[I]n the course of their reflections on the subject, they [the Annapolis trade commissioners] have been induced to think, that the power of regulating trade is of such comprehensive extent, and will enter so far into the general System of the federal government, that to give it efficacy, and to obviate questions and doubts concerning its precise nature and limits, may require a correspondent adjustment of other parts of the Federal System."

At one point in their address, the Annapolis delegates linked the "foreign and domestic" problems (which they termed "embarrassments") that only a revision of "system of Federal Government" could resolve: "That there are important defects in the system of the Federal Government is acknowledged by the Acts of all those States, which have concurred in the present Meeting; That the defects, upon a closer examination, may be found greater and more numerous, than even these acts imply, is at least so far probable, from the embarrassments which characterise the present State of our national affairs—foreign and domestic, as may reasonably be supposed to merit a deliberate and candid discussion."³⁷

It is probably worthy of note that neither Benson nor Hamilton was particularly motivated to recapture enslaved people so as to strengthen the institution of slavery. Like most patriots seeped in the liberal enlightenment, neither leader thought it defensible in theory. Benson criticized it in his *Memoirs* published thirty-five years later, saying that even the mildest forms of slavery, such as he believed was common among the old Dutch settlements, was such that a man was still "*subject* to the *will* of *another*" and "assanable" as a "beast," and he concluded, "it has been given to us in these latter days to see the injustice of the bondage."[38] Rather, both founders understood slavery as being hopelessly knotted with what they saw as more important and more immediate issues. National power and prestige were at the top of their list.

Another Annapolis delegate, Edmund Randolph, who represented Virginia, was elected governor of that state just a few months afterward. Randolph had the occasion to chair the state convention that considered ratification of the new U.S. Constitution in 1788. During a speech to the assembled delegates, Randolph recounted the importance of what transpired at Annapolis: "On a thorough contemplation of the subject, they found it impossible to amend that system. What was to be done? The dangers of America, which will be shown at another time by particular enumeration, suggested the expedient of forming a new plan."

Randolph listed how this ongoing neglect of Congress manifested—in quotas unpaid, public credit at a low, commerce languishing—but these issues were not the sources of the nation's problems, merely their symptoms. The taproot of America's political misery extended overseas: "We became contemptible in the eyes of foreign nations . . . [it] was found that Congress could not even enforce the observance of treaties."[39]

John Adams, who tended to write obtusely and thereby hedge his political risks, was clear about what changes he thought needed to be made in the charter of government for America. In the only volume of his three-volume history of constitutionalism that was published before the Philadelphia convention, Adams concluded that Congress needed additional powers to have the international standing an independent nation needed to negotiate agreements with other powers. "Full power in all foreign affairs, and over foreign commerce, and perhaps some authority over the commerce of the states with one another, may be necessary; and it is hard to say, that more authority in other things is not wanted: yet the subject is of such extreme delicacy and difficulty, that the people are much to be applauded for their caution."[40]

Rhode Island, the northern state most entangled with the Atlantic human trade, was deeply concerned with the questions surrounding the British treaty, as its economy was nearly entirely dependent on overseas trade. Rhode Island's representative in Congress, General James Varnum, had been moved by the issues swirling around the peace treaty to the position that the powers of Congress needed to be strengthened. Varnum informed that state's governor in April 1787 that Jay's report seemed to be making progress in moving this "important" issue to some resolution by denying "the power of individual States to vary in any measure, the conclusive act of the United States in Congress in matters confided to them by the articles of Confederation."[41]

The consequences of state violations of the Treaty of Paris had been made evident in the fall of 1786 when John Jay read his report detailing them to Congress. Was it a mere coincidence that less than six months after Jay made it clear that the prospect of reaching a new trade pact with England was practically nil as long as a handful of powerful states violated the only standing agreement the nation had with the Crown that Congress finally and decisively moved to fix this problem by calling for the Constitutional Convention? Do these very different time lines of perceived crises and action tell us something about the relative importance of each issue?

After Secretary Jay submitted his report to Congress, that body unanimously agreed in March of 1787 to exert all the powers it had to force the states to comply with the terms of the treaty. Such powers consisted of a stern statement explaining that the legislatures of the states "cannot of right pass any act or acts for interpreting, explaining or construing a national treaty . . . nor for restraining, limiting or in any manner impeding, retarding or counteracting the operation and execution of the same" and calling on the states to repeal such acts. As the Congress had no mechanism to enforce law over the states, all it could do was "recommend to the several

States to make such a repeal" by "declaring in general terms that all such acts . . . repugnant to the treaty of peace between the United States and his britannic Majesty . . . shall be and thereby are repealed."[42]

Little action was taken by the states over the next month, and Congress was compelled to unanimously issue another pleading resolution to the states that drew heavily from the constitutional principles John Jay had laid out in his speech on the British treaty: "we regret that in some of the States too little attention appears to have been paid to the public faith pledged by that treaty. Not only the obvious dictates of religion, morality and national honor, but also the first principles of good policy demand a candid and punctual compliance with engagements constitutionally and fairly made. . . . the 9th Article of the confederation most expressly conveys to us the sole and exclusive right and power of determining on war and peace, and of entering into treaties and alliances &c."[43]

Just as Congress's "recommendations" and "urging" of states to comply with the provisions of the peace treaty and remove legislative barriers to payment of claims to British creditors were issued in April 1787, Virginia adjourned its legislature until January of 1788. Madison recognized immediately the obstructionism that motivated this move. "Virginia we foresee will be among the foremost in seizing pretexts for evading the injunctions of Congress. S. Carolina is not less infected with the same spirit."[44]

In the spring of 1786, Congressman Charles Pettit of Pennsylvania expressed his concerns about the future of the country to his colleague Jeremiah Wadsworth, then in Paris, but who would soon return to his native Connecticut and serve in Congress and later play a role in ratifying the new U.S. Constitution in his home state. Pettit wrote, "Our political Situation, merely from want of [ar]rangement and Combination of our Strength, is indeed wretched—Our Funds exhausted, our Credit lost, our Confidence in each other and in the federal Government destroyed." These were vexing problems, but Pettit thought others even more urgent: "Instead of supporting the respectable Rank which we assumed among Nations, we have exposed our Follies to their View—they treat us accordingly, they severally shut the Door of commercial Hospitality against us, while ours being open they enter and partake with us at their Pleasure."

Pettit complained of how his fellow congressmen did not take their appointments seriously and how gathering a quorum was difficult. But the root cause of the nation's problems he attributed to the states refusing to pay British debts in retaliation for the loss of their fugitive human property. "Foreigners perceive our lethargic Imbecility. . . . They openly charge us with a Breach of the Treaty by obstructing the Recovery of british Debts by Legislative Acts in some of the States; in this, however, there is some Truth, tho' less than [the]y pretend; but I should suppose that their refusal to [pa]y for the Negroes they purloined and which they acknowledge [t]o be a failure on their Part, might have been a balance for this breach of ours, as it was in some Measure the Occasion or at least the Pretence for it."

Pettit worried that these problems could doom the republic: "Is it possible that a great political System, however wise[ly] formed, can be preserved and well conducted in this Manner [?]" He predicted that these problems would soon come to a head: "Such Disorders both within and without cannot fail to bring on a Crisis of some kind ere long—What will be the Result, or what Turn it will take, is uncertain. However we may dread the Event, it seems to be the only chance we have of restoration to political health."[45]

Pettit's analysis that the federal government suffered from a "lethargic imbecility" was shared by America's counterparties to the treaty across the Atlantic. When Parliament debated the Provisional Articles, Lord North rose to complain of the lack of protections for Loyal Britons in the treaty, saying they were "subject of an odious exception . . . those who deserved of this country every grace, every favour that it could bestow, should be abandoned to the impotent recommendation of a Congress, whose authority to levy money, was disputed and denied by every state in the confederacy."[46]

Congress's disorganization when it came to conducting foreign affairs, its "lethargic imbecility," was exposed further by the travails of Phineas Bond, England's first British consul to the United States. Bond was a Philadelphian who stayed loyal to the Crown through the war, was placed under house arrest and then detained with Quakers in the Freemason's lodge, but somehow escaped and fled to England. His own estate had been confiscated by the state of Pennsylvania. Bond arrived back in the city of his birth at the end of 1786 and had to wait months before Congress was able to assemble a quorum to confirm his credentials.[47]

Growing pessimistic about the prospects of Americans getting their government in order, Bond sent to London a gloomy assessment of the nature of the government he was supposed to conduct business with: "such is the present state of this country that I cannot discover any prospect of speedy or effectual relief for the many inconveniences the British merchants labor under."[48]

While unable to perform his official duties for lack of federal recognition, Bond spent his time compiling a comprehensive archive of all the state laws that conflicted with Articles Four and Five of the Treaty of Paris.[49] When Congress had yet to act on his commission that spring, Bond determined to pursue a different strategy and applied to various state legislatures for their official recognition. As he explained to his superior, "As the recommendations of Congress, My Lord, have proved ineffectual to obtain a compliance even with the stipulations of treaties, this mode of application to the different States seemed to be the only resort."[50] Pennsylvania's assembly promptly accepted his credentials, establishing diplomatic relations between that state and the English Crown.[51]

Congress still had not recognized Bond's commission by May, and Bond sent to Lord Carmarthen a copy of the circular sent by Congress to the states and insightfully diagnosed the nature of the government's sclerosis. Bond blamed the southern states for subverting American obligations and surmised Congress lacked the power to bring them to heel:

> From the recommendation of the Congress, my Lord, I fear little is to be expected; tho' nominally the great executive body of the continent, each individual State claims and exercises sovereign and independent rights over itself, consequently each State may adopt or reject whatever is consistent with local convenience, or interferes with particular advantages: there is a defect of energy in the Congress, they want means to enforce their requisition and tho' they claim "a general tho' limited sovereignty, for the general and national purposes specified in the confederation," yet, my Lord each State may

resist every federal measure, and the dissent of any one State may effectually mar the success of the most important recommendation: unless therefore the hands of the Congress be strengthened, by the enlargement of their powers and unless they be enabled to conduct the affairs of the Union, by a system of uniform measures, foreign powers can have no reliance upon the engagements of the Federal Government, nor can the Confederation exist.[52]

In the year following the declaration of peace, both influential English and French newspapers highlighted stories of troubles between American states and implied the American union was falling apart. Benjamin Franklin, then still in Paris, was particularly rankled by their slanders, and wrote so to David Hartley, the chief British negotiator of the peace treaty, and his old friend: "You have deceived yourselves too long with vain Expectations of reaping Advantage from our little Discontents. . . . Our domestic Misunderstandings, when we have them, are of small Extent; tho' monstrously magnified by your microscopic Newspapers. He, who judges from them that we are on the Point of falling into Anarchy, or returning to the Obedience of Britain, is like one, who, being shown some Spots in the Sun, should fancy that the whole Disk would soon be overspread with them, and that there would be an End of Day Light."[53]

Franklin then complained in similar terms to his close friend Richard Price in London: "Your Newspapers are full of fictitious Accounts of Distractions in America. We know nothing of them."[54] Thomas Jefferson too attempted to correct these sensational reports in an article he sent to the *Gazette de Leyde* pointing out the extraordinary innovation of Pennsylvania and Connecticut settling their disagreement over the western territory they both claimed by submitting their grievance to a federal court, convened for just this purpose. Jefferson gushed with praise for the wisdom of their decision: "Perhaps history cannot produce such another proof of the empire of reason and right in any part of the world as these new states now exhibit."[55]

Jefferson sent an early version of his letter to Franklin before submitting it to the French paper's editor, and Franklin then began planning a response to similar spurious accounts that were common in the English press. Franklin's draft only got as far as an outline, but its substance indicates that he too was eager to point out the strengths of the American confederation. Franklin's outline listed the "lies" he planned to counter:

> Lies since the Peace to encourage a Renewal of the Wars
> Showing that the United States are in the greatest Distress
> Want of Provisions
> . . . of Money and Credit
> . . . of Good Government
> That they are weary of the Constitution
> of Independence
> of Congress.[56]

Such letters, of course, were propaganda, intended to sway international policymakers into a rosy view of American prospects and wariness of American strength. But Franklin's more confidential remarks were not that different in tone except for one threat to the nation that he saw as paramount to all others. To the congressional secretary, Charles Thomson, Franklin expressed his opinion that upholding foreign agreements was the highest priority of the young Republic: "If we do not convince the World that we are a Nation to be depended on for Fidelity in Treaties; if we appear negligent in paying our Debts, and ungrateful to those who have served and befriended us; our Reputation, and all the Strength it is capable of procuring, will be lost."[57]

On the eve of the opening of the Constitutional Convention, *The American Museum,* the most influential periodical of its day, printed on its first page the text of General Washington's farewell letter that he submitted to all the state governors in June of 1783. Its republication at this pivotal moment was clearly calculated to influence the delegates and focus attention on the problems facing the union that the great general said were "of greatest importance" four years earlier.

Washington warned that the United States had arrived at a historic junction and faced a choice of the highest importance, a question that would

determine the "destiny of unborn millions" to come. What made this moment so critical? What caused him to ring all his alarm bells and prophesy
that the upcoming debate over the powers of the federal government would
"establish or ruin their national character forever"? Reading carefully into
his language reveals that his primary concern was the relationship of the
states to foreign governments, which determined the limits of the federal
government's control over foreign policy. The nation's ability to conduct its
foreign affairs in unity hung in the balance. Not granting the federal government additional powers was tantamount to "annihilating the cement of
the confederation" by "exposing us to become the sport of European politics, which may play one state against another, to prevent their growing
importance, and to serve their own interested purposes."

Applying his astute strategic mind to this problem, Washington laid out
his prescription for a remedy, warning that unless these steps were followed,
"everything must rapidly tend to anarchy and confusion." First, the states
had to "suffer congress to exercise those prerogatives they are undoubtedly
invested with, by the constitution." This required recognizing that Congress
had "a supreme power to regulate and govern the general concerns of the
confederated republic," and, conversely, "there must be a faithful and pointed
compliance, on the part of every state," with Congress's rulings and acts.

Among these measures, Washington detailed "but one or two, which
seem to me of the greatest importance." At the top of his list was the issue
of "treaties of the European powers, with the united states of America,"
followed closely by the problem of raising revenues from the states (which
were needed to fund soldiers' pay and pensions).[58]

The American Museum's editor reinforced Washington's emphasis on the
importance of allowing the federal government full control over foreign affairs by reprinting in the next column the circular sent from Congress to all
the state governors the previous month, demanding the repeal of those laws
in violation of the provisional treaty of peace with England. These demands
famously proved ineffectual.[59] This was followed by Lord Carmarthen's response to John Adams's request that all British posts be handed over from
the previous year. (Carmarthen answered curtly that Britain would do so

"when America shall manifest a real determination to fulfil her part of the treaty" followed by a state-by-state rundown of all the confiscatory laws passed in response to England's harboring of escapees from slavery.[60]

Later in the same issue, "Z" described clearly what the root issue was that the convention needed to rectify. All the country's problems began when "the several states began to exercise the sovereign and absolute right of treating the recommendations of congress with contempt." For Z there was one obvious example of this: "we have seen the great federal head of our union clothed with the authority of making treaties, without the power of fulfilling them."

Many people had suggested all manner of schemes of reorganizing Congress, including some who proposed simply doing away with the states altogether. But Z noted that all such "schemes, like many others, with which we have been amused in times past, will be found to be merely visionary, and produce no lasting benefit." The reason for this was evident: "The error is not in the form of congress. . . . The source of all our misfortunes is evidently in the want of sufficient power in congress." Z proposed allowing the states to legislate on "local and internal" matters but giving entirely to Congress "those things which alike concern all the states, such as our foreign trade, and foreign transactions," along with the "power of enforcing their regulations."[61]

Another columnist, an "Honest Cheerful Citizen" of Boston, published an essay on the faults of the current Congress that the upcoming convention could remedy and, like so many others, identified the need for supremacy in upholding foreign obligations as paramount. "Congress must be vested with larger powers—powers to carry into effect their requisitions, and fully to regulate commerce. . . . When congress have plenary power to support the national faith and honour, by wise measures—to do justice to foreign and domestic creditors—to regulate trade, without being counteracted by any partial adjustments of particular states—then commerce will flourish; all nations will seek to trade with us; we shall have a ready market, and a good price."[62]

Only a few months before the opening of the Constitutional Convention, Madison wrote to Edmund Randolph his assessment of the state of national politics. He listed what he saw as the most "interesting measures" that he expected Congress to tackle. They were, first, the question of the Mississippi, by which he meant the many issues related to the western territories, which notably required coming to diplomatic agreement with Spain. Second, the lingering issues regarding the peace treaty with Great Britain, namely, that "infractions on the part of the U.S. preceded in several instances even the violation on the other side in the instance of the Negroes." Madison recognized that the only lever Congress could pull to try and effect change was the weak one of moral suasion, a mere "summons of the States to remove all legal impediments which stand at present in the way."

Madison then discussed the "proposed Convention in May." Though he did not say it explicitly, his framing linked the British treaty, the "carried off negro" question, and the coming Constitutional Convention. They were closely connected, as obtaining recognition of the supremacy of foreign treaties over state laws and some legal mechanism to enforce this principle was clearly the only way to conduct foreign policy, especially at a moment in time when the future of the young nation depended heavily on careful and delicate diplomatic negotiations.[63]

Three days later, Madison repeated many of the same points in a letter to George Washington, though now he listed the priority of business facing the Congress as "1. Treaty of peace . . . I find what I was not before apprized of that more than one infraction on our part, preceded even the violation of the other side in the instance of the Negroes." His second "object" was "the proposed Convention in May." Madison noted with satisfaction that he had heard that the "mutiny" in Massachusetts was "nearly extinct."[64]

Madison's anxiety about the fate of the republic continued to rise, and a few days later, in another letter to Edmund Pendleton, he noted that "men of reflection [are] much less sanguine as to the new than despondent as to the present System." The current structure of government lacked powers to coerce states to fulfill their duties and to adhere to federal law: "no respect is paid to the federal authority," and unless "some very strong props are applied will quickly tumble to the ground."[65] A month later, Madison's tone in a letter to Jefferson was much the same: congressional ranks were too "thin" to undertake the needed business at hand, foremost being the report of

Secretary of Foreign Affairs Jay on the violations by both parties of the provisional peace treaty. Madison approved of Jay's report on the British treaty, which he thought asserted that "the Treaty having been constitutionally formed is the law of the land, and urges a repeal of all laws contravening it, as well to stop the complaints of their existing as legal impediments, as to avoid needless questions touching their validity." Madison did not have to highlight that the federal government's having to "urge" the repeal of state laws by sending a circular to offending states requesting them to do so was not the action of a powerful central government.[66]

Ultimately, Madison not only wished to protect the national government's authority by establishing executive and judicial branches of government, he wanted them to have a veto over state laws just as the king's councils had over colonial bills. Tellingly, when Madison provided examples of the sorts of pernicious legislation this would prevent, his mind immediately gravitated to the states' trampling of the Treaty of Paris: "Without this defensive power, every positive power that can be given on paper will be evaded & defeated. The States will continue to invade the national jurisdiction, to violate treaties and the law of nations & to harrass each other with rival and spiteful measures dictated by mistaken views of interest."[67]

Washington responded to Madison's letter linking the debts and fugitives from slavery to the constitution in like manner. Washington candidly observed that the federal system needed a complete overhaul rather than mere amendments and trimming around the edges.[68] It was likely Washington's military mind that allowed him to see clearly that the republic's problems required not specific grants of power to remedy, but power itself. "I confess however that my opinion of public virtue is so far changed that I have my doubts whether any system without the means of coercion in the Sovereign, will enforce obedience to the Ordinances of a Genl Government; without which, every thing else fails." He then offered a few examples of ordinances requiring obedience: the reluctance of states to pay their shares of the federal budget and the states' failing to abide by the terms of the treaty of peace, singling out New York and Massachusetts for their confiscations of loyalists' property.

Resistance to the calling of the Constitutional Convention came mostly from northern states (referred to at the time as the "eastern states"), who were protective of their own existing powers and autonomy. Congressman William Irvine observed as much in a letter to James Wilson: "It was with some difficulty Congress carried the recommendation for a Convention. the Eastern Delegates were all much against the measure, indeed I think they would never have come into it, but that they saw it would be carried without them, then they Joined."[69] Connecticut's representative William Samuel Johnson thought the proposed convention was "a very doubtful Measure at best."[70] New York's Rufus King noted the enthusiasm of southerners for the convention, saying that "many well disposed men from Southern States" would attend, but then used nearly the same words as Johnson to describe it: "What the Convention may do at Philadelphia is very doubtful . . . my fears are by no means inferior to my Hopes on this subject."[71]

William Grayson, though an enslaving Virginian, did not think the upcoming convention would do much, "I believe the whole will terminate in nothing." Grayson's reasoning was that "the more slack the government the better the people like it: of course they will not give up any power, which will prevent them from being compelled to make satisfaction to their Creditors." But Grayson was an astute listener and told an overseas friend that some of the delegates he had spoken with seemed "for going a great way: some of them are for placing Congress *in loco* of the King of the G.B.—besides their present powers." Grayson, however, thought such talk fantastical: "Figure to yourself how the States will relish the idea of a negative on their laws."[72]

While Grayson, seemingly a natural pessimist, remained skeptical that the upcoming convention could accomplish anything, he did put his finger directly on the problem that needed to be solved, a problem highlighted by the fiasco with Britain. Americans, he hoped, "will eer long . . . see the folly of a weak disjointed nation contracting with a strong one, who can explain the contract as he pleases."[73]

In late February of 1787, Jay wrote to his diplomat in London, John Adams, about the slow and halting movement for revising the powers of the federal government. Jay described what he saw as "the Changes which ought to take place," and these required more than reforming or amending the powers of the current Congress. Rather, an entirely new structure was required: "It is hard to say what those Changes should be exactly.—There is one however which I think would be much for the better, Vizt. to distribute the federal Sovereignty into its three proper Departments of executive, legislative and judicial, for that Congress should act in these different capacities was I think a great Mistake in our Policy."

Within the same paragraph, and immediately after offering this insight, Jay brought up the recent action of New York's legislature in repealing some of its laws disenfranchising and discriminating against loyalists. Jay commented, "I hope all Discriminations inconsistent with the Treaty of Peace will gradually be abolished, as Resentment gives place to Reason and good Faith." So, in Jay's mind, the prospect of calling a "Convention" to restructure the national government was connected to the long-running issue of states ignoring Congress and its treaties to seize Tory property and discharge debts to England.[74]

As the Constitutional Convention drew nearer, the problems exposed by the treaty controversies clarified both the stakes involved and the changes that would be required to avert disaster. In many cases the documentary record is a kinked chain with broken links, and the lines between the archived attitudes of founders and their actions in the convention do not tightly connect. In the case of congressman and future Supreme Court jurist James Wilson, there is at least one patriot who said the problem was the failure of Britain to uphold the Paris treaty by returning the enslaved and then did something about it in Philadelphia.

In January of 1786, James Wilson, who was also one of the directors of the Bank of North America, the first bank chartered by Congress, gave a highly publicized speech in defense of his bank to the Pennsylvania legislature, which was considering a bill to revoke its state incorporation. In just a few months Wilson would take his seat in the convention that would draft the nation's new constitution. Wilson stood in the state house chamber and began: "The present is an awful crisis in the American history. It is a matter of doubt whether we shall long continue to enjoy the peace we are in at present. Has the treaty been fulfilled in all its essential parts? Have the negroes been delivered up? Have the posts been surrendered?"[75]

The founders' conviction that the states had allowed their legislatures to accumulate what Alexander Hamilton termed an "excess of democracy" was the tipping point that led to restructuring the nation's fundamental law because such "excess democracy" made it impossible to conduct foreign affairs in a world of hostile and competing empires. In the days following the conclusion of the Philadelphia convention, Madison observed that it was particularly the "flagrant" "evils issuing" from state legislatures that "contributed more to that uneasiness which produced the Convention, and prepared the public mind for a general reform, than those which accrued to our national character and interest from the inadequacy of the Confederation to its immediate objects." So thoroughly did Madison think the state legislatures required checks and balances that he had unsuccessfully pushed during the convention for a specific federal veto over all state laws.[76]

While Madison was also deeply troubled by laws emitting paper currency and frustrating foreclosures of property, he seems to have viewed the state laws that conflicted with treaties to be the more pressing issue facing the delegates who would draft the constitution. Indeed, while a member of the Virginia assembly, Madison himself voted for a measure that would allow Virginians to pay their taxes with tobacco rather than specie. When Madison reminded his fellow Virginian Jefferson of "our own experience both during the war and since the peace" when states were too solicitous of popular moods and passed unwise laws, he termed these "Encroachments of the States on the general authority, sacrifices of national to local interests," pointing to laws that conflicted with federal authority rather than those that were, in his view, the unwise rule of the mob, but still local matters. Madison's fellow legislator William Grayson either reflected or stoked Madison's growing concerns about the treaty power when he wrote him the year before the Constitutional Convention complaining of "the striking impropriety of the interference of States as to the construction of a treaty in any case whatever."[77]

Madison's fixation with the problem of state legislatures trampling over federal powers is evident in the notes he accumulated that he eventually organized into a memorandum he titled "The Vices of the Political System of the U. States." In this outline, Madison listed twelve vices of the present Confederation government that had to be reformed. "Encroachments by the States on the federal authority" and "Violations of the law of nations and of treaties" ranked second and third on Madison's twelve-point list, trailing behind only "Failure of the States to comply with the Constitutional requisitions."[78]

The convention opened with its bare quorum on a Friday and occupied most of the day with organizing itself and delegating Charles Pinckney along with George Wythe and Alexander Hamilton to draft rules for their proceedings. Monday's session was again filled with credential-scrutinizing and rules-making. It was not until the next afternoon that anything of true importance occurred. Edmund Randolph rose and listed the problems the nation faced: "commercial discord" existed between the states, "rebellion" in Massachusetts, foreign debts had become "urgent," paper money created "havoc," and treaties had been "violated." The root of all of these lay in the "defects" of the present confederation. Interestingly, most of the "defects" Randolph proceeded to describe were connected to Congress's lack of power to force the states to respect foreign treaties: "First, that the Confederation produced no security against foreign invasion. . . . Of this he cited many examples; most of which tended to shew, that they could not cause infractions of treaties, or of the law of nations to be punished; that particular States might by their conduct provoke war without control; and that, neither militia nor drafts being fit for defence on such occasions, enlistments only could be successful, and these could not be executed without money."[79]

Randolph's list of faults continued through several more points, most of these having to do with Congress's lack of power over the states: that the federal government could not resolve a "quarrel between the states," "defend itself against encroachments from the States," or put down a rebellion within them because it did not have "means to impose according to the exigency." Congress did not need more powers, it just needed more power.

Randolph then proposed the plan that he and the other Virginians, Madison and James McClurg, had agreed upon—that the Articles of Confederation should be "corrected and enlarged." He proposed fifteen revisions, including splitting Congress into two houses, the lower house proportioned by population ("free inhabitants" or a "rule [as] may seem best"), and the members of the second house to be elected by the other. Randolph's plan added executive and judiciary branches, and a "Council of Revision" that was empowered to overrule state laws. Except for the tripartite frame of government with its bicameral legislature, nothing in this so-called "Virginia Plan" looked anything like the government that would be hammered out over the next three months.

Immediately upon Randolph taking his seat, Charles Pinckney rose to introduce his plan of government. While Randolph's speech is only known in outline from Madison's notes (though Madison revised his notes with a summary Randolph later provided), Pinckney's rhetoric is preserved.

Perhaps he felt entitled and piqued because he could not hold the floor and deliver all of his planned speech, or maybe he was just a rule-breaker, but Pinckney, who had written the rules, which included utter secrecy both during and after the convention, published the speech he was not able to finish almost immediately after the convention closed. It is, if as billed, one of the few verbatim records of remarks delivered on the convention floor. Pinckney began by reviewing why they were there in the first place: "It is, perhaps, unnecessary to state to the House the reasons which have given rise to this Convention." Which, of course, meant he would, and the reasons he highlighted all pointed to the trouble with the British and the enslaved people they sheltered: "There is no one, I believe, who doubts there is something particularly alarming in the present conjuncture. There is hardly a man, in, or out of office, who holds any other language. Our government is despised—our laws are robbed of their respected terrors—their inaction is a subject of ridicule—and their exertion, of abhorrence and opposition—rank and office have lost their reverence and effect—our foreign politics are as much deranged, as our domestic economy—our friends are slackened in their affection,—and our citizens loosened from their obedience."[80]

It is not difficult to locate the causes of America's "deranged" foreign politics, its "despised" government with its "inaction" and ignored laws. The federal government was simply "destitute of that force and energy, without which, no government can exist." As that government currently consisted of nothing more than a national legislature, dependent on its constituent governments to carry out its will, it "might therefore to be said, in some measure, to be under the control of the State legislatures." While not men-tioning the issue of the "carried off" directly, Pinckney alluded to it in a way that everyone in the chamber would have understood. The "laws of the several States" had "interfered" with Congress's "objects or operations."

Step by logical step, Pinckney marched to his radical conclusion: the whole charter needed to be scrapped and the structure of both state and federal governments needed to be reinvented. Unlike Randolph's Virginia Plan, whose suggested fifteen amendments to the existing Articles presented the appearance of improving rather scrapping the original, Pinckney boldly stated what everyone in the room knew was happening. The old government was being overturned.

Like Randolph's plan, Pinckney envisioned a bicameral legislature and a government with three branches.[81] Peppered throughout Pinckney's list of governmental powers were mechanisms that, had they existed a few years earlier, would have prevented the breakdown of the Peace of the Paris. Where the old Articles merely attempted to restrain states from trespassing on federal prerogatives ("No State shall lay any imposts or duties, which may interfere with any stipulations in treaties"), Pinckney's plan clearly stated the legal supremacy of treaties, created a federal judiciary, and re-quired federal judges to interpret them that way. Of course, these were just legal principles, the real power came from the business end of a gun. Pinck-ney vested authority in the federal government to nationalize state militia, an authority necessary because, as he explained publicly, militia "are in fact the only adequate force the Union possess, if any should be requisite to coerce a refractory or negligent Member, and to carry the Ordinances and Decrees of Congress into execution."[82]

Randolph's detailing of the faults of the confederation began with those related to its inability to enforce its international agreements upon the states. The first evil of the present charter was "1st It does not provide against foreign invasions." This reads as though he was referring to some weakness of the common defense, such as Congress's perennial difficulty in raising troops and provisions from the states. But when Randolph ex-plained in more detail what he meant by this, it became clear that he was referring specifically to the problem of states not respecting the treaties that

Congress had agreed to: "If a State acts against a foreign power contrary to the laws of nations or violates a treaty, it cannot punish that State, or compel its obedience to a treaty. It can only leave the offending State to the operations of the offended power. It therefore cannot prevent a war. . . . A State may encroach on foreign possessions in its neighbourhood and Congress cannot prevent it."[83]

Randolph's insistence on the "absolute necessity of a more energetic government" required a radical reengineering of the basic structures of both Congress and the states. From the outset, Randolph "candidly confessed" that his fifteen resolutions "were not intended for a federal government," by which he meant a confederation as then existed, but that he "meant a strong *consolidated* union, in which the idea of the states should be nearly annihilated." Charles Pinckney then read his "ideas of a new government," and when he was finished "confessed that it was grounded on the same principle" as Randolph's.[84]

What is most significant at these early, indeed opening steps of the convention, is that the idea of trashing the existing structure of the confederation so as to vest more powers in the national government was approved with relatively little debate or controversy. Randolph's plan's first test came two days later when Delaware's George Read and South Carolina's General C. C. Pinckney, Charles's more conservative cousin, tried to water down its defining element, the supremacy of the federal government, by dropping the word "supreme" from Randolph's motion "Resolved, that a national government ought to be established consisting of a supreme legislative, judiciary and executive." The general asked Randolph if it was his intention to "annihilate state governments?" Randolph replied, "only so far as the powers intended to be granted to the new government should clash with the states, when the latter was to yield."[85]

General Pinckney, along with Massachusetts's Elbridge Gerry, was reluctant to consider refashioning the whole system because he thought this overstepping their charge. Pierce Butler initially shared these hesitations but swung over quickly to Randolph's view when he realized these new awesome powers would not be gathered into one body but divided between different branches of government.[86] In the end, Read and General Pinckney's attempt to preserve state sovereignty failed badly on a vote of six states to one (with one other delegation divided).[87]

Two days later the details of the powers of the legislative branch were debated, and it was agreed on the first reading that Congress would have the power to "negative all laws passed by the several States contravening in the opinion of the national legislature the articles of union." Benjamin Franklin, certainly drawing on his experience returning home from Paris after concluding a successful treaty of peace with England, only to find it subverted and disregarded by several states, including his own, offered the following addition: "or any treaty subsisting under the authority of the union." Franklin's proposal was adopted without "debate or dissent."[88]

After Randolph and Charles Pinckney's framework was agreed upon, Wilson noted that the "true reason why G. Britain has not yet listened to a commercial treaty with us has been, because she had no confidence in the stability or efficacy of our Government." He then argued for longer terms for Senators so that America would project the stability and continuity needed to convince foreign powers to trust its international commitments. Questions of foreign relations drove the fleshing out of the federal structure. "Every nation may be regarded in two relations 1. to its own citizens. 2 to foreign nations." Wilson thought the Senate the best instrument to secure such relations and, as such, "ought therefore to be made respectable in the eyes of foreign Nations."[89]

Perhaps one of the reasons that the importance of the issue of international treaties in the making of the U.S. Constitution has been largely overlooked is that it provoked so little controversy and was settled so quickly at the outset of the meeting. The swift adoption of the Virginia Plan, which revolutionized all levels of government by vesting the federal sphere with both legal supremacy and the means to enforce it, impoverished the documentary record by leaving much unsaid.

The same was true when the delegates quickly and largely without debate agreed to deny states the power to provide sanctuary to those fleeing slavery in other states. More than any other provision of the Constitution, the so-called Fugitive Slave Clause nationalized slavery by implicating every state in the policing and enforcing of slavery as long as there was one state that protected the idea of human property in its laws. Not only was this clause a powerful protection for slavery, it was a novel addition to America's governmental system, as the existing Articles of Confederation contained no such specific language (though, as George Van Cleve points out, the expansive wording of its Privileges and Immunities Clause accomplished the same purpose).[90]

It was late in August when C. C. Pinckney rose to demand that an additional "provision should be included in favor of property in slaves," and his fellow delegates from South Carolina, Pierce Butler and his cousin Charles moved that a clause requiring the interstate return of fugitives be amended to "require slaves and servants to be delivered up like criminals." Only two northerners pushed back, James Wilson of Pennsylvania objecting to the public expense of hunting runaways, and Roger Sherman of Connecticut, who "saw no more propriety in the public seizing and surrendering a slave or servant, than a horse."[91] In short order, the clause stating "If any Person bound to service or labor in any of the United States shall escape into another State, He or She shall not be discharged from such service or labor in consequence of any regulations subsisting in the State to which they escape; but shall be delivered up to the person justly claiming their service or labor" was adopted by a vote of eleven to none.[92]

If ever there was a glaring example of what William Wiecek called the "Federal Consensus," the general agreement that slavery must be supported where it was established in law, this is it. While it was slavery-state southerners who called for the addition of a clause expressly guaranteeing the return of their fugitive human property, it was northerners who crafted its language. Ironically, it was northerners who worded this clause so as to avoid all mention of the word slavery. The wording was borrowed from a provision of the draft of the Northwest Ordinance authored by Massachusetts's Rufus King that guaranteed that none of the western territories created by this law would provide sanctuary to runaways from slavery. King, it should be noted, served simultaneously as a member of Congress and a delegate to the Philadelphia convention. Moreover, the committee that voted to include this fugitive clause in Article VI of the Northwest Ordinance was chaired by another Yankee from Massachusetts, Nathan Dane.[93]

When the convention was finally adjourned, Madison wrote a famous and lengthy summary of its achievements and failures to Jefferson in Paris. At one point, Madison ruminated upon the factors that had led up to the convention and surmised that it was the lack of a "constitutional negative on the laws of the States" that made it happen: "The mutability of the laws of the States is found to be a serious evil. The injustice of them has been so frequent and so flagrant as to alarm the most stedfast friends of Republicanism. I am persuaded I do not err in saying that the evils issuing from these sources contributed more to that uneasiness which produced the Convention, and prepared the public mind for a general reform, than those which accrued to our national character and interest from the inadequacy of the confederation to its immediate objects."

While these remarks could indicate that Madison was referring to the sort of stay laws and paper money pushed by poor farmers that infringed upon the rights of merchants and bankers, they could equally reflect the long record of states trampling on Congress's ratified Treaty of Paris. While Madison certainly viewed the sort of populist debtor laws the Shaysites demanded in Massachusetts as trampling on individual rights, they did not necessarily violate federal prerogatives the way that loyalist confiscation laws did, and in other portions of his letter Madison seemed far more concerned with such transgressions.

Madison began his letter by noting that no delegate had suggested dividing the nation, or what Madison termed "a partition of the Empire," and then immediately headlined what he must have seen as the convention's greatest work: overcoming the "evil of imperia in imperio," the "encroachments of the States on the general authority" that had been "a great part of the history of our political system." At least, he observed, it "was generally agreed that the objects of the Union could not be secured by any system founded on the principle of a confederation of sovereign States" or the "voluntary observance of the federal law by all the members." While Madison fell short in pulling the body toward granting the federal government a veto over state laws, he took comfort that the central government was strengthened and, at last, given *power*.[94]

It was just this prospect of enhanced centralized power that could shield

against the enticing away of their human property that swung southern enslavers to support of the Constitution. One Virginian linked all these issues
together in a letter he sent a friend in Scotland:

> We are at present in a very miserable situation; neither money nor credit to be
> had. I have tried to sell all my landed property on purpose to pay my debts; but
> I cannot get it sold unless for credit, and then I could not recover the money.
>
> Our Assembly has been sitting ever since last October. They have agreed
> to pay the British debts as soon as Britain will deliver up the western forts,
> and pay for the negroes carried off, &c. We are to have a Convention in May
> next, which, I hope, will give full powers to Congress, otherwise Virginia will
> be forever lost, or torn to pieces by one another, and it is only by giving full
> power to Congress that will save us from destruction.[95]

Similar sentiments were expressed by Governor Randolph in his grand
oration to the Virginia assembly on the importance of ratification. "The
Confederation . . . on which we are told we ought to trust our safety, is totally void of coercive power and energy. Of this the people of America have
been long convinced; and this conviction has been sufficiently manifest to
the world. . . . The General Government ought to be vested with powers
competent to our safety, or else the necessary consequence must be, that we
shall be defenceless."

The issue of the "carried off" had by this time grown so knotty that both
sides, federalists and anti-federalists, could find ways to weld it to their
cause. James Monroe, for example, argued that the British posed no threat
to American interests that required such drastic reshaping of the government. Curiously, his example of British amity was their dispute over disposition of the "negroes which had been carried away contrary to the treaty."
While conceding that Britain "committed the first breach" of the treaty, he
did not think this amounted to a "hostile intention towards us" because "a
compliance with the treaty on our part must precede it on theirs."[96]

Likewise, others chiefly interested in how a resolution of the issue of
carried-off fugitives would harm the financial interests of those indebted to
British merchants were swayed to oppose the Constitution because a more

powerful GENERAL government would force southerners to pay up. Archibald Maclaine, writing as "Publicola" in the *State Gazette* of North Carolina warned, "There is an objection made to the new constitution, which I believe originated in this state. . . . It is I believe a very powerful reason with many among us, for opposing any alterations in the federal government; in some from mistaken zeal, in others from interested motives.—The objection is this—that if the new government takes place, the debts due to British subjects will be recoverable." Maclaine was unsympathetic to these arguments and bemoaned that such had "given a plausible pretext for one breach on the part of the British, and for not making compensations for another."[97]

Likewise, South Carolinian David Ramsey explained to Yankee general Benjamin Lincoln at the time that his state had begun to favor ratifying the Constitution because Carolinians had come to believe that "Eastern states can soonest help us in case of invasion." Ramsey particularly praised Massachusetts's delegates for agreeing to a twenty-year moratorium on legal restrictions on the human trade. "Your delegates never did a more political thing than in standing by those of South Carolina about negroes."[98]

British consul Phineas Bond observed these developments with great satisfaction and optimism. Clearly a diplomat who kept his ear close to the ground, by that July Bond had caught news of some of the doings in Independence Hall. He wrote Lord Carmarthen about what he learned they were doing behind closed doors: "nothing is known with accuracy but that their drift is to endeavour to form such a federal constitution, as will give energy and consequence to the union. Whether this is to be done by improving the old governments or by substituting new ones—whether by continuing a power in each State to regulate its internal policy, or to abolish all separate establishments, and to form one grand federal authority, is a matter of consideration which creates much doubt and animadversion."[99]

Bond sent Carmarthen a copy of the freshly drafted U.S. Constitution on September 20, 1787.[100] As it became clear that the requisite number of states would ratify and that the Constitution would go into force, Bond hailed it as a boon for the United States: "It will be a fortunate thing for this country and for those whose interests are connected with it to enjoy a system of Government whose energy may correct the present relaxed situation of the laws and restore public faith and private credit."[101]

Bond, having compiled the most complete inventory of state laws that violated the Treaty of Paris on either side of the Atlantic, kept note that with the public promulgation of the draft U.S. Constitution, state legislatures began repealing their old laws that conflicted with the treaty. Even New York's legislature reversed itself after the Constitutional Convention was concluded, and on February 22, 1788, it passed a bill repealing all laws conflicting with the treaty of peace. Virginia's House of Delegates passed a similar measure on December 12, 1787. Ten days later North Carolina proclaimed the peace treaty "to be part of the law of the land."[102]

Though Virginia had hedged its bets by predicating its act of repeal on Britain giving up the forts and "delivering up the negroes belonging to the citizens of this State," Bond could happily report that "The establishment of judiciary courts under the New Constitution promises some relief in the controul of local laws which press hard upon the interests of British creditors and in correcting a system of delay which has been highly oppressive: indeed my Lord if a more summary mode of proceeding in the recovery of Brit: debts does not prevail the spirit of the Treaty of Peace cannot be said to be fulfilled—some more expeditious mode seems essentially necessary to secure the debts already subsisting and to put the future com. intercourse between the two countries upon any tolerable footing of certainty."[103]

America's new constitution had just been ratified when Lord Grenville, whose London office oversaw "colonial affairs," dispatched a special emissary to New York to discuss future commercial agreements. Lieutenant-Colonel George Beckwith arrived in New York as the federal government was just preparing for its first meeting of Congress. Beckwith knew the city well, as he had served under General Carleton during his time preparing for the evacuation of soldiers, loyalists, and refugees from American slavery from the city.

Beckwith was unable to meet with America's new secretary of state, Thomas Jefferson, who had not yet returned from France, so instead he arranged a series of meetings with Alexander Hamilton, the secretary of the treasury. Hamilton assured Beckwith that he spoke for "the most enlightened men in the this country" and that his views were also "those of General Washington . . . as well as of a great majority in the Senate." More importantly, Hamilton emphasized that he spoke for a central government that now had the power to enforce its will upon the states and was a reliable partner to any agreements the two countries would reach. "We have lately established a Government upon principles, that in my opinion render it safe for any nation to enter into Treaties with us . . . which has not hitherto been the case," he boasted.

The two men spoke extensively of trade policies and the future of their respective "empires," but Hamilton soon cautioned the English emissary that there were still outstanding issues to be settled from the old treaty of peace. "There are two points only that occur to me as being complained of," Hamilton said. He then explained that the laws confiscating English property and disadvantaging English creditors were effectively "done away by the present Government" with the "formation and establishment of its Judiciary branch" and the organization of a "supreme court very shortly."

Having established that those British complaints would soon be swept away by the powers of the new federal system, Hamilton then pivoted to America's complaints, of which there were only two. "On our side there are also two points still unadjusted, the Western Forts and the Negroes." Hamilton then confided in Beckwith that personally he approved of General Carleton's policy, saying, "To have given up these men to their masters, after the assurance of protection held out to them, was impossible." The official summary of Beckwith's memoranda of these discussions, prepared for dispatch to London, omitted Hamilton's support of London's sanctuary policy and simply read that "a government is now established in the United States with which it is safe to enter into treaties" and that the conversation added some other "considerations respecting the confiscation and other Acts, the cession of the western posts, and the giving up of negroes."[104]

Hamilton's frank conversation with Beckwith revealed that in the mind of this leading Federalist the strong central government had all along been propelled by the necessity for this young, aspiring nation to play the great game of empire by upholding its agreements. Congress's failure and paralysis in enforcing the terms of its most important international agreement—the one that recognized its sovereignty and independence, secured its trade, and opened the door to the conquest of a vast hinterland—had been brightly illuminated by the tangle of patriot demands knotted around British refusals to hand over the men and women under their protection, and their popular retaliation against English Tories and merchants in response.

Patriot leaders had only a short time to bask in the glory of their great constitutional achievement before the seemingly greater power of the new federal government had to test itself in the hard truths of the diplomatic world. Almost immediately newfound contradictions of this power were exposed by the new centralized governments' renewed efforts to recapture the long lost fugitives from American slavery.

FIVE

Jay's Treaty and
the Politics of Recapture

In the span of the decade between the end of the War for Independence and the signing of the peace treaty with England, none of America's famed diplomats had succeeded in forcing the Crown to either relinquish the thousands of African Americans it sheltered or to pay restitution to their former owners. Public concern with Article 7 of the Treaty of Paris seemed to have waned once the U.S. Constitution was ratified and George Washington took his oath of office as the nation's first president. But the absence of congressional debate, petitions, or street protests did not signify that the issue had burned out, only that its coals smoldered, waiting for new air to blaze forth. While there was little public discussion of the issue in the years since the time of various meetings to debate ratification of the Constitution, Article 7 remained a frequent topic at the highest levels of government.

England's diplomatic agent in Philadelphia, Phineas Bond, was a careful observer of American politics and attitudes. In the spring of 1791, he sent to his superior, the Duke of Leeds, a clear-eyed breakdown of the partisan landscape. America's federal government was divided between three factions. The New England states had a commercial interest in barring English vessels from carrying the trade of the United States. Southern states had the opposite interest, as they were "desirous of participating in the Benefits of our carrying Trade" with England "by whose Merchants they are well served, whose Manufactures they prefer, & whose Credit affords them a Convenience, they can not look for elsewhere." Against both were a nationalist "third Party, unactuated by Motives of local Benefit" whose primary concern was establishing the "Credit of the Country" and the "Revenue of the Country" to better the "Circumstances of the People."

Given this distribution of interests, Bond warned that the incoming Congress would "favor a commercial Connexion with France" and that this tendency was worsened by the lingering issue of the fugitives from slavery carried off nearly a decade earlier. "Already my Lord, the Refusal of Great Britain to make Compensation for the Slaves, taken from the southern States, has been pressed, with no small address, upon the Minds of the Southern Members, as an Act of national Injustice—& some without duly considering the broad Ground Great Britain stands on, in this Respect, have suffered this Refusal to reconcile them to Regulations, which they, heretofore, reprobated, as militating against the Interest & Convenience of the States they represent."[1]

Bond's analysis proved accurate, and when he was recalled and the first British ambassador to the United States of America under its new constitution, George Hammond, arrived in Philadelphia on October 21, 1791, the issue of the "carried off" continued to haunt negotiations.[2] Hammond was well versed in the history of the negotiations that had produced the disputed Treaty of Paris, as he had previously served as David Hartley's secretary while he concluded its negotiations with the American delegation. In this, Jefferson was at a disadvantage, as he did not participate in the treaty's deliberations.

Jefferson and Hammond had vastly different priorities. Hammond's first order of business was to press the case of Thomas Pagan, a British subject languishing in Boston's debtor prison after being found liable for damages caused by a war privateer he had owned. Boston's judges ruled it was a simple case of debt, while the Crown viewed it as a violation of international maritime law and the standing peace treaty. (Jefferson and other national leaders refused to intervene in the case.) Jefferson's priority was to complain that England had not yet addressed the matter of the those "carried off" and the forts still garrisoned.[3] "In recalling your attention to the Seventh article of the Definitive Treaty of Peace . . . I need not observe to you that this article still remains in a state of inexecution. . . . Permit me then, Sir, to ask whether you are instructed to give us explanations of the intentions of your court as to the execution of the article above quoted?"[4]

When Jefferson brought up the issue of "carry away any Negroes," Hammond replied curtly: "With respect to the non-execution of the seventh article . . . which you have recalled to my attention, it is scarcely necessary for me to remark to you, Sir, that the King my master was induced to suspend the execution of that article on his part, in consequence of the non-compliance, on the part of the United States."[5]

Jefferson resolved then to set his clerks to compiling a file of reports documenting the true state of American and British compliance with the treaty. Assuring Hammond that he wished to "lessen difficulties, by passing over whatever is of smaller concern, and insisting on those matters only which either justice to individuals, or public policy render indispensable," Jefferson thought the each of them should "begin by specifying, on each side, the particular acts which each considers to have been done by the other in contravention of the treaty." He thought to "set the example" by beginning, and his first complaint was of the "carried off" and the forts, writing that:

> On withdrawing the troops from New York, 1. a large embarcation of negroes, of the property of the inhabitants of the U.S. took place, before the Commissioners, on our part, for inspecting and superintending embarcations had arrived there, and without any account ever rendered thereof. 2. Near three thousand others were publicly carried away by the avowed order of the British commanding officer, and under the view and against the remonstrances of our Commissioners: 3. a very great number were carried off in private vessels, if not by the express permission, yet certainly without opposition on the part of the commanding officer, who alone had the means of preventing it, and without admitting the inspection of the American commissioners: and 4. of other species of property carried away.

According to America's highest diplomatic official, these were the most serious points of disagreement between the two nations. Everything else Jefferson termed "other smaller matters between the two nations" that he thought should be handled by "ordinary channel(s)" rather than "embarrass the present important discussions with them." Having set the example of specifying his grievances, Jefferson invited Hammond to do the same, asking which "particular acts" of the Americans were considered infringements of the treaty's fourth, fifth, and sixth articles.[6] It took Hammond and his clerks the entire winter to complete their inventory of American violations of the treaty. Meanwhile, having presided over the convention that created a strong executive and an independent federal judiciary that could exert a check on state's abilities to ignore duly ratified treaties, George Washington went on as president to assert these powers with vigor.

Recapturing runaways continued to be a priority for American foreign relations under the new constitution. The first treaty concluded under Washington's first administration required the Creek nation to return all escapees from slavery to their American owners. As negotiations with Spain continued over East Florida, the president instructed his diplomats to arrange for the recovery of all fugitives from slavery who sheltered within Spanish borders. Spanish officials had little interest in being America's slavery patrollers, so the American commissioner in St. Augustine offered to pay a St. Augustine jailor for his services and to provide bounties and payments to Spanish soldiers who assisted in conveying the recaptured men and women to American officials in Georgia.[7]

Under pressure from a coalition of international merchants and staple planters to finally secure a treaty with Great Britain that would open European markets to American goods carried in American ships, Washington interpreted his newfound license to conduct diplomacy in the most expansive terms. Washington chose to interpret the Senate's power to provide "Advice and Consent" to his treaty-making authority to mean only reviewing an agreement once it had been reached. Prior practice had long been that the Congress established a set of detailed instructions to guide diplomats in their talks and then later approved the agreements that had been signed.

Early in his administration Washington established an unofficial back channel to begin negotiations to settle the issues still lingering from the old peace treaty. Washington tapped Gouverneur Morris to act as his liaison and sent him secret instructions that included ascertaining what the British intended to do about the Americans' human property. Morris was to stress that the newly centralized federal structure should dispel all British doubts as to America's ability to uphold the agreements: "Your inquiries will commence by observing, that as the present Constitution of Government and the Courts established in pursuance of it remove the objections heretofore made to putting the United States in possession of their frontier posts, it is natural to expect from the assurances of his Majesty and the national good faith, that no unnecessary delays will take place." Washington then tied these developments to the lingering issue of the fugitives from slavery: "Remind them of the article by which it was agreed that negroes belonging to our Citizens should not be carried away; and of the reasonableness of making compensation for them. Learn with precision, if possible, what they mean to do on this head."[8]

Six months later Morris reported back on his discussions with the British minister for foreign affairs, the Duke of Leeds, at Whitehall. Morris had opened his meeting with the duke by reassuring him that the problems that had stymied American compliance with the treaty were now all overcome by the nation's new constitution. "I observed that by the Constitution of the United States which he had certainly read all Obstacles to the Recovery of british Debts are removed, and that if any Doubts could have remained they are now done away by the organization of a federal Court which has Cognizance of Causes arising under the Treaty," Morris reported. In fact, this was all yet theoretical, as few aggrieved loyalists had been compensated.

Morris then moved to his main concern, compensation for lost humans, dredging up Franklin's old argument that British seizure of American slaves had destroyed the means of repaying the very debts England now demanded. "[H]ere I took occasion to observe that the Southern States who had been much blamed in this Country for obstructing the Recovery of british Debts, were not liable to all the Severity of Censure which had been thrown upon them—that their Negroes having been taken or seduced away, and the Payment for those Negroes having been stipulated by Treaty they had formed a Reliance on such Payment for Discharge of Debts contracted with british merchants both previously and subsequently to the war." Up to this point in his nearly verbatim recounting of his conversation with the foreign secretary, Morris had not mentioned the issue of the western forts. When Morris finally turned to it, he wondered if it were possible that this issue had already been cleared up, admitting that he did not know if Washington had sent out orders to do just that, something Morris thought "very probable."

The duke reacted, Morris thought, "a little embarrassed" when he replied that he did not know exactly what orders had gone out to the fort commanders. As for "the affair of the Negroes," the duke said "he had long wished to have it brought up and to have Something done, but Something or other had always interfered."[9]

A few weeks later Morris advised Washington that prospects for settling these issues were dim. "I have some Reason to believe that the present administration intend to keep the Posts, and withhold Payment for the Negroes. If so they will color their Breach of Faith by the best Pretexts in their Power." Even the inducement of a new commercial treaty did not seem to interest his counterpart, as England seemed to have decided that the status quo was the most profitable alternative.[10]

Morris's backdoor diplomacy had reached an impasse until events handed the Americans a new lever to pry open negotiations. British warships had intercepted and boarded a number of American merchant ships and carried off seamen who they claimed were British citizens. Tasked with protesting to Whitehall, Morris was received not only by the foreign secretary but by Prime Minister William Pitt (the younger) as well. Morris used the occasion to raise the issue of the "carried off" again and, for the first time in the seven years of the two countries' negotiations, formally renounced any claims to the physical return of the escapees and demanded only payment. Morris expressed sympathy "for the Situation they were in of being obliged either to break Faith with the Slaves whom they had seduced by the Offer of Freedom, or to violate the Stipulations they had made with us upon that Subject." And, as a result, informed Pitt that "we were willing therefore to w[ave] our literal Claims, but had every Right to insist upon Compensation."[11]

The prime minister responded by pointing to the British debts that remained blocked by American states and suggested that it might be best if the two sides simply start over and negotiate a new treaty, rather than attempting to settle the old one. Morris then pushed the issue of compensation for evacuated fugitives again: "I said that even on that Ground I did not see what better could be done than to perform the old one—'as to the Compensation for Negroes taken away; it is too trifling an Object for you to dispute; so that Nothing remains but the Posts.'" Pitt did not give ground on either subject at this meeting, but in the coming days Morris heard from various informants that "it seemed probable that they would give up the Posts," and he assured Washington that "My Information is good."

Morris's assessment of the British government's posture was proved wrong by the swiftly shifting political situation in Europe. Revolution in France reshuffled the delicate latticework of alliances that governed an expanding colonial world system. In rapid succession the French Republic was declared, Louis XVI was beheaded, and war broke out between France and an alliance of Austria, Prussia, the Netherlands, and Britain. President Washington attempted to keep the United States out of the growing conflagration by tearing up its agreements with its closest ally, France, and suffering without response British seizures of American ships and sailors. Washington's policy of neutrality and passivity in the face of British provocations was rapidly dividing the nation into factions favoring either a pro-British or pro-French posture. The arrival of the new French minister from revolutionary France, Citizen Edmond-Charles Genet, exposed the depth of this political fracturing and gave opportunity for common citizens to demonstrate their newfound political allegiances in pro- and anti-Genet parades and "disorders."

Against this backdrop of looming questions of war, disunion, and economic collapse, the lingering issues from the Treaty of Paris, namely the wartime debts, the loyalist confiscations, and the uncompensated damages for liberated people, should have lapsed into relative obscurity. But surprisingly they lived on in the broadsheets of an expanding number of newspapers and journals and, most importantly, in the streets. "Agricola," writing in Richmond's *Virginia Gazette and General Advertiser*, aired these grievances in the fall of 1793:

> The government has now been in motion for more than five years and in the course of this time have permitted, and the courts been open, for the recovery of British Debts. . . . In fact, the treaty was executed by the adoption of the constitution, if it was ever violated before. But what has been the conduct of Great Britain in this respect during this same period of time? Have the posts been surrendered or the negroes paid for? The contrary is well known to be the case. . . . What then, under these circumstances, has been the conduct of the Executive? Has any bold or magnanimous council been suggested by that department to the legislature, or has even an example of that kind been exhibited to the community at large, which might inspire our citizens with a confidence in the wisdom and fortitude of our rulers?[12]

The puzzle of the resilience of this issue was solved in part by Alexander Hamilton, who wrote what was perhaps the most detailed and insightful confidential brief sent to President Washington at this crucial moment. Ongoing British seizures of American ships in the Caribbean was tipping Congress in favor of punitive actions against England, risking renewed war. Hamilton opened his letter with a warning: "The present is beyond question a great, a difficult & a perilous crisis in the affairs of this country." He apologized for submitting his ideas "without an official call" but thought he was excused due to the "great importance that the chief Magistrate should be informed of the real state of things."

Hamilton warned Washington that "in our councils three considerable parties" had emerged, one for peace, one for war, and one only inclined "to excite and keep alive irritation and ill humour between the UStates and Great Britain." The latter two parties, especially the war party, "say and . . . do every thing which can have a tendency to stir up the passions of the people and beget a disposition favourable to war—to make use of the inflamation which is excited in the community for the purposes of carrying through measures calculated to disgust Great Britain and to render an accommodation impracticable." Here, then, was the key to unlocking the secret persistence of patriot anger over the British harboring of escapees from slavery, even a decade after the signing of the terms of peace. Throughout his briefing report to the president, Hamilton stressed how the leaders of these new "parties" targeted their appeals not to other national leaders, but, radically and dangerously, to the people themselves. They preyed on the "public mind" by stirring up "angry and perverse passions." Already, the republican ideal that the nation would be steered by virtuous men reasoning together was crumbling: "the symptoms are strong of our being readily enough worked up into a degree of rage and phrenzy, which goes very far towards silencing the voice of reason and interest." War demagogues excited "the strongest passions" against Great Britain by recalling the injuries of the past: "Their animosity against [Britain] . . . is inflamed by the most violent resentment for recent and unprovoked injuries—in many instances by personal loss and suffering or the loss and suffering of intimate friends and conections." Was Hamilton here alluding to patriots' loss of their human property? Certainly, such unresolved grievances were encompassed in this observation.

As would be evident in the angry meetings and street protests that would erupt when the terms of a new peace treaty were leaked later that year, Hamilton well understood that the "carried off" issue was one capable of "inflaming" the "public mind." Like the issue of the western forts that was entangled with popular hatred of Indians and hunger for America's future westward empire, so the issue of British harboring of American slaves reverberated far beyond the personal property interests involved. At stake was the security of slavery itself, for if any officer in time of war could liberate people from slavery, not only was slavery undermined, but the future safety of the American nation was endangered. Foreign nations would be tempted to enlist Americans held in bondage to their banners—or worse, entice them to rise up and overthrow their masters.

Hamilton's solution to the looming threat of war was "to nominate a person, who will have the confidence of those who think peace still within our reach, and who may be thought qualified for the mission as envoy extraordinary to Great Britain." Only one person, in Hamilton's view, besides himself, could accomplish this mission. "Mr. Jay is the only man in whose qualifications for success there would be thorough confidence and him whom alone it would be adviseable to send."[13] Washington immediately followed Hamilton's advice and appointed his chief justice of the Supreme Court to this duty.

Over the following week Hamilton prepared a list of negotiating goals for Jay that he sent to the president in a memo titled "Points to be Considered in the Instructions to Mr. Jay, Envoy Extraordinary to G B." The top level considerations all had to do with protecting American shipping by limiting British seizures to actual contraband, to "instrumenta belli" (guns, powder, and so forth), and requiring payment for American ships and cargoes confiscated outside of this category. A second set of negotiating goals, titled "Grounds of adjustment with regard to the late Treaty of Peace on the part of the British," was an inventory of unresolved business from the previous treaty. The most important unfinished business, at least judging by its being the first in this series, was "Indemnification for our negroes carr[i]ed away." The second item was "Surrender of our Posts."[14]

Hamilton did not explain his thinking behind prioritizing "Indemnification for our negroes" over "Surrender of our Posts." But as his rough memo was refined as it was passed among cabinet members, something of the outlines of an explanation emerged in the final product.

It was Secretary of State Edmund Randolph who sent the final set of secret instructions to John Jay. Over the course of an extensive list of issues, including concerns about British high-seas seizures of American-flagged ships and suspicions the British were holding on to their western forts to encourage native attacks on American settlements, Randolph asked Jay to ask the British "to reconsider the compensation of the negroes" and explained: "The reason, why I again brought up the negroes was, that, as the amount would to the British nation be small; so the King might, upon reconsideration, be desirous of giving the best chance for conciliation by removing one of the chief irritations."[15]

A dozen years after the British pledged to not "carry off" fugitives from slavery, this memory remained "one of the chief irritations" among the two nations in the eyes of many patriots. Even if Hamilton and the other hardcore Federalists had little personal interest in recovering the escapees or forcing payment for their liberation, they keenly understood the political power of the issue to mobilize the masses. Removing this "chief irritation," they certainly hoped, would lower the temperature of the debate and make whatever agreement was reached with the Crown that much more palatable to the American people.

In taking Hamilton's advice and asking John Jay to represent American interests in reopening negotiations on a new treaty of peace, Washington was punctuating the international powers of the Constitution. Picking Jay as his special envoy to London symbolized the idea that treaties were the supreme law of the land and that the federal government had the power to enforce this principle. Jay was, after all, the sitting chief justice of the Supreme Court. It did not escape his critics' notice that by choosing Jay, Washington guaranteed that the person who drafted whatever agreement was reached with Lord Granville would also later decide what it legally meant. This was only one of the reasons that Jay's appointment was contentious, as evidenced by the eight Senators, a third of the total, who voted against him.[16]

Just before Jay boarded a ship bound for London with a man he claimed as his property, and whom Jay had taken from his wife and family, Alexander Hamilton sent him a personal letter with his best advice for leveraging the most beneficial agreement from the Crown. Shrewdly, Hamilton suggested how the various issues could be sequenced and how obtaining one would impact English positions on others. Hamilton seemed to suggest that resolving the lingering issues from 1783 would pave the way for new agreements regarding questions of neutral shipping and trading privileges in the West Indies. "It will be worth the while of the Government of this Country," Hamilton urged his friend, "to satisfy, itself & its own citizens, who have suffered."[17]

At first Jay dutifully followed his instructions and pressed the issue of compensation for fugitives from slavery with his British counterparts. In his report of his first round of negotiations to George Washington, Jay indicated he and Lord Grenville had detailed discussions about the topic of the "Negroes," as he clearly outlined their two positions: "They contend that the article about the Negroes, does not extend to those who came in on their Proclamations; to whom (being vested with the Property in them by the Rights of War) they gave Freedom; but only to those who were bona fide the property of americans when the war ceased."[18] After Grenville presented Jay with a draft treaty, Jay prepared a memo listing dozens of objections, including "the Silence of the Treaty as to the Negroes carried away."[19]

But over the course of his feting and dining in the salons of London's elite, including those of such antislavery luminaries as William Wilberforce and Edmund Burke, Jay's commitment to insisting on a specific indemnification for lost American human property waned. When Grenville submitted a draft treaty that contained no provisions for paying damages to American claimants of lost human property, Jay offered only a meek protest. Jay wrote that its "preamble, connected with the silence of the treaty as to the negroes carried away, implies that the United States have been the aggressors," an objection that could be addressed by tweaking the language of the preamble rather than conceding any ground on the issue of the "carried away." Grenville responded with an addendum in which he declared himself willing "to consider any form of words which Mr. Jay may suggest for those articles, as better suited to the two objects to which they are directed," but Jay did not seize upon this invitation to reopen the question of the "carried off."[20]

In a September 13 letter, which must have caused his superior in America, Secretary of State Edmund Randolph, to spit up his tea, Jay intimated that he had been won over to the British view of the fugitive issue. Jay recounted that after a "number of informal conversations" he stated once again the longstanding American position that the keystone to several outstanding points was what "constituted the first violation of the Treaty of Peace;—The carrying away of the Negroes contrary to the 7th Article." Jay "insisted" that this was "the *first* aggression." Jay then repeated Grenville's response in a manner that seemed to have struck Randolph as too sympathetic. He seemed to concede that the British were interpreting that clause "in the obvious sense of the Words which expressed it"—that is, that their military evacuation was to have been made without taking away "*any Negroes or other Property* of the American[s]." The British position was that by running to their camps, American escapees from slavery became British property and not subject to this restriction. As Jay characterized the argument: "That every Slave like every Horse which escap'd or stray'd from within the American lines, & came into the Possession of the British Army, became by the Laws & Rights of War *British* Property;—and therefore ceasing to be *American* Property, the exportation thereof was not inhibited by the Stipulation in question."

Had Jay stopped there and merely concluded as he did later in his letter that "On this point we could not agree," he might have retained Randolph's confidence in him. After all, this position was old news and one that Jay himself had repudiated in the report he made to Congress on the matter back in October 1786 when he concluded, "They could not by merely flying or eloping extinguish the right or title of their Masters—nor was that title destroyed by their coming into the enemy's possession, for they were received, not taken, by the enemy . . . by no Act therefore either of their own or of their friends was the right of their Masters taken away, so that being, the property of american Inhabitants, it was an infraction of the 7th. Article of the treaty to carry them away."[21]

But instead, Jay continued and described how Grenville took a higher moral ground. Grenville argued that "to extend" Article 7 "to the Negroes who under the Faith of Proclamations, had come in to them . . . and to whom, according to promise, Liberty had been given; was to give to the Article a greater Latitude than the Terms of it would warrant, & was also *unnecessarily* to give it a construction which being *Odious*, could not be supported by the known & established rules for construing Treaties." As David Gellman insightfully observed, employing the word "odious" in this context raised the specter of what to Randolph and other southerners was the infamous *Somerset* decision of 1772, in which the high court had ruled that only formal positive legal language enforcing slavery could uphold such "odious" interpretations of the rights of British subjects and, because there were no such specific statutes in England, effectively ended chattel slavery in the homeland.[22]

Certainly, Randolph would have been irked at what he would have read as the moral arrogance of abolitionists, but this discomfort would have turned to rage as he came to the bottom of the page and Jay admitted his sympathies for it. As the "Affair of the Negroes emerg'd—and was insisted upon . . . I confess however that his Construction of that Article has made an impression upon my Mind, & induced me to suspect that my former opinion on that Head may not be well founded." Jay then informed Randolph that in light of this he had unilaterally decided that it had become "adviseable to quit those Topics." Instead, Jay and Grenville pulled out their sketchy maps of the largely uncharted western territories and argued over where to draw the boundary between the states and Canada.

Randolph received this letter two months later, on November 11, the usual swiftness of even the highest priority diplomatic messages in the era of wood and sail. Randolph fired off a response and sent it with William Penn, who was just embarking. He said little about Jay's about-face on the "Affair of the Negroes," but what did he write spoke volumes: "I must . . . trouble you with a few remarks on those points which attract notice on the first view. The reasoning of Lord Grenville, in relation to the negroes, is so new to me, as are his observations on the *first* aggression, that their accuracy cannot be assented to without the fullest reflection."[23]

Randolph was less cryptic in his next letter. "I must, in the hurry of the moment, take the liberty of suggesting that I am extremely afraid that the reasoning about the negroes will not be satisfactory." The former governor of Virginia and sponsor of the Virginia Plan at the Constitutional Convention admitted, "Indeed, I own that I cannot myself yield to its force." Randolph then prophetically warned, "if you omit mentioning them *at all*, will not some quarters of the Union suppose themselves neglected?"[24]

Before sending his full analysis and criticisms of Jay's actions, Randolph shared them with Washington and let Jay know that what they contained was "under the correction of the President." Randolph conceded that it was "immaterial" and a "mere point of honor" to squabble further about who was responsible for the "first violation" of the Paris treaty. But that was not really the issue—the fugitives were. It will be recalled that Grenville argued that once fugitives from slavery entered a British camp, they ceased to be "American property" and therefore were not prohibited from being "carried away." One can almost hear the exasperation in Randolph's voice when he wrote, "But really, sir, the force of Lord Grenville's reasoning appears to fall very short of its object." "That a property is acquired in moveables as soon as they come within the power of the enemy, is acknowledge. But it will not be denied that rights, even in moveables, acquired by war, may, by the treaty of peace, be renounced. In this instance, there was great reason for such a renunciation. Negroes were not, like moveables in general, difficult to be distinguished. They carried an infallible mark."

What Jay had described as the British understanding of the "obvious sense" of the Paris treaty's wording regarding fugitive "negroes" was to Randolph and Washington pure sophistry. Randolph noted that its "reasoning appears to fall very short of its object. . . . The essence of Lord Grenville's argument seems to consist in a refinement of interpretation which he gives to the words *'other property of American inhabitants,'* as if they confined the word 'negroes' to those negroes who should be thereafter captured from the Americans by the British arms, and excluded such as were then denominated, by the rights of war, British property." Ironically, this was precisely the argument Jay himself had made to Congress eight years earlier.

This probably should have been enough to illuminate their displeasure with Jay's sympathy for Grenville's position. But Washington and Randolph seemed compelled to confront the British presumption of moral superiority wrapped up in Grenville's use of the word "odious." To them it rather reeked of hypocrisy. There was no "mathematical precision" in the "moral reasoning" employed in interpreting treaties. Grenville was merely "sheltering himself from the true construction of the article . . . by branding it with the epithet 'odious.'" "The construction is not odious, because the British Government hate slavery. No, sir, they established it in the United States, while colonies; they continued the importation of slaves against the will of most of the States; it exists, by their authority, in many of their foreign dominions. The odium, then, of the business, must be in depriving the slaves of the liberty granted to them, that is, in first giving, and then taking away."

Here the two Virginians, each the owner of hundreds of beings kept as chattel, had walked themselves to the precipice of abolition. Was not taking away a man's liberty something "odious"? Neither Randolph nor Washington thought so in this case, because they refused the principle that one nation could legally or legitimately free the slaves of its enemy. "There might be some countenance to this plea, if we should insist that slaves, originally belonging to the British, and afterwards manumitted by them, were now demanded by us to return to their former condition," the pair conceded. "But those in question belonged to our citizens: the war only presented the chance of liberation." And such "liberation" was, in fact, illegitimate because even the person fleeing from their master during the war "must have been conscious (and such is the law of nations) that, if they had been regained by their former proprietors, in the course of the war, they would have reverted to the condition of slaves; and that what the war gave, might, by a peace, be taken away." In other words, slavery that was properly grounded in the workings of the law and of private property could not be "odious."

Having chastened their envoy's logic, perhaps even his apostasy, before departing from this topic and critiquing other proposals dealing with forts, Indians, and trade negotiations, Randolph and Washington appealed to him as a pragmatic politician. "You must be too sensible of the anxiety of many parts of the United States, upon this subject, to pass it over unnoticed." Both the former governor and the sitting president understood the political importance of at least appearing to represent the property interests of southerners. This may have been the moment when the pair realized that Senate confirmation would be a bloody battle.[25]

Randolph's criticisms were written about the time Jay was putting seal to his concluded treaty in London. Randolph's letters were entrusted to friends sailing across the ocean but would not arrive until just before Jay was packing to return to America once the winter ice retreated later the next spring. This means that Jay did not have the opportunity to reflect on Randolph's views or incorporate any of his points into the final round of negotiations. This is evident in the fact that Jay's summary and commentary on the treaty that he wrote before Randolph's letter to him had passed Long Island contained no mention of the "carried off" issue except for the afterthought that "Various articles, which have no place in this treaty, have from time to time, been under consideration, but did not meet with mutual approbation and consent."[26]

Jay's first response came in February of 1795, when he excused himself by claiming it was simply not possible to obtain compensation for the "Negroes" and tried to sugarcoat his failure: "In considering the Treaty, it will doubtless be remembered that there must be two to make a Bargain. We could not agree about the Negroes. was that a good Reason for breaking up the negociation? I mentioned in a former Letter that I considered our admission into the Islands as affording compensation for the Detention of the posts, and other Claims of that nature—in that way we obtain Satisfaction for the Negroes, tho' not in express words."[27]

Thirteen months later, the *Severn* arrived back in New York harbor from Bristol. An "immense concourse of citizens" cheered its docking as John Jay disembarked, and then accompanied him to his home "amidst repeated acclamations."[28] If the crowd was hoping to learn the details of the agreement Jay brought with him, they were sorely disappointed, as these were kept secret and entrusted only to the president and members of the Senate. Some details had leaked over the past months: that the new treaty was agreed to at the end of January, that a firm deadline had been set for the British surrender of its remaining forts, that commercial shipping between America and the British West Indies was to be opened, and that the question of what American ships could carry to belligerent nations would be referred to a commission. None of these details excited much controversy, given the greater number of unknowns.[29]

Senators immediately got to work debating Jay's Treaty in complete secrecy. On Wednesday, June 17, a vote to approve the treaty failed. Two days later, a majority of senators agreed to request that the president provide for their scrutiny all of Jay's reports and all correspondence between Washington and Carleton "on the subject of the 7th Article of the Treaty of Peace," which primarily dealt with enslaved property and the British forts. Then, on the following Monday, the vice president carried into the Senate chamber the full "Book of Negroes," or as the Senate secretary referred to it, "the list of Negroes, to which the correspondence between the Commander-in-Chief of the American Army and Sir Guy Carleton relates."[30]

Several senators opposed the treaty on the grounds that there was no compensation offered for those liberated and evacuated by the British army. After some debate, Senator Aaron Burr moved that the treaty be laid aside and the president instructed to seek modifications, including that the "value of negroes and other property carried away" be paid for. Debate on Burr's motion spilled over into the next day, and when the question was called it failed on a strict party line vote of 20–10. It is interesting to note that while all ten Democratic-Republican senators voted against the bill, this caucus was not strictly sectional. Three of the ten senators voting against the treaty were northerners, John Langdon from New Hampshire, Aaron Burr from New York, and Moses Robinson from Vermont. Only two state delegations, Virginia, and North Carolina, cast both their votes against the treaty.[31]

Debate on the topic of the "negroes and other property carried away" continued the following day and culminated when Senator Jacob Read, a South Carolina Federalist who had voted to sustain the treaty against Burr's attempt to sink it, proposed to approve the treaty but with an additional condition of "obtaining adequate compensation for the negroes." While still falling far short, the ground seemed to be shifting in favor of the Jeffersonians, as this time Humphrey Marshall, a Federalist from the new state of Tennessee, joined with Read to increase the oppositions' total to twelve.

Virginia's Senator Henry Tazewell then thought to test the strength of the anti-treaty forces by moving to table the treaty entirely. Tazewell read into the record seven reasons why the "Treaty of Amity" was unacceptable, and his first reason was "because the Treaty hath not secured that satisfaction from the British government, for the removal of negroes, in violation of the Treaty of 1783, to which the citizens of the United States were justly entitled."[32] Tazewell's motion lost, and also failed to win Read's and Marshall's votes. This cleared the way for a vote on the treaty itself, minus Article 12, which governed America's commerce with the British West Indies, and this squeaked through without a vote to spare, 20–10.

But this was not the end of the debate over the unfinished business of America's refugees from slavery. James Gunn, a Federalist of Georgia, moved that the Senate recommend to the president a renewal of negotiations over "the claims of the American citizens, to compensation for the negroes and other property, so alleged to have been carried away."

Debate on Gunn's motion to continue negotiations to obtain payment to Americans for lost slaves carried on into the following day, until a compromise was reached to vote separately on the main resolution and also on postponing the issue until after all the remaining points of disagreement had been overcome. This then became, first, a vote on whether to abandon claims to patriots' lost human property, and then on whether those negotiations should be put on hold until the issues of Caribbean trade had been resolved. All but one senator voted to both divide the issue and to approve the first principle part of the resolution. That left only the question of whether these negotiations should move forward in parallel with the disagreements over trade policy or should be shelved until those were completed. After some parliamentary maneuvering that had to be resolved by a procedural ruling by Washington himself, the idea of negotiating all these issues together lost 17–11.[33]

It is important to note that adding this qualification to the previous ratification vote required the same two-thirds majority that the treaty itself required. When the question was called to approve Gunn's original amendment, eighteen senators voted in favor of reopening negotiations with England to gain compensation for the enslaved people England had protected and liberated after the other trade issues were resolved. The eleven who voted against were all the hard-liners who had earlier voted in favor of dumping the treaty on the grounds of its silence on the issue of the "carried off." Among these were Timothy Bloodworth, John Brown, Aaron Burr, Pierce Butler, James Jackson, John Langdon, Humphrey Marshall, Alexander Martin, Stevens Mason, Moses Robinson, and Henry Tazewell. All the votes taken together reveal that every member of the Senate voted at one time or another to demand compensation from England for expatriated American fugitives from slavery.

South Carolina's Pierce Butler and New Jersey's Frederick Frelinghuysen, realizing that if the last vote stood, then there would be no Senate negotiations on the fugitive issue, then joined forces to call for the reconsideration of the previous vote, which was significant, given that Butler had just voted against the measure. But in the end they could not find one more vote and their last-ditch attempt failed, leaving the resolution toothless. A final vote was then taken on this dismembered resolution, which now satisfied neither side, and it predictably went down in flames, falling one vote short of a bare majority.[34] In the end, the Senate approved the treaty with no margin to spare, 20 to 10, except for Article 12, which limited American trade with the British West Indies.

Only after it was approved by the narrowest of margins was a copy of the treaty leaked by Senator Stevens Mason to the publisher Benjamin Franklin Bache, who printed it in his *Philadelphia Aurora* newspaper. In the South, where large land owners and merchants were invested in slavery as a matter of profit and poor farmers and artisans viewed it mostly as a matter of public safety, political opposition to Jay's Treaty cut across class lines. But in the North, where the merchant class had no stake in slavery, other than profiting from the transatlantic trade in people and the goods made by those in bondage, support for the treaty was elite and opposition arose from the streets.[35]

Philadelphia's Independence Day celebrations were overtaken by popular protests against Jay's Treaty. According to one eyewitness, the Kensington shipwrights were the core of a mob numbering about five hundred who marched through the city streets armed with clubs. They were led by someone holding aloft a "transparent painting" depicting Jay handing to the Senate the treaty while holding the scales of justice, the higher pan labeled "Virtue, Liberty, and Independence" while the heavier one was "British Gold." Before the crowd could grow to dangerous numbers, it was confronted by a "small party of the Light Horse" who tried to disperse them, but the cavalry was itself scattered by stones.[36]

Later that week, a more orderly meeting was held and shouted their huzzahs in approval of a set of resolutions to be sent to President Washington. Listed first among their objections to the treaty was that "it does not provide a fair and effectual settlement of the differences that previously subsisted between the United States and Great Britain," as it provides no compensation for the "Western Posts" and "inasmuch as it waves a just claim for the value of the negroes, who were carried off at the close of the war."[37]

About the same time, a town meeting held in Portsmouth, New Hampshire, sent a formal address to President Washington expressing "our most hearty disapprobation" of the treaty Jay negotiated and the Senate recently ratified. They listed their "general reasons" for denouncing the treaty. The

first of their list of six was "Because that part of the treaty of 1783, securing payment of debts due to British subjects, is rigorously enforced; while
an important article in the treaty, requiring compensation for negroes and
other property unjustly removed, is placed wholly out of view."[38]

New Yorkers gathered on July 20, 1795, and shouted their approval for
resolutions denouncing the treaty for being "injurious to the agriculture,
manufactures, and commerce of the United States, derogatory from their
national honour, and dangerous to their welfare, peace and prosperity." Like
other mass meetings, this one's first cause of complaint pointed directly to
passions aroused by the treaty's silence on the issue of escapees from slavery. This meeting's first charge was that Jay's Treaty had elevated the "vague
and ill founded claims of Great Britain . . . upon the same footing as the
numerous, important, and just demands of the United States; and while the
former, unsupported as they were, are amply provided for, many of the latter are either entirely overlooked, or placed upon a footing, from which no
adequate redress or compensation can reasonably be expected." While this
language was general, the resolutions provided detail to what was alluded:

> By the treaty of Peace, Great Britain was to cause no destruction, nor to
> carry away any negroes or other American property. In direct violation of
> this promise, several thousand negroes were carried off long after the treaty
> was known. Many of those negroes were registered with a view to future
> compensation. The claim, on this account, which amounted to a least two
> millions of dollars, although hitherto a matter of extreme solicitude with
> America, has not only been abandoned and consigned to oblivion, but Great
> Britain is thereby justified for her inexecution of the treaty of peace, and an
> indelible stain is fixed upon our national faith.[39]

A similar protest meeting took place in Boston, and the third of this
gathering's resolutions condemned the treaty for providing "no indemnification . . . to the citizens of the United States for property taken from them
at the close of the war." One critic pointed out the obvious omission in this
wording in a letter to the *Providence (R.I.) Gazette:* "You do not mention
what this *property* is.—I have heard no complaints on this ground, save that

of carrying away a number of negroes by the British, at their evacuation of New-York, which I suppose you undoubtedly allude to."[40]

Boston's town meeting angered Stephen Higginson, one of the grand merchants of Boston and a member of the "Essex Junto" that ran the state's political machinery. Higginson instinctively recognized the lower-class origins of protest against the treaty. He called treaty opponents "Jacobins" and made no effort to disguise the class interests behind Jay in his correspondence to other Federalists.[41] Resolutions against the treaty were "not countenanced by any merchant of eminence, not by ten in all."[42]

Higginson alleged that opposition was whipped up by "Mr Franklin Bache," who "came on here with Masons Copy of the Treaty, with Burrs and Tazewells motions, and with a large collection of Lies, of Riots in Phil in New York &c, to creat a flame here and to urge on our common people to excesses. all he could affect with the aid of our previous Incendiaries."[43]

Further south, the reaction was even more vociferous. A mass meeting at the capitol building in Richmond, Virginia, denounced the treaty as "Insulting to the dignity, Injurious to the interest, [and] Dangerous to the security" of the United States. These Virginians linked the issue of the "carried away" fugitives to the payment of British debts, protesting that Jay's Treaty failed, "not even deigning to speak of compensation, or to apologize for the immense robbery committed in carrying away negroes, and other property, contrary to treaty; and yet having the effrontery to demand a guaranty of British debts." A letter continuing their detailed objections, drafted by a committee chaired by George Wythe, former speaker of the Virginia House and since the days of the Revolution one of the three judges on the state's highest court, was entrusted to Richmond's mayor to send to George Washington that very night.[44]

Likewise, a "numerous meeting" held in Caroline County, Virginia, tied the issue of payment for their lost human property to payment of British debts: "Because no compensation is stipulated for, either on account of the negroes plundered or the posts detained, both of which are as confessedly infractions of the treaty of peace, as legal obstructions to the recovery of British debts would have been; whereas the existence of the latter is far from being ascertained, whilst the former are avowed."[45] Further south in the state, a gathering of "numerous & respectable . . . Inhabitants Land-holders" at the Amelia County Courthouse were also angered that the treaty established a commission to assess payment to British creditors out of the public treasury, "by which means a vast addition will undoubtedly be made to the public Debt," but "not the least notice is taken, nor is any compensation provided for the damages sustained by our citizens in being deprived of their Negroes & other property carried off by the Brittish Army, in direct violation of the 7th Article of the said Treaty."[46]

In Charlestown, denunciations of the treaty were more structured and formal. On July 16, St. Michael's church was filled with interested "Citizens," and after discussion it was decided to elect a committee of fifteen "to take into consideration the impending treaty." A secret vote was arranged, the ballot box to be available to anyone at the mercantile exchange during business hours for the next two days. Once the 822 votes were counted, a committee of the most powerful and well-known names in state politics was seated, including three Rutledges, Christopher Gadsden, David Ramsay, Charles Cotesworth Pinckney, and Aedanus Burke.

A second meeting to hear the committee's recommendations overflowed St. Michael's and heard the select committee's report that condemned the treaty because it "has not that reciprocity which ought to be the basis of all contracts;—that it contains no provisions in favour of the United States, in any manner proportionate to the various concessions made to Great-Britain." Rather than state which feature was most objectionable, as there were so many, it critiqued them, one by one in order of their official numbering in the treaty. Articles one and two restated the rights of loyalists to return and apply for citizenship, which effectively "establishes a British colony within our limits" that would combine "their most bitter and irreconcilable enemies" with the "savages [who] have lately waged war against us." Other articles threatened the trade with Indians and impaired American shipping rights. But the sixth article seemed particularly onerous, as it forced the Americans to "make good such losses on debts, to British creditors . . . although the first infraction of that treaty, was made on the part of Great-Britain, by carrying away from these states many thousands of negroes" and "no compensation is stipulated to be made to the citizens, whose negroes, and other property, have been illegally carried off; their right of recovery being passed over in silence." It was noted bitterly that "We are precluded from exporting in our own vessels, not only foreign cotton, but the cotton of our growth," which can be carried only in British ships.[47]

Then former governor Charles Pinckney gave a speech that began not by criticizing the treaty but by condemning the appointment of John Jay as being unconstitutional. Pinckney, one of the architects of the Constitution, soberly observed that "the spirit of the constitution" was that the judiciary should be independent of the other branches, and that "the same man should not have it in his power to form a treaty, and afterwards, as a judge, prejudiced as he must be by being concerned in its negotiation, to decide upon its meaning." Pinckney chalked this breach of the nation's charter to "a determination in a party in our government to force a connection with Great Britain." Likewise, Washington refused to share his instructions to Jay with the Senate, an action Pinckney viewed as an infringement of the Senate's role to provide "advice and consent" to treaties. "He cannot be said to advise with them upon a measure, if he forms a treaty without their knowledge, and merely leaves to them the power of determining whether they will ratify it or not."

Even if such powers were granted to the president, even if it were deemed appropriate to appoint the nation's chief justice to negotiate a treaty, Pinckney found Jay the worst choice for the job. Pinckney reminded his audience of how Jay had attempted to "barter away the rights of his country, in sacrificing the interests, and of course dissevering the western territory from the union," by agreeing to allow Spain to close the Mississippi to American shipping. Pinckney roused the crowd by asking, "Has he obtained complete satisfaction for the depredations in the West Indies, the delivering of the posts, compensation for their detention, and payment for the negroes carried away?" Not only did the crowd acclaim the committee's scathing report, one man in the crowd moved that their resolution include a request to impeach John Jay.[48]

At a public meeting in Williamsburg, South Carolina, the proceeding's declaration regretted that the public had been deceived by Jay's mission: "we were told that he was sent to demand delivery of the western posts and compensation for our domestics, carried away by the British plunderers, as the former treaty of peace gave us a right to demand." Instead of winning these points and compensation for the ships plundered in the West Indies, they were presented with a treaty "insulting to our national honor, prejudicial to our domestic happiness, and injurious to our rights and interests, as citizens of a free nation."[49]

As soon as the Senate approved the Jay Treaty on June 24, 1795, and the public protests flared across the breadth of America, George Washington asked the members of his cabinet to prepare a full analysis of the document: "my wishes are, to have the favorable, and unfavorable side of each article stated, and compared together; that I may see the bearing and tendency of them: and, ultimately, on which side the balance is to be found." Washington was then preparing to respond to the letters and petitions pouring into his office and needed as plain a breakdown of the pros and cons of the agreement as possible before he formulated his replies.[50]

Alexander Hamilton took to this task most determinedly. He returned to his president a brief of 11,256 words that broke down every facet of the treaty in exhaustive detail. He even provided an extensive discussion of the elephant not in the room, the fact that the Jay Treaty lacked any provision for compensation for Americans' evacuated human property. Here, Hamilton was most interested in the question of whether the British had broken the treaty by "carrying away of the negroes" contrary to Article 7.

Perhaps because he well knew of Washington's own clash with Carleton and the English commander's refusal to surrender the thousands of Black people in his protection, Hamilton stated his new position as plainly as he could: "Great Britain has much to say with Truth & Justice." And he placated by conceding that Britain's "seducing away our negroes during the War were to the last degree infamous—and form an indelible stain in her annals." But, in the end, Hamilton argued, "it would have been still more infamous to have surrendered them to their Masters."

From a legal perspective, Hamilton parses out the language of Article 7, arguing that "his Britannic Majesty shall with all convenient speed, and *without causing any Destruction, or carrying away any Negroes or other Property* of the American Inhabitants, withdraw all his Armies, Garrisons &

Fleets from the said United States" is ambiguous in general and positively unclear in its reference to "Negroes or other Property." Hamilton identifies the source of confusion in the question of whose property the "Negroes" were at the time the treaty was signed. Had they been taken as "booty" by the enemy and therefore by the laws of war as laid down by the philosophers Vattel and Grottius become English property? Or were slaves somehow exempt from ever being considered a prize of war? Assuming this article obligated the British to restore property that they had legally seized, could the British "stipulate the surrender of men made free to slavery?"

It is here where we first see Hamilton reconsider his earlier outrage at General Carleton's stubborn refusal to surrender the people he sheltered. Initially, Alexander Hamilton viewed Britain's evacuation of escapees from American slavery as did most all his fellow patriots, as a clear violation of the terms of the peace treaty. On the first day of June in 1783, Hamilton wrote to New York's Governor Clinton a legal analysis of the treaty in which he commented that General Carleton's refusal to return the people enjoying his protection was "a doubtful construction of the treaty." But now, a decade on, his position had reversed, and he knew it, admitting to Washington, "I have at different times viewed the matter in different lights."[51]

Like the sharp lawyer he was, Hamilton found a means of avoiding a definitive judgment as to which of these interpretations of Article 7 was correct. Rather, he concluded that *both* had merit, and since "there is really a well founded doubt as to the true legal construction . . . the acting of the other party on a construction different from ours could not be deemed such a clear manifest breach of Treaty as to justify retaliation." In other words, as Article 7 was legally ambiguous, it was essentially a dead letter, at best subject to "amicable discussion and negotiation."[52]

Hamilton closed by assuring Washington that the United States was right to drop the whole matter. "Compensation for the negroes, if not a point of doubtful right, is certainly a point of no great moment. It involves no principle of future operation. It terminates in itself—and the actual pecuniary value of the object is in a national sense inconsiderable & insignificant."

Before Secretary of State Edmund Randolph submitted his interpreta-

tions of the treaty, Washington gave him Hamilton's lengthy legal disqui-
sition. Between Randolph's lines can be heard echoes of his grumbling, as
he had consistently fallen on the other side of the question of the "carried
off." Randolph prefaced his analysis by complaining that Hamilton's letter
forced him to change his entire outline: "My first purpose was to class the
articles of the treaty under these different heads. . . . But the paper, which
you did me the honor of shewing to me, having gone into this detail, I shall
speak of them separately, only where I differ from its writer." Randolph
listed what he termed "rights surrendered," and the first item on this list
was "satisfaction for the negroes." Randolph reminded the president that,
as secretary of state, just six months earlier, he had officially instructed his
special negotiator in London, Jay, to drop the matter "if it is necessary,
in order to accomplish the negotiation amicably," though Randolph then
wrote at length about why the Americans' claims for the return of "negroes"
was legal and just.[53]

While street protests and town meetings registered the intensity of popular feeling toward Jay's Treaty, the pamphlet and newspaper war that en-
sued revealed that the issue of fugitives from slavery continued to preoccupy
the minds of patriot leaders and resonate with the American public. Both
Federalist and Republican ideologues seized their quills, charged into battle, and used the issue of escapees from slavery as a means of bludgeoning
their opponents.

Clearly the issue of fugitive recapture was a central element of this debate. One Federalist letter writer who appeared simply as "A Citizen" indicated the importance of the question when he accused his opponents of
harping on the lost slaves. "The real grounds of complaint against the late
treaty," Citizen observed, is "that it is silent on the subject of Negroes; that
while the old British debts are taken notice of, no compensation is provided
for the negroes carried away at the evacuation of New-York."[54] Likewise,
another defender of the treaty, who penned "Vindication of the Treaty of
Amity, Commerce and Navigation," thought "the carrying away of the negroes" was a "subject [that] has occasioned as much altercation, as any point
between the two countries." To this observer it was obvious that "the silence
of the present treaty on that subject, is the ground of violent clamor."[55]

Federalist champions were arguably the more accomplished rhetoricians: Alexander Hamilton penned at least two dozen essays under the pen name "Camillus," and Noah Webster drafted a dozen polemics under the name "Curtius" for his *American Minerva*. Benjamin Russell's *Columbian Centinel* became the mouthpiece for Boston's elite. On the other side, Republicans had authors of lesser note but not lesser tenacity. Robert Livingston as "Cato," Brockholst Livingston as "Decius," and A. J. Dallas as anonymous all drove hard the presses of Republican editor Benjamin Franklin Bache.[56]

While this rhetorical war ranged widely over a variety of international and domestic policies, the issue of America's fugitives from slavery, while not the most discussed issue, was ever present. Purely as a matter of politics, Republicans had the upper hand on the issue of fugitives, as it took little explanation or philosophical gyrations to argue that slaves were property, that Britain agreed in writing to return them, and that it then broke the promise and "carried them away." Jay simply failed to uphold American power and dignity and surrendered these claims unnecessarily and unjustly.

Probably the most detailed rebuttal came from the pen of Alexander Hamilton's one-time assistant, Tench Coxe of Philadelphia, who attended the Annapolis Convention, served a term in the Confederation Congress, and wrote under the pen name "Juricola" for the influential *Philadelphia Gazette*. Much of his essays were dedicated to dismantling the lawyerly English justifications for retaining the runaways and refusing compensation, arguments that had now passed on to the Federalist apologists themselves. Coxe took added delight in poking his old boss and pointing out that Hamilton moved a resolution in Congress in 1783 complaining that "negroes . . . have been carried off contrary to the true intent and meaning" of the Paris treaty. At times Coxe was clearly sympathetic to the humanity of the fugitives themselves, as when he noted that the "negroes themselves would prove strong, though simple remonstrants" against the treaty that demanded their return, and he admitted their "case was serious and hard, and it was humane and prudent to let them go, under the idea of a compensation in money."[57]

Federalist ideologues had no clear or straight path to rebut these criticisms without adopting the British excuse that the African Americans evacuated from Savannah, Charlestown, and New York were no longer enslaved and therefore not property subject to the terms of Article 7. How exactly it was they did not count as "property" was a tangled and fraught subject.

The fact was that no matter how Federalists cared to spin the meaning of the treaty, it was an abandonment of principles laid down ten years before by John Jay himself, first as a member of the team negotiating the terms of peace and then as a foreign secretary who carefully laid out his nation's interpretation of it in his famous report to Congress of October 13, 1786. In that report, Jay had divided all the enslaved people transported away by the British into three classes. Those who were taken as "booty" during the war, those who were property of Americans and inside the areas of British control at the time peace was declared, and those who fled to the Union Jack in response to promises of liberty in exchange for military service.

Jay argued that the British promise "not to carry away any Negroes or other property of the American Inhabitants" did not apply to those persons who were seized by Redcoats, as it was well established by the laws of war that when armies confiscated such "booty" it ceased to be private property. It is not clear whether Jay believed that in carving out this exception to American policy he was theoretically emancipating very few people, if any, as every surviving record of the era indicates that enslaved people eagerly and willingly fled patriot bondage and viewed the English army as liberators.

As for the vast majority, who, "confiding in Proclamations and Promises of freedom and protection, fled from their Masters without, and were received," they remained subject to reenslavement because such military emancipations were illegitimate. Enslaved Americans "could not by merely flying or eloping extinguish the right or title of their Masters" even if the British received them "not as Slaves but as friends and freemen."[58] In 1795, Federalists argued exactly the opposite, that because the British had freed these refugees, they were no longer slaves under the meaning of Article 7.

While Madison and Jefferson chose not to jump into the fray directly, Alexander Hamilton seized his pen and produced a dozen articles under the pseudonym "Camillus" in defense of the treaty. In doing so, he reversed his initial views of the Treaty of Paris. After Congress learned of Carleton's refusal to hand over fugitives who he argued were not covered by Article 7 because the proclamations of British commanders had freed them, Hamilton called his actions "contrary to the true intent and meaning" of the article and moved that Washington be instructed to "continue his remonstrances to Sir Guy Carleton, respecting the permitting of negroes belonging to the citizens of these states to leave New York, and to endeavor to prevail with him to discontinue" and that America's diplomats be instructed "to use their utmost endeavor to obtain . . . such reparation as the nature of the case will admit."[59]

Now Hamilton, as Camillus, detailed these same British arguments and found them sound, persuasive, and in full accordance with the laws of war. "Let me now ask this question of any candid man. Is our construction of the article respecting the negroes so much better supported than that of Great Britain, as to justify our pronouncing with positiveness that the carrying them away was a breach of the treaty?"[60]

Opponents of Jay's Treaty had their second opportunity to wrench the gears of government when the House took up a resolution to provide funds for implementation of the controversial agreement. When the House took up the question of providing appropriations to carry the already ratified treaty into effect, the first objections raised arose from the issue of fugitives.[61] One after another, congressmen emphasized that the issue of the fugitive Black Americans was the centerpiece of their fight. John Williams, a Democratic Republican congressman representing New York, observed that the "great objection against the Treaty was, that payment for the negroes which were carried away by the British, at the close of the war, was not provided for."[62] James Hillhouse, a Connecticut Federalist, even conceded that "The first, and if well-founded, the most important objection which he had heard made against the [present] Treaty was, that a claim for negroes and other property carried away from New York had been wholly overlooked or given up by our Minister." Hillhouse had to unfurl a lengthy speech to sink this common objection.[63]

Representative William Maclay of Pennsylvania claimed to have originally been "rather inclined in favour of the treaty," as he once thought that "there was nothing in it which would warrant the outcries made against it" and suspected that the treaty's opponents had "sinister motives" or that the "people had not had proper information on the subject." But over the course of gathering more details about it and studying the issue closely, "the result left an unfavorable impression" upon his mind. Why? Because "it appeared . . . the treaty did not give satisfaction for past injuries; that it did not provide for the loss of negroes."[64] This sparked an extensive discussion over whether it was appropriate for the House to hold a debate on a treaty, which was the Senate's prerogative. Some wanted to hold a snap vote, while others pushed to have a full and lengthy debate on the treaty's merits. Back and forth on that point carried over into the next day, when the debaters prevailed, and James Madison took the floor first.

Madison warmed up by emphasizing that the question was one of a larger "extent and importance" than he would be able to "go through all the observations that might be applicable to it." But he would try.

Madison outlined for his audience the subjects of his remarks: first, how the treaty of peace of 1783 had been executed, then the general international laws of nations, and finally, the state of trade between England and the United States. He wasted no time cutting to the heart of the issue of the old treaty of peace—"the arrangements for carrying that treaty into effect . . . were founded on the grossest violation" of the principle of "exact and scrupulous reciprocity." In particular:

> There were two articles which had not been executed by Great Britain; that which related to the negroes and other property carried away, and that which required a surrender of the posts. The article unexecuted by the United States was, that which required payment of all bona fide debts . . . this article is now to be carried into the most compleat effect by the United States, and damages to the last fraction are to be paid for the delay. Is there a reciprocal stipulation by Great Britain with respect to the article unexecuted by her? Nothing like it. She is wholly absolved from the obligation to fulfil one of the articles, viz. that relating to the negroes &c. and she is to make no compensation whatever for delaying to fulfil the other, viz. the surrender of the posts.[65]

Madison had no doubts that the treaty actually covered the men, women, and children who the British claimed had been freed by fiat and therefore were not "property" at all. He observed that the British did not even dispute that point until just recently in these negotiations.

With a spirit of conciliation, Madison allowed that there was one potential reading of Jay's Treaty that did not surrender American claims to compensation for spiriting away their human property. It could seem from the order of the articles in the new treaty that "the compensation for the spoliations on our trade had been combined with the execution of the treaty of peace, and might therefore have been viewed as a substitute for the compensation for the negroes &c." But even allowing this generous reading of the treaty's text through its form, Madison argued such terms were unfair because the right of Americans to enslave people was too well established: "It was impossible that any claims could be better founded than those of the sufferers under the 7th article of the treaty of peace; because they were supported by positive and acknowledged stipulation, as well as by equity and right."

Imagine, Madison proposed, that the tables had been reversed and the claims of merchants for compensation for their intercepted cargoes and seized ships had been swapped for payment of the old slave masters' claims? Do you not suppose "the complaints of the merchants would not have been as universal and as loud as they would have been just"?[66] Madison's dissertation on international law then continued for what was probably hours.

Madison had provided what was probably the strongest, and certainly the longest, Republican refutation of Federalist abandonment of America's enslavers as anyone in his party ever had. Tapped to respond was one of Connecticut's representatives, Zephaniah Swift, who hewed close to the new Federalist line that America never had a right to those people liberated under the English flag of war, but to do so had to maintain the fiction that the thousands of African Americans were taken, not welcomed; booty "carried off" and not men and women claiming their freedom. Swift argued that the article "was intended only to prevent their carrying away negroes and property that should be taken in future, and could have no reference to those captured during the war and before the treaty, the property of which had vested in the captors."[67]

Debate continued the next day, April 18, with Virginia's William Giles noting the vast importance of the decision before them, a controversy whose "extreme sensibility excited on the public mind by the agitation of the treaty question." According to Giles, the "first object of the negociation respected the inexecution of the treaty of peace" and the new treaty declared that "either both parties were equally culpable or equally blameless, in respect to the inexecution of the treaty of peace." Giles "thought with great force, that the stipulations in the present treaty do not correspond with the principle professed as its basis" because Great Britain failed to fulfill the "restoration of certain property in possession of the British at the close of the war, and the surrender of the Western posts." For their part, Giles admitted, the United States had failed to respect "the promise that no legal impediments should be thrown in the way to the recovery of debts due to the British subjects." But while the Treaty of Amity bound the United States to complete its obligations under the old treaty, Americans' "claim of compensation for the property carried away in contravention of the treaty of peace is wholly abandoned."[68]

Few congressmen defended the treaty on the grounds that Americans never actually had a right to reclaim their fugitives, as Hamilton had anonymously done in the popular press of the day. In the end, the appropriation bill passed, the treaty passed into law, and the partisan bickering that would continue for generations found other dry tinder to engulf.

In the end, the British never returned any of the thousands of men, women, and children they liberated from American slavery. England never paid any compensation to enslavers who made claims against them. Only one fugitive property claim arising from the British evacuation was ever granted by Congress. In the 1850s, during a time when southerners moved to firm up the bulwarks of slavery on every side, Congress paid the grandson of a Revolutionary War major $38,757 in compensation for the ninety-six enslaved people who were seized by the British while holding a patriot hero, Major William Hazard Wigg, as a prisoner of war.[69]

EPILOGUE

Thirty years after Benjamin Franklin, John Adams, John Jay, and Henry Laurens demanded on behalf of their new republic the return of thousands of men, women, and children who had fled American slavery and found sanctuary under British protection, these two nations warred again. This time the Americans were quickly overpowered by an empire most of whose forces were fighting a continental war with France. After just two years of conflict, the British army had occupied much of Massachusetts and burned the nation's capitol, and its navy controlled the sea coasts. The federal government was nearly bankrupt, Congress was fractured to the point of paralysis, and New England states threatened secession. When Americans sued for peace and drew up instructions to guide their negotiators drafting a peace treaty, they again placed near the top of their list of priorities the return of the thousands of people who had run away from slavery.

In America's war with England in 1812, history repeated as British fleets again controlled all of America's coasts and British commanders invited enslaved Americans to flee and join their ranks. The only difference, perhaps, was the much greater efficiency with which those who took up this offer were drilled, uniformed, and formed into regiments and sent to fight their former enslavers. Just as they had done in their Revolution, American generals and patriot leaders displayed great reluctance to follow suit, tabling proposals to recruit enslaved soldiers with offers of freedom or to even form regiments composed of Black freedmen.[1]

Just as in the 1780s, by the time a truce had been declared the British harbored thousands of escapees from American slavery. As in the earlier war, American peace negotiators, including John Adams's son, vigorously attempted to force the British government to return to slavery those they had promised freedom, pushing this demand into the first article of their treaty of peace. In both conflicts the issue of "slaves carried off" was tied to greater concerns than merely the private interests of enslavers who had lost their fortunes in human property.

As has been documented here, in the years following American triumph at Yorktown, the "carried off" became entangled in the politics of southern indebtedness to British merchants and the confiscation of loyalist property. As these entanglements tightened, the "carried off" controversy revealed the deficiencies in the structure of federalism and clarified the choice between forming a republic that was to be a loose confederation of independent states or a unitary government of divided powers and defined jurisdictions. By the time Jay negotiated America's second treaty of amity with Great Britain in 1794, he all but conceded that the Treaty of Paris had failed to pressure England to return escapees back to their chains or, in effect, to pay for what the Americans insisted was just property.

America's third attempt at drafting language that would require the British to return slavery's fugitives proved more successful. This was not because the Treaty of Ghent, signed in the last days of 1814 and swiftly ratified as soon as the sealed copy reached Washington, had more ironclad wording than its predecessor, but due to the greater power of the centralized and expanding federal state that was the Treaty of Paris's legacy. Simply put, by 1815 the Americans' determination to enforce its claim to the forced return of fugitives was more resolute than it had been when its ideals were untested and shiny.[2]

It was Secretary of State James Monroe at the beginning of 1814 who first explicitly directed America's negotiators in Belgium to negotiate for the return of enslaved people liberated from America. Because he assumed that many of these fugitives had been sold into slavery in the British West Indies by unscrupulous British officers, he divided them into two classes: those who should be physically returned and those who should be paid for. As only those who had been reenslaved—or as Monroe put it, considered "as property"—were to be paid for, the end result would be the return of all fugitives into their chains.[3]

More than a year before the signing of the Treaty of Ghent, America's top diplomat, John Quincy Adams, complained to his English counterpart, Lord Castlereagh, of British admirals offering "inducements" to enslaved Americans to abscond with their fleets. Adams charged that many of these fugitives were later sold in the West Indies, causing Castlereagh "some apparent agitation" as he rushed "to deny it in the most unqualified terms," saying it was "impossible" and "totally destitute of foundation." Castlereagh thought that such claims were "one of those charges . . . originating only in the spirit of hostility" and praised the character of his naval officers, declaring that "their generosity and humanity could not be contested." Castlereagh informed Adams that since 1811 "the act of selling any man for a slave" had been a "felony without benefit of clergy," or, in other words, one punishable by death.

Was Adams stung by Castlereagh's positioning of his forces on the side of humanity and, by implication, the Americans on the other? Adams could only weakly respond that "there would be in all classes individuals capable of committing actions of which others would be ashamed" and that he had been "instructed" to convey these concerns.[4]

Ultimately, the British government demanded proof that freed people had been sold back into slavery and asserted that any officer guilty of such an act would be "punished in an exemplary manner." Adams found this "negro note" insufficient, as it "confounds together the two acts of seducing the slaves and afterwards selling them, and promises only to punish the whole." To the Americans, Adams candidly revealed, the act of reenslavement was not an issue, "It is the seduction of the slaves that constitutes the offence against us." Adams demanded that the British "indemnify the owners of the negroes for the loss of them."[5]

Adams knew that his claims about American proof that British naval officers sold freed people back into chains was just bluster. He had been told personally by Albert Gallatin that "our proof is weak," and he doubted "whether the fact can be proved" as all they had was a single affidavit from an Irishman. Gallatin also wondered if it might be better to drop their demand for the British to disavow the "seduction" of enslaved people because "all the opponents of the slave-trade would approve and justify the act." In other words, at least Gallatin worried that America would place itself on the wrong side of humanity by doing so.[6]

John Quincy Adams, when serving as "Minister Plenipotentiary" to Great Britain, was well aware of what being returned to their enslavers meant to the men and women who had fled to British protection. While in London, Adams offered his advice on what a ship captain should do if he discovered a stowaway fugitive from slavery on board his ship that had sailed to a foreign port. Adams observed that the laws of his nation were clear: "slaves are property" and any "slaves escaping from their masters into a state where slavery does not exist, are to be restored them on demand." Adams advised the captain that even if he sailed to Boston, he was to surrender the man to the district marshal. It was, however, in the captain's right, when surrendering his prisoner to his erstwhile master, "to call upon his sense of justice and humanity most earnestly for a promise that he will exercise no personal rigor towards the slave by way of punishing him for this elopement." Knowing that punishment was the escapees' lot, all Adams could do was suggest an appeal to the enslaver's morality. Likely it was he also knew this was unlikely to succeed, but it may have soothed both his and the ship captain's consciences.[7]

The treaty that was agreed upon in December of 1814 placed the issue of the runaways "carried off" in its first of eleven articles. That article's third sentence included the relevant clause: "All territory, places, and possessions, without exception, taken by either party from the other during the war, or which may be taken after the signing of this treaty, shall be restored without delay and without causing any destruction, or carrying away any artillery or other public property, or any slaves or other private property."[8] Such verbiage was very close to the wording of the Treaty of Paris signed in 1782: "his Britanic Majesty shall with all convenient speed, and without causing any Destruction, or carrying away any Negroes or other Property of the American inhabitants, withdraw all his Armies, Garrisons & Fleets from the said United States, and from every Post, Place and Harbour within the same; leaving in all Fortifications, the American Artillery that may be therein." The chief difference being the use of the term "Negroes" in the earlier document and "slaves" in the later. The significance of this shift is mitigated somewhat by the simple fact that in both cases such categories of people are equated with property.

When Andrew Jackson received word that a peace treaty had been signed, his first communication with his British counterpart demanded the return of fugitives from slavery. Major-General Lambert, who had risen to command of British forces after both his superiors had fallen in battle at New Orleans, complied by abandoning Fort Bowyer in Mobile Bay and exchanging prisoners of war, but he refused Jackson's directive to return those who had escaped bondage. Lambert tried to placate the American commander by denying he was any sort of an abolitionist, writing, "I have from the first, done all I could to prevent, and subsequently . . . have given every facility, and used every persuasion, that they should Return to their Masters, and many have done so." Rather, Lambert painted his denial as being compelled by the language of the treaty itself: "If those Negroes (the matter now in Question) belonged to the territory or City we were actually in occupation of, I should conceive we had no right to take them away; but by their coming away, they are virtually the same as Deserters or property taken away at any time of the War." To this Jackson seemed honestly confused: "As it respects the Negroes, I do not clearly perceive the distinction between their being carried away and their being taken."[9]

Had he been a diplomat rather than a military man, Lambert might have stopped there. But he apparently could not resist claiming a moral high ground over the Americans. Lambert confessed, "I could not reconcile it to myself to abandon any, who from false reasoning perhaps, joined us during the Period of Hostilities, and have thus acted in violation of the laws of their Country and besides become obnoxious to their masters." Once again, peeking through the stilted official communications is the reality that the worth of those who were to be returned lay not only in their exchange value, but in the demoralizing effect upon other enslaved peoples of the failure of their flight for freedom and the demonstrative horror of their torture or even murder.

As British fleets prepared to evacuate the sea islands and forts they occupied, federal agents were sent to reenslave the people given English sanctuary. Three American commissioners were dispatched to meet with Royal Captain James Clavelle aboard his flagship, the *Orlando,* anchored in the Patuxent River of Maryland. Clavelle refused to turn over any of the many formerly enslaved people sheltering on Tangier Island, as, according to his reading of the treaty, he was only obligated to surrender "private property originally captured in the said forts or places." Clavelle continued, "As none of the slaves now in Tangier were captured there, I cannot feel myself at liberty to deliver them up; far less can I give up those now serving on board His Britannic Majesty's ships, as by entering into the service they made themselves free men." The Americans protested, of course, sending a flurry of notes and messages to both Clavelle and Washington, but on April 15 Clavelle and his fleet hauled up their anchors and sailed for Bermuda, Clavelle sending one last letter that said simply, "In reply to your communication . . . I beg to state that my determination is not to restore any slaves, private or public property, captured before the exchange of the ratifications of the treaty of peace . . . agreeably to my instructions from Rear Admiral Cockburn."[10]

American captain Thomas Newell was dispatched to Cumberland Island, Georgia, to demand of British admiral George Cockburn the restitution of the people freed by the British there. As Major-General Lambert had done for Andrew Jackson, Cockburn allowed the Americans to enter his camp and appeal to the Black refugees to voluntarily return to their masters. Pressed further, Cockburn begrudgingly handed the agents a list of seventy-seven fugitives who came into his camps after the peace treaty came into force and who he agreed to surrender. A month later, the American commissioners complained that ten of these men and women had never appeared as agreed, and two or three others that had been surrendered had already absconded. The Americans lamely asked the British officers to be on the lookout for them, as they assumed they would attempt to once more clamber onto their ships.[11]

America's determined commissioners pursued the British fleet to the Bahamas. Thomas Spalding presented his credentials, apparently signed by the president, to Britain's Admiral Edward Griffith, who then informed him with "much regret" that most of the fugitives had been sent on to Halifax. The following day Spalding met with the colony's governor, Sir James Cockburn, the brother of the rear admiral, who "instantly lost his temper; denied my authority" and "declared he would receive nothing from any one but the Secretary of State." When Spalding persisted, Cockburn "vehemently added, that he would rather Bermuda, and every man, woman, and child in it, were sunk under the sea, than surrender one slave that had sought protection under the flag of England."[12]

The extraordinary importance of these official missions to reclaim and return escapees from slavery was evident in the provisions made by Secretary of State Monroe when he learned that thousands of fugitives had sailed for Nova Scotia. Monroe dispatched a special agent, Augustine Neale, to pursue these escapees, affording him use of a vessel from the navy and $2,000 that he knew was given with thin legal authority. Monroe told his agent: "Knowing the Presidents disposition & earnest desire, to make every effort in his power, to recover back the Slaves of our fellow Citizens, I have confidence that the plan will be approved by him. I think therefore you may proceed to execute it without a moments delay, advising me repeatedly of the measures you may adopt, as no legal provision has been made for this expenditure, and it must be defrayed from the Contingent fund, or laid before Congress and provided for by a future law."[13]

Landing in Halifax, Neale could neither pressure Canadian officials to relinquish any freed people who had taken sanctuary there, or persuade any fugitives from slavery to return "home," where they would not suffer the "winter's frost." Rather, Neale reported, the refugees could not be assuaged of their "horrors of anticipated punishment."[14]

President Madison pushed Secretary of State Monroe to not relax his insistence on the return of the men and women who had fled to British sanctuary, telling him in April of 1815 to keep "the principle admitted in the article, that negroes or slaves, under certain circumstances, are to be restored" in "prominent view." This in spite of the fact that in the very same letter Madison admitted that the British stood on the moral high ground. Madison characterized his own government's insistence on the return of fugitives as "in every view extremely reproachful," as "a perfidious surrender of them to their masters can never be palliated, especially whilst that nation professes to be the champion of their Cause." Nevertheless, Madison saw that upon this tender point he could apply painful pressure, as he had "no doubt that every sophistical exertion will be made by the B. Govt. to evade the obligation to restore negroes." Pressing this point "fastens on the B. Ministry the charge on which they will doubtless be arraigned; at the same time that it confirms a construction which is necessary to make the effect real and not merely nominal, to the U.S." In other words, in spite of his own qualms, Madison was quite willing to leverage the freedom of thousands of Black men and Black women who had fled American slavery for a stronger hand in the negotiations.[15]

In the months that followed, it became clear that the Americans expected that the British would both pay compensation for some of the enslaved people they had rescued and return others back into their chains. In May of 1815, Adams complained to Castlereagh that a "British Admiral stationed in the Chesapeake had declined restoring slaves he had taken." When no action had been taken in the matter, Adams repeated his objections the following month.[16] In August, Castlereagh's successor, Lord Liverpool, informed Adams that their reading of the treaty obligated them to only return the enslaved in forts and places that had been seized on American soil. Adams responded that he construed the article (which he reminded Liverpool the British side had written) to mean that the British were obligated to return "slaves, which had been in any manner captured on shore during the war." Liverpool then took the high ground, saying that his government would never have agreed "that persons who, from whatever motive, had taken refuge under the protection of the British forces should be delivered up to those who, to say the least, must feel unkindly towards them and might treat them harshly."[17]

Whether by some sense of duty to his nation, his office, and his charge, or whether Liverpool's embrace of benevolence provoked Adams to employ his lawyerly instincts rather than his humanitarian ones, the man who would in a few years passionately argue before the Supreme Court for the freedom of enslaved rebels who had taken over the Spanish schooner *Amistad* responded that "Slaves were private property." This then gave Lord Liverpool the opportunity to lecture Adams that this was absurd. "A table or chair, for instance, might be taken and restored without changing its condition; but a living and a human being was entitled to other considerations." Adams was forced to concede that yes, "a living, sentient being, and still more a human being, was to be regarded in a different light from the inanimate matter of which other private property might consist." But, Adams noted, this distinction was not made in the wording of the treaty and therefore did not carry the force of law. Adams then fell back to a compromise position: if England "felt bound to make good the promises of her officers to the slaves, she might be willing to do an act of justice, by compensating the owners of the slaves for the property which had been irregularly taken from them."[18]

Following this chronology, it is clear that the American position from the beginning had been one of demanding the bodily restoration of great numbers of fugitives and payments of compensation for those beyond reach. Only months after the treaty had been signed and the details of its implementation negotiated did the American demands soften to compensation alone. Because of American intransigence in demanding the physical return of escapees, the issue lingered another year, with notes and meetings finally culminating in referring the whole matter to an independent commission. Years later this process culminated in the British payment of $1,204,960 in compensation for the loss of Americans' human property of 3,601 souls. This sum eventually trickled back into enslavers' pockets, and, undoubtedly, in many cases, was used to purchase more human property.[19]

While the parallels between these two episodes of peacemaking are fascinating, their different outcomes reveal more about the direction the institutions of American federalism had taken since their birth. Contrasting these two periods, the inability of the first generation of patriot leaders to squeeze a similar sum from the Royal Treasury can be seen as a result of two factors: their lack of unity on the issue and the inability of their government to speak with one authoritative voice. Though John Adams, Benjamin Franklin, John Jay, and Henry Laurens dutifully wheedled language into the Treaty of Paris that appeared to require the return of slavery's fugitives who had been "carried off," none of them fought nearly as hard for this clause's fulfillment as did Madison, Monroe, or even John Quincy Adams. When John Jay had his second bite at the apple in negotiating a knock-on agreement, he failed completely, sidestepping his instructions and raising the ire of his secretary of state for his obvious sympathy with the humanitarian arguments posed by the other side.

Initially, though, the Treaty of Paris's failures, particularly the seemingly obvious violation of Article 7's agreement to return fugitives to slavery, brought Americans into a new consciousness of the foundational flaws and fissures inherent in their structure of government. Britain deftly exploited these cracks to interpret the agreement as favorably and flexibly as circumstances demanded. In a sense, in a sort of dialectic, Americans were led to see themselves in a profoundly new and powerful way and to use this knowledge to leverage a fundamental change in government while denying to themselves that they were, in effect, reimagining and reconstructing what was a failed state. It was this new, nascently modern and embryonic bureaucratic state that, thirty years later, even in the midst of military defeat, was powerful enough to enforce a degree of its will over the victor.

In both eras, national unity had been purchased with the coin of enslaved people. In the fervor of the Revolution, many Americans looked harshly upon the slavery in their midst, not so much out of a newfound sense of human empathy and benevolence for the enslaved, but out of a sure knowledge that slavery was a sin and God's providence or retribution was just and sure, or because slavery corrupted the master and the republic just as surely as it steadily drew into the nation an increasing number of Blacks whose presence undermined the dreams of a white republic.[20] Patriots readily sacrificed their desire to extinguish slavery so as to secure their independence and establish their state. This included demanding the return of thousands of Black Americans whose fate violated the Revolution's soaring liberal ideals of equality and democracy.

Thirty years later, when the ancient patriots and young politicians who had whooped up a war fever against the world's most powerful empire were brought to the edge of ruin and disunion in just two years of fighting, they understood that the price of keeping the republic unified was to be paid with recaptured runaways. New Englanders viewed the war as a partisan attack upon their own way of life by a political faction empowered by the Constitution's artificial inflation of southern voting strength. Southerners felt betrayed by Yankees who did not volunteer to fight, Yankee military commanders who did not prioritize defending the Chesapeake, and Yankee congressmen who dragged their feet at war requisitions. Anything less than a robust pursuit of those who had escaped American bondage in the bottoms of English ships would have raised further doubts among southerners about the continuing usefulness of having traded state sovereignty for federal protection in the Constitution.[21]

In this, like so many other things about the War of 1812, what was lost or eroded in the war was won in peace. Madison, Monroe, and John Quincy Adams all understood that by stridently and firmly demanding the return of fugitives from slavery they were reassuring the minority of white Americans who held the balance of power that the compromises made in Philadelphia in 1787 still served their interests. White unity and political stability had been, once again, purchased with Black bodies.

NOTES

INTRODUCTION

1. For accounts tying southern independence to slavery, see Woody Holton, *Unruly Americans and the Origins of the Constitution* (New York: Hill and Wang, 2007); Gerald Horne, *The Counter-Revolution of 1776: Slave Resistance and the Origins of the United States of America* (New York: New York University Press, 2014); Robert G. Parkinson, *The Common Cause: Creating Race and Nation in the American Revolution* (Chapel Hill: Univ. of North Carolina Press, 2016); Donald L. Robinson, *Slavery in the Structure of American Politics* (New York: Harcourt Brace Jovanovich, 1971); Simon Schama, *Rough Crossings: Britain, the Slaves and the American Revolution* (New York: HarperCollins, 2009); Douglas R. Egerton, *Death or Liberty: African Americans and Revolutionary America* (New York: Oxford Univ. Press, 2009); Don Fehrenbacher, *The Slaveholding Republic: An Account of the United States Government's Relations to Slavery* (New York: Oxford Univ. Press, 2001).

2. Phillip D. Morgan and Andrew Jackson O'Shaughnessy, "Arming Slaves in the American Revolution," in *Arming Slaves: From Classical Times to the Modern Age*, ed. Christopher Leslie Brown, Philip D. Morgan (New Haven: Yale Univ. Press, 2006).

3. Natsu Taylor Saito, *Settler Colonialism, Race, and the Law: Why Structural Racism Persists* (New York: New York Univ. Press, 2020).

4. Henry Laurens to George Washington, March 16, 1779, in *The Papers of George Washington, Revolutionary War Series*, vol. 19, *15 January–7 April 1779*, ed. Philander D. Chase and William M. Ferraro (Charlottesville: Univ. of Virginia Press, 2009), 503–505; see also Philip M. Hamer et al., eds., *The Papers of Henry Laurens*, vol. 12 (Columbia, S.C., 1968–2003), 392; George Washington to Henry Laurens, March 20, 1779, in *The Papers of George Washington, Revolutionary War Series*, 19:542–543.

5. Morgan and O'Shaughnessy, "Arming Slaves in the American Revolution," 185; Justin Iverson, *Rebels in Arms: Black Resistance and the Fight for Freedom in the Anglo-Atlantic*

(Athens: Univ. of Georgia Press, 2022); Gregory Massey, *John Laurens and the American Revolution* (Columbia: Univ. of South Carolina Press, 2000).

6. L. Scott Philyaw, "A Slave for Every Soldier: The Strange History of Virginia's Forgotten Recruitment Act of 1 January 1781," *Virginia Magazine of History and Biography* 109, no. 4 (2001), 367–386.

7. Aline Helg and Lara Vergnaud, *Slave No More: Self-Liberation before Abolitionism in the Americas* (Chapel Hill: Univ. of North Carolina Press, 2019), 117. See also Thomas B. Allen, *Tories: Fighting for the King in America's First Civil War* (New York: HarperCollins, 2010), 152–153; Peter Wood, "'Taking Care of Business' in Revolutionary South Carolina: Republicanism and the Slave Society," in J. William Harris, *The Hanging of Thomas Jeremiah: A Free Black Man's Encounter with Liberty* (New Haven: Yale Univ. Press, 2009); William R. Ryan, *The World of Thomas Jeremiah: Charles Town on the Eve of the American Revolution* (New York: Oxford Univ. Press, 2010).

8. James W. St. G. Walker, *The Search for a Promised Land in Nova Scotia and Sierra Leone, 1783–1870* (Toronto: Univ. of Toronto Press, 1992), 2.

9. Alan Gilbert, *Black Patriots and Loyalists: Fighting for Emancipation in the War for Independence* (Chicago: Univ. of Chicago Press, 2012), 205, 173–176.

10. See Benjamin Quarles, *The Negro in the American Revolution* (Chapel Hill: Univ. of North Carolina Press, 1961); Sylvia R. Frey, *Water from the Rock: Black Resistance in a Revolutionary Age* (Princeton, N.J.: Princeton Univ. Press, 1991); Simon Schama, *Rough Crossings: The Slaves, the British, and the American Revolution* (New York: Harper Collins, 2006); Gilbert, *Black Patriots and Loyalists;* Egerton, *Death or Liberty.*

11. One of the common ways the issue of fugitives was downplayed was by portraying them not as people who had successfully fled to sanctuary, but as booty stolen by the British. In that representation, no change was made to their status as enslaved or free persons, they were simply property transferred from one owner to another. John Fisk, who wrote the first scholarly book investigating the causes of the Constitution, noted that the Americans opposed restoring the property of loyalists because of the "damage they had done in burning houses and kidnapping slaves." Later in Fiske's account, he does concede that "Many negroes had left the country with the British fleet: some doubtless had sought their freedom; others, perhaps, had been kidnapped as booty." John Fiske, *The Critical Period in American History, 1783–1789* (Boston: Houghton Mifflin, 1888), 32, 73. 131; see also Henry Steele Commager, "John Fiske: An Interpretation," *Proceedings of the Massachusetts Historical Society,* 3rd series, vol. 66 (October 1936–May 1941): 332–345. Andrew C. McLaughlin, who contributed volume 10, *The Confederation and the Constitution,* to the prestigious and quasi-official twenty-six-volume series *The American Nation: A History,* also denied the agency and humanity of enslaved people by portraying them passively as property to be "stolen" or "carried off." Andrew C. McLaughlin, *The Confederation and the Constitution, 1783–1789* (New York: Harper and Bros., 1905), 75, 30. See also Herman Belz, "Andrew C. McLaughlin and Liberal Democracy: Scientific History in Support of the Best Regime," *Reviews in American History* 19, no. 3 (September 1991): 445–461. Merrill Jensen wrote that the "British

had plundered Carolina of its Negroes and silver plate." Merrill Jensen, *The New Nation: A History of the United States During the Confederation, 1781–1789* (New York: Knopf, 1950), 16. Another common method of clouding the issue of fugitive slaves was picturing the desire to recapture escaped slaves as a policy limited to the evil South. John Bach McMaster, who, like McLaughlin, served as president of the American Historical Association, wrote, "The carrying off of the negroes was another matter yet to be adjusted. The injury done by this act was little felt north of the Potomac." John Bach McMaster, *A History of the People of the United States* (1883; reprint, New York: Appleton, 1914), 117, 235; Andrew C. McLaughlin, "Western Posts and British Debts," *Annual Report of the American Historical Association* (Washington, D.C.: Government Printing Office, 1895), 421. Likewise, Frederick Ogg of Indiana University, who innovated what became known as "Diplomatic History," downplayed the issue of fugitive slaves in the peace negotiations between the United States and Britain in 1782 by describing the demand for the return of such people as being the sole interest of the one southerner among America's diplomats, South Carolinian Henry Laurens. Ogg wrote that "the incorporation of the negro clause was purely the result of the chance arrival of Henry Laurens at Paris on the closing day of the negotiation." Frederic A. Ogg, "Jay's Treaty and the Slavery Interests of the United States," *American Historical Association Annual Reports*, vol. 1 (Washington, D.C., 1901), 273–298.

Histories from the mid-twentieth century commonly simply avoided mentioning the diplomatic impasse over the people who escaped American slavery. Carl Van Doren is entirely silent about fugitive African Americans and even notes that Virginia "refused to carry out the treaty's stipulations in regard to the treatment of loyalists and the debts owed by Virginians to their British creditors" without saying why. Carl Van Doren, *The Great Rehearsal: The Story of the Making of the Constitution of the United States* (New York: Viking, 1948), 80. There is not a word about the controversy over British harboring of American fugitives from slavery in Gordon Wood's masterpiece, *The Creation of the American Republic, 1776–1787* (Chapel Hill: Univ. of North Carolina Press, 1969), 399, 404.

Neither Forrest McDonald, Catherine Drinker Bowen, nor Clinton Rossiter writes a word about the controversy over British evacuation of fugitives from slavery. Forrest McDonald, *Novus Ordo Seclorum: The Intellectual Origins of the Constitution* (Lawrence: Univ. Press of Kansas, 1985); Catherine Drinker Bowen, *Miracle at Philadelphia: The Story of the Constitutional Convention* (Boston: Little, Brown, 1966), 33, 246; Clinton Rossiter, *The Grand Convention* (New York: Macmillan, 1966). Books published around the time of the Constitution's bicentennial also kept the issue of fugitives under wraps. Christopher Collier and James Lincoln Collier, *Decision in Philadelphia: The Constitutional Convention of 1787* (New York: Ballantine Books, 1987), 4–5, 7; William Peters, *A More Perfect Union* (New York: Crown Publishers, 1987); Richard B. Bernstein, *Are We to Be a Nation?: The Making of the Constitution* (Cambridge, Mass.: Harvard Univ. Press, 1987); Robert Middlekauff, *The Glorious Cause: The American Revolution, 1763–1789* (New York: Oxford Univ. Press, 1982, 2005), 594.

This long history of scholarly neglect of the role of fugitive slaves in the negotiations was first broken by Arnett G. Lindsay, a Howard University graduate student writing his dissertation under the direction of Carter Woodson. Arnett G. Lindsay, "Diplomatic Relations between the United States and Great Britain Bearing on the Return of Negro Slaves, 1783–1828," *Journal of Negro History* 5, no. 4 (October 1920): 391–419. Fifty years later, Ralph Lowry significantly broadened the subject of fugitives from patriot slavery to include a much more thorough discussion of what was happening in Paris and London during the year of negotiations after Yorktown. Ralph J. Lowry, "The Black Question in Article Seven of the 1783 Peace Treaty," *Negro History Bulletin* 38, no. 5 (June/July 1975): 415–418.

12. Typical of more recent popular works is Joseph J. Ellis, who studiously avoids any mention of the fugitive slave issue even when his narrative leads him directly into its thickets. Joseph J. Ellis, *Quartet: Orchestrating the Second American Revolution, 1783–1789* (New York: Knopf, 2015), 103–105; Joseph J. Ellis, *American Creation: Tragedies and Triumphs at the Founding of the Republic* (New York: Knopf, 2007), 86–87. Similarly, Jack N. Rakove, in his Pulitzer Prize-winning book, *Original Meanings*, goes to great lengths not to mention the patriots' crisis over British harboring of their runaway human property. Jack N. Rakove, *Original Meanings: Politics and Ideas in the Making of the Constitution* (New York: Vintage, 1996), 24–27. David O. Stewart's *The Summer of 1787: The Men Who Invented the Constitution* (New York: Simon and Schuster, 2007) also skirts around the issue. Richard Beeman in *Plain, Honest Men* never mentions that Britain had liberated thousands of American slaves or that American leaders demanded their return. Richard Beeman, *Plain, Honest Men: The Making of the American Constitution* (New York: Random House, 2010). Pauline Meier, in her prize-winning account of the Constitution's ratification, in highlighting Congress's inability to cajole the states to abide by the Treaty of Paris, only mentions British retention of frontier forts as the source of disagreement. Pauline Maier, *Ratification: The People Debate the Constitution, 1787–1788* (New York: Simon and Schuster, 2010), 13. Carol Berkin's *A Brilliant Solution: Inventing the American Constitution*, also gives only the unembarrassing side of the story by mentioning forts, not fugitives. Carol Berkin, *A Brilliant Solution: Inventing the American Constitution* (New York: Harcourt, 2002), 20–21.

13. More recent works continue this trend. Melvin Yazawa in *Contested Conventions* includes a section in his chapter detailing the problems that led to the Constitutional Convention titled "Irregularities and the Treaty of Paris" that makes no mention of the issue of escaped slaves or the requirement in the treaty that they be returned. Melvin Yazawa, *Contested Conventions: The Struggle to Establish the Constitution and Save the Union, 1787–1789* (Baltimore: Johns Hopkins Univ. Press, 2016), 4–6. Woody Holton does not discuss Article 7 in *Unruly Americans and the Origins of the Constitution;* nor does Max Edling in his *A Revolution in Favor of Government* indicate that the return of escapees from slavery was an article of the peace treaty or mention this issue at all. Max Edling, *A Revolution in Favor of Government: Origins of the U.S. Constitution and the Making of the American State* (New York: Oxford Univ. Press, 2003). Michael Klarman's *The Framers' Coup* disconnects the eagerness of states to pass confiscation laws and debtor relief laws from the issue of fugitive slaves, only mentioning in passing that in 1783 "the British had violated the treaty provi-

sion in which they promised not to carry away American-owned slaves in their possession when their military forces departed." Michael Klarman, *The Framers' Coup: The Making of the United States Constitution* (New York: Oxford Univ. Press, 2016), 46. In *We Have Not a Government,* George William Van Cleve goes somewhat further in writing that "southern planters . . . were angry about the fact that departing British military forces had taken several thousand slaves" and that Virginia's legislature used "slave removals as its pretext" to violate the peace treaty. George William Van Cleve, *We Have Not a Government: The Articles of Confederation and the Road to the Constitution* (Chicago: Univ. of Chicago Press, 2017), 71–72. Jeff Broadwater in his study of the Constitution that was focused on the friendship of Jefferson and Madison once brushes against the issue of British harboring of fugitives in describing how Madison was "no abolitionist," as, among other things, he once "excoriated British commanders for taking fugitive slaves with them, in violation of the Treaty of Paris, when they withdrew from American cities at the end of the war." Instead, he too obscures the issue of fugitive slaves by the usual means of mentioning only the question of forts. Jeff Broadwater, *Jefferson, Madison, and the Making of the Constitution* (Chapel Hill: Univ. of North Carolina Press, 2019), 115, 92. A similar elision of critical facts are found in Gerald Leonard's *The Partisan Republic: Democracy, Exclusion, and the Fall of the Founders' Constitution, 1780s–1830s* (New York: Cambridge Univ. Press, 2019), 11.

Only a handful of recent works forthrightly face the fact that America's founders prioritized recapturing slave fugitives from England and spent the better part of a decade agitating for their return. One is Eliga Gould's *Among the Powers of the Earth.* Gould accurately recounts the efforts of congressmen, statesmen, and diplomats from both the North and South to pressure the British government. Eliga H. Gould, *Among the Powers of the Earth: The American Revolution and the Making of a New World Empire* (Cambridge, Mass.: Harvard Univ. Press, 2012), 19–154, 161–165. David Gellman's *Liberty's Chain: Slavery, Abolition, and the Jay Family of New York* insightfully chronicles John Jay's central role in the controversy of the "carried off," from his being commissioned to draft a report on state infractions of the treaty in 1786 to his surrendering of American claims to compensation in the treaty that carried his name nearly a decade later.

14. There are a fair number of fine histories of the struggles of enslaved people who took advantage of the chaos and opportunities afforded by the war with Britain to liberate themselves. Quarles, *The Negro in the American Revolution;* Frey, *Water from the Rock;* Graham Russell Hodges, ed., *The Black Loyalist Directory: African Americans in Exile After the American Revolution* (New York: Garland, 1996); Schama, *Rough Crossings;* Alan Gilbert, *Black Patriots and Loyalists;* Egerton, *Death or Liberty;* Maya Jasanoff, *Liberty's Exiles: American Loyalists in the Revolutionary World* (New York: Knopf, 2011); Karen Cook Bell, *Running from Bondage: Enslaved Women and Their Remarkable Fight for Freedom in Revolutionary America* (Cambridge: Cambridge Univ. Press, 2021), 105.

15. Thurgood Marshall, "The Constitution's Bicentennial—Commemorating the Wrong Document," *Vanderbilt Law Review* 40, no. 6 (1987): 1337–1342.

16. Jack Valenti, "Despite Slavery, a Constitution That Built a Nation," *New York Times,*

June 6, 1987; Clarence Thomas, "An Afro-American Perspective: Toward a 'Plain Reading' of the Constitution—The Declaration of Independence in Constitutional Interpretation," *Howard Law Journal* 30, no. 4 (September 22, 1987): 983.

17. Paul Finkelman, *Slavery and the Founders: Race and Liberty in the Age of Jefferson,* 2nd ed. (New York: Sharpe, 2001); George William Van Cleve, *A Slaveholders' Union: Slavery, Politics, and the Constitution in the Early American Republic* (Chicago: Univ. of Chicago Press, 2010). The secret draft of the Jay-Gardoqui treaty swapped favorable American access to the markets of the Spanish empire (a priority of northern merchants) in exchange for surrendering to Spain control of the West's greatest artery of commerce, the Mississippi River, for thirty years (an unacceptable idea to the expanding slave South). Parkinson, *The Common Cause.*

18. Sean Wilentz, *No Property in Man: Slavery and Antislavery at the Nation's Founding* (Cambridge, Mass.: Harvard Univ. Press, 2018); David Waldstreicher, *Slavery's Constitution: From Revolution to Ratification* (New York: Hill and Wang, 2009), 154.

19. William M. Wiecek, *The Sources of Antislavery Constitutionalism in America, 1760–1848* (Ithaca: Cornell Univ. Press, 1977).

ONE. *Recapture of Slavery's Fugitives in the Early Republic*

1. "Seasonable Thoughts," *Pennsylvania Journal,* January 3, 1776, in *Diary of the American Revolution: From Newspapers and Original Documents,* vol. 1, ed. Frank Moore (New York: C. Scribner, 1860), 188–189.

2. William Gordon, *The History of the Rise, Progress, and Establishment of the Independence of the United States of America,* vol. 4 (London: Charles Dilly and James Buckland, 1788), 196.

3. Jared Sparks, ed., *The Diplomatic Correspondence of the American Revolution,* vol. 8. (Boston: N. Hale and Gray and Bowen, 1829), 320.

4. Quarles, *The Negro in the American Revolution,* 159–161. Governor Harrison to Count Rochambeau, June 26, 1782, in *Official Letters of the Governors of the State of Virginia,* vol. 3, ed. H. R. McIlwaine (Richmond: Virginia State Library, 1929), 257.

5. "General Orders, 25 October 1781," Founders Online, National Archives, https://founders.archives.gov/documents/Washington/99-01-02-07264.

6. Edmund Pendleton to James Madison, July 29, 1782, in *The Papers of James Madison,* vol. 4, *1 January 1782–31 July 1782,* ed. William T. Hutchinson and William M. E. Rachal (Chicago: Univ. of Chicago Press, 1965), 442–444. "We have heard . . ." quote in Edmund Pendleton to James Madison, August 19, 1782, in *The Papers of James Madison,* vol. 5, *1 August 1782–31 December 1782,* ed. William T. Hutchinson and William M. E. Rachal (Chicago: Univ. of Chicago Press, 1967), 63–65.

7. James Madison to Edmund Pendleton, August 6, 1782, in *The Papers of James Madison,* 5:27–28.

8. James Madison to Edmund Pendleton, September 3, 1782, in *The Papers of James Madison,* 5:101–103.

9. Edmund Pendleton to James Madison, September 24, 1782, in *The Papers of James Madison,* 5:157–158.

10. Edmund Pendleton to James Madison, September 2, 1782, in *The Papers of James Madison*, 5:96–98.

11. Edmund Pendleton to James Madison, September 24, 1782, in *The Papers of James Madison*, 5:157–158. See also Edmund Pendleton to James Madison, August 19, 1782, in *The Papers of James Madison*, 5:63–65.

12. Jean-Baptiste Donatien de Vimeur, Comte de Rochambeau (1725–1807). Jean-Baptiste Donatien de Vimeur, Comte de Rochambeau, to Patrick Henry, correspondence, March 28, 1782, GLC04837.01, The Gilder Lehrman Institute of American History, New York.

13. David Ross Jr. to George Washington, October 25, 1781, Founders Online, National Archives, https://founders.archives.gov/documents/Washington/99-01-02-07271.

14. Quarles, *The Negro in the American Revolution*, 165. Jerome Nadelhaft, "Ending South Carolina's War: Two 1782 Agreements Favoring the Planters," *South Carolina Historical Magazine* 80, no. 1 (January 1979), 50–64.

15. Walker, *The Search for a Promised Land*, 8; Allen D. Candler, ed., *The Revolutionary Records of the State of Georgia*, vol. 3 (Atlanta, Ga., Franklin-Turner, 1908), 119–120; Quarles, *The Negro in the American Revolution*, 163. Allan Kulikoff estimates that five thousand enslaved people reached British camps in the upper south and perhaps thirteen thousand in the Carolinas and Georgia. Allan Kulikoff, "Uprooted Peoples: Black Migrants in the Age of the American Revolution, 1790–1820," in *Slavery and Freedom in the Age of Revolution*, ed. Ira Berlin and Ronald Hoffman (Charlottesville, Va.: Univ. Press of Virginia, 1983); Allan Kulikoff, *Tobacco and Slaves: The Development of Southern Cultures in the Chesapeake, 1680–1800* (Chapel Hill: Univ. of North Carolina Press, 1986); *Pennsylvania Gazette* (Philadelphia), September 4, 1782, 2.

16. The Virginia Delegates to the Governor of Virginia, September 10, 1782, in *Letters of Members of the Continental Congress*, vol. 6, ed. Edmund C. Burnett (Washington, D.C.: Carnegie Institute, 1933), 468; Schama, *Rough Crossings*, 149.

17. A. J. Bowen, ed., *The Unpublished Revolutionary Papers of Major-General Edward Hand* (New York: George H. Richmond, 1907), 30.

18. Ordinance of March 21, 1784. See petition of Taliaferro et al., December 1792, Document Number: 1792 #214, Records of the General Assembly, South Carolina, Department of Archives and History, Columbia, South Carolina, Race and Slavery Petitions Project Series 1, Legislative Petitions, University of North Carolina Greensboro.

19. *Pennsylvania Gazette*, December 29, 1784, 1.

20. Brigadier General William Irvine to George Washington, November 11, 1779, in *The Papers of George Washington, Revolutionary War Series*, vol. 23, *22 October–31 December 1779*, ed. William M. Ferraro (Charlottesville: University of Virginia Press, 2015), 245.

21. George Washington to Rufus Putnam, February 2, 1783; David Humphreys to Rufus Putnam, February 4, 1783; Rufus Putnam to George Washington, February 4, 1783; Rufus Putnam to David Humphreys, February 7, 1783; Jonathan Hobby to George Washington, February 7, 1783, all at Founders Online, National Archives, https://founders.archives.gov/documents/Washington/99-01-02-10551, 10565, 10566, 10595, 10588.

22. James McHenry to George Washington, February 2, 1783; George Washington to James McHenry, February 18, 1783, both at Founders Online, National Archives, https://founders.archives.gov/documents/Washington/99-01-02-10550 and 10665.

23. A. Van Doren Honeyman, ed., "The Revolutionary War Record of Samuel Sutphin [*sic*], Slave," *Somerset County Historical Quarterly* 3 (1914): 186–190.

24. Helen Catterall, ed., *Judicial Cases Concerning American Slavery and the Negro*, vol. 4 (Washington, D.C.: Carnegie Institution of Washington, 1936), 422.

25. Sidney S. Rider, *An Historical Inquiry Concerning the Attempt to Raise a Regiment of Slaves by Rhode Island* (Providence, R.I.: Sidney S. Rider, 1880), 57–58, 71; Judith L. Van Buskirk, *Standing in Their Own Light: African American Patriots in the American Revolution* (Norman: Univ. of Oklahoma Press, 2017), 188.

26. Van Buskirk, *Standing in Their Own Light*, 178, 187. Armistead's petition can be found in *Journal of the House of Delegates of the Commonwealth of Virginia*, December. 4, 1784 (Richmond, Va., 1828), 57. Eva Sheppard Wolf observes that "though Virginia masters petitioned and received permission from the colonial assembly to substitute their slaves for their own service, upon the promise that they would be freed upon the conclusion of their enlistment, few actually honored their promises. Only a handful of the several hundred enslaved fighters promised their freedom in exchange for serving in the Continental Army or Virginia Militia were actually manumitted after 1783." Eva Sheppard Wolf, *Race and Liberty in the New Nation: Emancipation in Virginia from the Revolution to Nat Turner's Rebellion* (Baton Rouge: Louisiana State Univ. Press, 1982), 39.

27. Anthony Benezet to Joseph Phipps, May 28, 1763, in *Am I Not a Man and a Brother: The Antislavery Crusade of Revolutionary America, 1688–1788*, ed. Roger Bruns (New York: Chelsea House Publishers, 1977), 97–99.

28. Benjamin Vaughan to Benjamin Franklin, August 9, 1783, in *The Papers of Benjamin Franklin*, vol. 40, *May 16 through September 15, 1783*, ed. Ellen R. Cohn (New Haven: Yale Univ. Press, 2011), 449–450.

29. Richard K. Murdoch, "The Return of Runaway Slaves 1790–1794," *Florida Historical Quarterly* 38, no. 2 (1959): 97.

30. *Journals of the Continental Congress, 1774–1789*, vol. 34, ed. Worthington Chauncey Ford (Washington, D.C.: Government Printing Office, 1937), 431.

31. James Seagrove to Pierce Butler, August 8, 1790, in *The Documentary History of the First Federal Congress of the United States, March 4, 1789–March 3, 1791*, vol. 20, ed. Charlene Bangs Bickford, Kenneth R. Bowling, William C. diGiacomantonio, and Helen E. Veit (Charlottesville: Univ. of Virginia Press, 2019).

32. Note 1, Thomas Jefferson to William Carmichael, May 31, 1790, in *The Papers of Thomas Jefferson*, vol. 16, *30 November 1789–4 July 1790*, ed. Julian P. Boyd (Princeton: Princeton Univ. Press, 1961), 450–451.

33. John Jay to William Carmichael, October 2, 1789, in *The Selected Papers of John Jay*, vol. 5, *1788–1794*, ed. Elizabeth M. Nuxoll (Charlottesville: Univ. of Virginia Press, 2017), 148–149; Thomas Jefferson to William Carmichael, May 31, 1790, in *The Papers of Thomas Jef-*

ferson, 16:450–451; Thomas Jefferson to William Carmichael, August 29, 1790, in *The Papers of Thomas Jefferson,* vol. 17, *6 July–3 November 1790,* ed. Julian P. Boyd (Princeton: Princeton Univ. Press, 1965), 472–473.

34. Edward Telfair to Thomas Jefferson, January 12, 1791, in *The Papers of Thomas Jefferson,* vol. 18, *4 November 1790–24 January 1791,* ed. Julian P. Boyd (Princeton: Princeton Univ. Press, 1971), 491–492.

35. George Washington to James Seagrove, May 20, 1791, in *The Papers of George Washington, Presidential Series,* vol. 8, *22 March 1791–22 September 1791,* ed. Mark A. Mastromarino (Charlottesville: Univ. Press of Virginia, 1999), 198–200.

36. "Enclosure II: Juan Nepomuceno de Quesada to James Seagrove, 6 August 1791," in *The Papers of Thomas Jefferson,* vol. 22, *6 August 1791–31 December 1791,* ed. Charles T. Cullen (Princeton: Princeton Univ. Press, 1986), 407–408.

37. Kathryn E. Holland Braund. "The Creek Indians, Blacks, and Slavery," *Journal of Southern History* 57, no. 4 (1991): 601–636; Colin G. Calloway, *Pen and Ink Witchcraft: Treaties and Treaty Making in American Indian History* (New York: Oxford Univ. Press, 2013), 48.

38. William Crawford to George Washington, September 20, 1774, in *The Papers of George Washington, Colonial Series,* vol. 10, *21 March 1774–15 June 1775,* ed. W. W. Abbot and Dorothy Twohig (Charlottesville: Univ. Press of Virginia, 1995), 162–164; William Crawford to George Washington, November 14, 1774, in *The Papers of George Washington, Colonial Series,* 10:181–185.

39. *American State Papers: Public Lands,* 1:52.

40. Charles Joseph Kappler, ed., *Indian Affairs: Laws and Treaties,* vol. 2 (Washington, D.C.: Government Printing Office, 1905), 3.

41. Anthony Wayne to George Washington, November 1, 1783, Founders Online, National Archives, https://founders.archives.gov/documents/Washington/99-01-02-12007.

42. Kappler, ed., *Indian Affairs: Laws and Treaties,* 2:3, 5, 6, 9, 11, 14, 16.

43. "Instructions to the Commissioners for Southern Indians, Aug. 29, 1789," in *The Documentary History of the First Federal Congress of the United States, March 4, 1789–March 3, 1791,* vol. 2, ed. Linda Grant De Pauw, Charlene Bangs Bickford, and LaVonne Marlene Siegel (Baltimore: Johns Hopkins Univ. Press, 1974), 206.

44. Pierce Butler to Roger Parker Saunders, August 26, 1790, in *The Documentary History of the First Federal Congress of the United States, March 4, 1789–March 3, 1791,* vol. 20, ed. Charlene Bangs Bickford, Kenneth R. Bowling, William C. diGiacomantonio, and Helen E. Veit (Baltimore: Johns Hopkins Univ. Press, 2012), 2459.

45. Henry Knox to George Washington December 31, 1794, in *The Papers of George Washington, Presidential Series,* vol. 17, *1 October 1794–31 March 1795,* ed. David R. Hoth and Carol S. Ebel (Charlottesville: Univ. of Virginia Press, 2013), 345–346.

46. "Notes of a Conversation with George Hammond, 4 June 1792," in *The Papers of Thomas Jefferson,* vol. 24, *1 June–31 December 1792,* ed. John Catanzariti (Princeton: Princeton Univ. Press, 1990), 26–33.

47. My argument that eighteenth-century white abolitionism was rooted in the desire to maintain white supremacy is developed more fully in *The Patriots' Dilemma: White Aboli-*

tionism and Black Banishment in the Founding of the United States of America (London: Pluto Press, 2024).

TWO. *America's Broken First Treaty of Peace*

1. Peter M. Bergman and Jean McCarroll, eds., *The Negro in the Continental Congress* (New York: Bergman Publishers, 1969), 56–57.

2. Journals of Congress for September 1782, in Bergman and McCarroll, eds., *The Negro in the Continental Congress*, 56–57.

3. Franklin to Oswald, November 26, 1782, *The Diplomatic Correspondence of the United States of America*, vol. 4 (Washington, D.C.: Francis Preston Blair, 1833), 40–41; Arthur Zilversmit, *The First Emancipation: The Abolition of Slavery in the North* (Chicago: Univ. of Chicago Press, 1967), 130–131. James Oakes claims that, prior to signing of provisional treaty, Congress "threatened to demand compensation for emancipated slaves if the British did not drop their own demand that American loyalists be compensated for the property they had lost during the war," and when the "British backed down, the congressional threat was withdrawn" (109). His wording here is meant to reinforce his thesis that Americans at this time generally viewed the British freeing or at least harboring escapees from patriot slavery as a legitimate act of war. This is an inaccurate representation of what Congress agreed to in September of 1782.

Congress's action followed immediately after the British evacuation of Savannah, in which the navy sailed off with thousands of formerly enslaved people. Congress resolved, with just seven no votes out of thirty-five, to instruct the secretary of foreign affairs to "as speedily as possible" gather "authentic returns of the slaves and other property which have been carried off" and send them to America's diplomats in Paris, who were "negotiating a peace." Understanding that compiling such a list would take time, the congressmen added that America's ministers in the meantime be informed that "many thousand of slaves and other property to a very great amount have been carried off . . . and that in the opinion of Congress the great loss of property . . . will be considered by the several states as an insuperable bar to their making restitution . . . to the former owners of property which has been or may be forfeited to or confiscated by any of the states." Franklin to Oswald, November 26, 1782, in *The Papers of Benjamin Franklin, vol. 38, August 16, 1782, through January 20, 1783*, ed. Ellen R. Cohn (New Haven: Yale Univ. Press, 2006), 350–356. At no time from the beginning of evacuations of emancipated people from Savannah to their conclusion in New York did Congress, as Oakes claims, back down on their demand for the return of all persons claimed as the property of loyal Americans. James Oakes, *The Scorpion's Sting: Antislavery and the Coming of the Civil War* (New York: National Geographic Books, 2015).

4. Hartley to Franklin, October 4, 1782, in Sparks, ed., *The Diplomatic Correspondence of the American Revolution*, 4:24.

5. *The Revolutionary Diplomatic Correspondence of the United States*, vol. 5, ed. Francis Wharton (Washington, D.C.: Government Printing Office, 1889), 843.

6. *The Revolutionary Diplomatic Correspondence of the United States*, vol. 6, ed. Francis Wharton (Washington, D.C.: Government Printing Office, 1889), 466.

7. See, for example, Richard B. Morris, *The Peacemakers: The Great Powers and American Independence* (New York: Harper and Row, 1965), 378–379; Robinson, *Slavery in the Structure of American Politics*, 124; Fehrenbacher, *The Slaveholding Republic*, 25; Schama, *Rough Crossings*, 136–137; Egerton, *Death or Liberty*, 199; Charles R. Ritcheson, *Aftermath of Revolution: British Policy Toward the United States, 1783–1795* (Dallas, Tex.: Southern Methodist Univ. Press, 1969), 71; Parkinson, *The Common Cause*, 564; Andrew Delbanco, *The War Before the War: Fugitive Slaves and the Struggle for America's Soul from the Revolution to the Civil War* (New York: Penguin, 2018), 75–76.

The mistaken idea that the stipulation that the British not "carry away" American slaves in their camps was snuck into the peace treaty by Henry Laurens has a long pedigree that rests on a desire to position the founders as abolitionists. A version of this story appears in William Gordon's 1788 history of the United States, where Gordon writes that Laurens "proposed the insertion of a paragraph against carrying away any negroes or other property, belonging to the American inhabitants." Gordon's scholarly rival, David Ramsey, who borrowed liberally from Gordon's work, left all references to escaped slaves in the peace treaty out of his books. David Ramsay, *History of the American Revolution* (1789; reprint, Lexington, Ky: Downing and Phillips, 1815). See Orin Grant Libby, "A Critical Examination of William Gordon's History of the American Revolution," *Annual Report of the American Historical Association* 1 (1900): 382; Elmer Douglass Johnson, "David Ramsay: Historian or Plagiarist?" *South Carolina Historical Magazine* 57, no. 4 (1956): 189–198; Gordon, *The History of the Rise, Progress, and Establishment of the Independence of the United States of America*, 4:340. Later, one of the most influential of all American historians, George Bancroft, sharpened Laurens's responsibility for this clause by describing him as demanding it. "On the demand of Laurens, a clause was interlined, prohibiting, on the British evacuation, the 'carrying away any negroes or other property of the inhabitants.'" George Bancroft, *History of the United States*, vol. 10 (Boston: Little, Brown, 1874), 521. Bancroft, like a majority of the socially elite amateur historians of the nineteenth century, was a New Englander who saw slavery as a threat to the nation and depicted the founding fathers as patient heroes doing what they could to set slavery on a course for extinction. See Edgar Johnson, "George Bancroft, Slavery, and the American Union" (Ph.D. diss., Auburn University, 1983). Bancroft simply could not depict Washington's fury at the British for harboring slaves, or Franklin's insistence at the negotiating table for the return of escapees, without tarnishing the halo he had so carefully placed upon their heads.

A notable exception to the rush to blame Laurens is the insightful analysis of David Waldstreicher, who observes that during the negotiations "Franklin countered demands that loyalists be reimbursed for their property losses with resolutions from the state of Pennsylvania 'that all losses of Negro or mulatto slaves . . .' should be compensated." David Waldstreicher, *Runaway America: Benjamin Franklin, Slavery, and the American Revolution* (New York: Hill and Wang, 2004), 221. David N. Gellman's *Liberty's Chain: Slavery, Abolition, and the Jay Family of New York* (Ithaca: Three Hills, Cornell Univ. Press, 2022) dispels the myth that Laurens smuggled the clause prohibiting carrying off human property and documents that all four American commissioners lobbied the British for their return. In the end, Gellman concludes that "Jay and his colleagues set aside antislavery inclinations and aspirations in their talks with the British to pursue specific American material interests" (65).

8. David Duncan Wallace, *The Life of Henry Laurens* (New York: G. P. Putnam's Sons, 1915), 191; Sparks, ed., *The Diplomatic Correspondence of the American Revolution*, 3:390–393.

9. Wallace, *The Life of Henry Laurens*, 191.

10. David R. Chesnut, C. James Taylor, Peggy J. Clark, and Thomas M. Downey, eds., *The Papers of Henry Laurens*, vol. 16 (Columbia: Univ. of South Carolina Press, 2003), 534–535.

11. Chesnut et al., eds., *The Papers of Henry Laurens*, 16:559.

12. Laurens to William Drayton, February 23, 1783, in Chesnut et al., eds., *The Papers of Henry Laurens*, 16:155–156.

13. John Adams to Robert R. Livingston, November 11, 1782, in *The Adams Papers: Papers of John Adams*, vol. 14, *October 1782–May 1783*, ed. Gregg L. Lint, C. James Taylor, Hobson Woodward, Margaret A. Hogan, Mary T. Claffey, Sara B. Sikes, and Judith S. Graham (Cambridge, Mass.: Harvard Univ. Press, 2008), 51–56.

14. Richard Oswald to Thomas Townshend, November 15, 1782, in *The Selected Papers of John Jay*, vol. 3, *1782–1784*, ed. Elizabeth M. Nuxoll (Charlottesville: Univ. of Virginia Press, 2013), 222–225.

15. Entries for November 17, 28, 30, 1782, in *The Adams Papers, Diary and Autobiography of John Adams*, vol. 3, *Diary, 1782–1804* (Cambridge, Mass.: Harvard Univ. Press, 1961); L. H. Butterfield, ed., *Autobiography, Part One to October 1776* (Cambridge, Mass.: Harvard Univ. Press, 1961), 40–85.

16. Francis Dana to Robert Livingston, June 17, 1783, *The Revolutionary Diplomatic Correspondence of the United States*, 6:496.

17. Jared Sparks in his *Life of Franklin* says that it was Franklin who demanded compensation for "negroes that had been plundered" and who also told Oswald that Congress had no power to restrain the states from confiscating loyalist property and if the English wished to tie the two issues together, they should establish an independent commission to tally up the damages on each side and lay any difference to whom it belonged. Jared Sparks, *Life of Franklin*, rev. ed. (Philadelphia: Childs and Peterson, 1859), 486–487.

18. Waldstreicher, *Runaway America*, 221.

19. *Journals of the Continental Congress, 1774–1789*, vol. 23, ed. Worthington Chauncey Ford (Washington, D.C.: Government Printing Office, 1936), 562–563.

20. Robert R. Livingston to Benjamin Franklin, August 9, 1782, in *The Papers of Benjamin Franklin*, vol. 37, *March 16 through August 15, 1782*, ed. Ellen R. Cohn (New Haven: Yale Univ. Press, 2003), 717–719.

21. Benjamin Franklin to Robert R. Livingston, October 14, 1782, in *The Papers of Benjamin Franklin*, 38:219–223.

22. Adams to Robert Livingston, November 11, 1782, in *The Emerging Nation: A Docu-*

mentary History of the Foreign Relations of the United States under the Articles of Confederation, 1780–1789, 3 vols., ed. Mary A. Giunta et al. (Washington, D.C., 1996), 1:656.

23. See Chesnut et al., eds., *The Papers of Henry Laurens,* 16:73.

24. Laurens to Gervais, August 9, 1783, in Chesnut et al., eds., *The Papers of Henry Laurens,* 16:255.

25. Laurens to Gervais, December 14, 1782, in Chesnut et al., eds., *The Papers of Henry Laurens,* 16:73.

26. Gervais to Laurens, September 27, 1782, in Chesnut et al., eds., *The Papers of Henry Laurens,* 16:31.

27. Bergman and McCarroll, eds., *The Negro in the Continental Congress,* 57.

28. Chesnut et al., eds., *The Papers of Henry Laurens,* 16:363–364.

29. Laurens to Gervais, March 4, 1784, in Chesnut et al., eds., *The Papers of Henry Laurens,* 16:403.

30. John T. Rutt, *Life and Correspondence of Joseph Priestley . . .* 2 vols. (London, 1831–32), 1:227n.

31. B. Zorina Khan, *Inventing Ideas: Patents, Prizes, and the Knowledge Economy* (Oxford Univ. Press, 2020), 352.

32. See Chesnut et al., eds., *The Papers of Henry Laurens,* 16:254, 260, 264, 267–268. Bernard Bailyn, *The Ideological Origins of the American Revolution* (Cambridge, Mass.: Belknap Press of Harvard Univ. Press, 1967); Gordon S. Wood, *The Radicalism of the American Revolution* (New York: Knopf, 1992); Sean Wilentz, *No Property in Man: Slavery and Antislavery at the Nation's Founding* (Cambridge, Mass.: Harvard Univ. Press, 2018).

33. James E. Bradley, *Religion, Revolution and English Radicalism: Non-conformity in Eighteenth-Century Politics and Society* (Cambridge Univ. Press, 2002), 292–293; see also B. Zorina Khan, *Inventing Ideas: Patents, Prizes, and the Knowledge Economy* (Oxford Univ. Press, 2020), 352.

34. The *Public Advertiser* (London), December 8, 1775, 2. Hartley's proposal in Parliament is covered in Christopher Leslie Brown, *Moral Capital: Foundations of British Abolitionism* (Chapel Hill: Univ. of North Carolina Press, 2006), 146–148. See also George H. Guttridge, *David Hartely, MP An Advocate of Conciliation, 1774–1783* (Berkeley: Univ. of California Press, 1926). The first news of Hartley's speech reached America via daily London newspapers that had reported Hartley's plan imprecisely and did not quote any of Hartley's words. The first reference to it may have been in the *Philadelphia Gazette* for February 28, 1776, which noted that "Mr. Hartley made a motion, the purport of which was, to address his Majesty, that he would be graciously pleased to withdraw his troops from Boston; that the colonists should be restored to their constitutional right of trial by jury, and that all the grievances which they complain of, on the score of taxation, should be redressed; at the same time he proposed a plan for establishing the supremacy of the legislature of Great-Britain in all other cases; But after some debate the motion was totally rejected, by 123 to 21." This was clearly cribbed from any of several London newspapers. *Pennsylvania Gazette,* February 28, 1776, 2. See, for example, the *Public Advertiser* (London), December 8, 1775,

2. The nearly exact wording was in the item carried in the competing Philadelphia paper, the *Pennsylvania Packet* and the *Maryland Gazette* a few days later. *Pennsylvania Packet,* March 4, 1776, 4; *Maryland Gazette* (Annapolis), March 7, 1776, 2.

Hartley's motion, though rejected by the House of Commons, only provoked more animosity against Parliament, as it came from the supposed friends of America. News of the details of Hartley's plan took months to make its way to the American colonies. The full text of the Hartley Plan was published in the *Pennsylvania Ledger.* Hartley's speech was also printed in the *Parliamentary Register,* number 14, which was a monthly compendium of the most important business of the government. *The Public Advertiser* (London), December 21, 1775, 1. The *Maryland Gazette* of Annapolis printed Lord Saville's speech in support of Hartley's plan in the first column of its front page on June 13, 1776. This speech included Saville describing Hartley's motion as "lightening the chains of slavery in America, recommended by my honourable friend" and urging it as a test of America's sincerity and loyalty, a "test of living obedience." *The Maryland Gazette* (Annapolis), June 13, 1776, 1.

35. C[harles] J. Fox to David Hartley, April 10, 1783, David Hartley Papers, vol. 1, 3–6, William L. Clements Library, University of Michigan.

36. Laurens to Franklin, April 4, 1783, *The Revolutionary Diplomatic Correspondence of the United States,* 6:358.

37. "Draft Articles to Supplement the Preliminary Anglo-American Peace Treaty, [circa April 27, 1783]," in *The Adams Papers: Papers of John Adams,* 14:448–450.

38. Giunta et al., eds., *The Emerging Nation,* 2:127.

39. C[harles] J. Fox to David Hartley, June 10, 1783, David Hartley Papers, vol. 1, 102–103, William L. Clements Library, University of Michigan.

40. Emer de Vattel, *The Law Of Nations : Or, Principles Of The Law Of Nature, Applied To The Conduct And Affairs Of Nations* (Philadelphia :T. and J. W. Johnson, 1853), 356–359; T. Rutherford, *Institutes of Natural Law* (Cambridge: J. Bentham, 1756), 114; Hugo Grotius, *The Most Excellent Hugo Grotius, His Three Books Treating the Rights of War and Peace* (London: M.W., 1782), 116, 159.

41. "Article Proposed and Read to the Commissioners . . . ," in *The Revolutionary Diplomatic Correspondence of the United States,* 5:842. Elizabeth M. Nuxoll, editor of the John Jay papers, concluded that American leaders conceded no ground to their British counterparts who made a distinction between fugitives from slavery who fled to their flag under promises of sanctuary and freedom and those who happened to areas in their control at the conclusion of the war. Nuxoll writes that Congress and America's diplomats "pressed for the return of all slaves regardless of how they had come under British control and when they had been taken." "Anglo-American Relations: Editorial Note," in *The Selected Papers of John Jay,* vol. 4, *1785–1788,* ed. Elizabeth M. Nuxoll (Charlottesville: Univ. of Virginia Press, 2015), 33–41.

42. Bergman and McCarroll, eds., *The Negro in the Continental Congress,* 14, 49, 53–54; *Pennsylvania Gazette,* December 12, 1781, 1.

43. Bergman and McCarroll, eds., *The Negro in the Continental Congress,* 58.

44. "To the honorable the General Assembly of the State of North Carolina," November 25, 1788, Brunswick County, North Carolina, General Assembly, Session Records, North Carolina Department of Archives and History, Raleigh, North Carolina.

45. Washington to Burwell Bassett Jr., August 11, 1799, in *The Papers of George Washington, Retirement Series,* vol. 4, *20 April 1799–13 December 1799,* ed. W. W. Abbot. (Charlottesville: Univ. Press of Virginia, 1999), 237–238. Erica Armstrong Dunbar, *Never Caught : The Washingtons' Relentless Pursuit of their Runaway Slave, Ona Judge* (New York: 37 Ink/Atria, 2018).

46. "A Conversation on Slavery, 26 January 1770," in *The Papers of Benjamin Franklin,* vol. 17, *January 1 through December 31, 1770,* ed. William B. Willcox (New Haven: Yale Univ. Press, 1973), 37–44.

47. Theodore Bland to Jacob Morris, July 17, 1783, *The Bland Papers, Vol. 1,* Charles Campbell, ed. (Petersburg, Va.: Edmund and Julian C. Ruffin, 1840), 111.

48. *Newcastle Weekly Courant* (Newcastle upon Tyne), August 9, 1783, 4.

49. *Newcastle Weekly Courant* (Newcastle upon Tyne), August 9, 1783, 4.

50. C[harles] J. Fox to David Hartley, August 9, 1783, David Hartley Papers, vol. 3, 53–54, William L. Clements Library, University of Michigan.

51. "Extracts from John Jay's Report on Violations of the Treaty of Peace," October 13, 1786, in *The Selected Papers of John Jay,* ed. Elizabeth M. Nuxoll (Charlottesville: Univ. of Virginia Press, 2014), 424.

52. Leslie to Carleton, August 10, 1782, Gen. Leslies Letterbook, Thomas Addis Emmet Collection, New York Public Library.

53. Henry Lee, *Memoirs of the War in the Southern Department of the United States* (Philadelphia: Bradford and Inskeep, 1812), 450.

54. Quarles, *The Negro in the American Revolution,* 167.

55. Franklin to Laurens, July 6, 1783, in Sparks, ed., *The Diplomatic Correspondence of the American Revolution,* 4:113.

56. "The Retort Courteous," *The Writings of Benjamin Franklin,* Albert Henry Smyth, vol. 10 (New York: Macmillan, 1907), 112–113; Verner W. Crane, "Franklin's 'The Internal State of America' (1786)," *William and Mary Quarterly* 15, no. 2 (April 1958), 214–227.

57. The American Peace Commissioners to Robert R. Livingston, December 14, 1782, in *The Adams Papers: Papers of John Adams,* 14:128–131.

THREE. *The "Carried Off" and American Protest*

1. Greene to R. R. Livingston, December 19, 1782, Papers of the Continental Congress, Record Group 360, National Archives; see also William Floyd to George Clinton, January 16, 1783, in *Letters of Delegates to Congress, 1774–1789,* vol. 7, ed. Paul Smith (Washington, D.C.: Library of Congress, 1995), 18.

2. South Carolina Delegates to Carleton, March 27, 1783, in *Letters of Delegates to Congress,* 7:110.

3. Morris, *The Peacemakers*, 441; *Journals of the Continental Congress, 1774–1789*, vol. 24, *Jan. 1–Aug. 29, 1783*, ed. Gaillard Hunt (Washington, D.C.: Government Printing Office, 1922), 249, 242–243.

4. South Carolina Delegates to Washington, May 19, 1783, in *Letters of Delegates to Congress*, vol. 20, ed. Paul H. Smith (Washington, D.C.: Library of Congress, 1993), 256; Chesnut et al., eds., *The Papers of Henry Laurens*, 16:363–364.

5. Benjamin Harrison to Virginia Delegates, August 30, 1782, in *The Papers of James Madison*, 5:90.

6. "Thomas Walke's Account of Capturing his Runaway Slaves in New York City," May 3, 1783, in Papers of the Continental Congress, 1774–1789, Records of the Continental and Confederation Congresses and the Constitutional Convention, Record Group 360, National Archives, Washington, D.C.; "William Byrd to Jonathan Walke, May 29, 1689," *Virginia Magazine of History and Biography* 26 (1918), 24; "Notes from the Records of Princess Anne County," *Virginia Magazine of History and Biography* 26 (1918), 413.

7. "Memoirs of the Life of Boston King, a Black Preacher (1798)," in *I Belong to South Carolina: South Carolina Slave Narratives*, ed. Susanna Ashton (Columbia: Univ. of South Carolina Press, 2010), 26.

8. Carleton to Clinton, June 18, 1783, in *Public Papers of George Clinton*, vol. 8, ed. Hugh Hastings (Albany: Oliver A. Quayle, 1904), 207–208.

9. Clinton to Carleton, July 1, 1783, in *Public Papers of George Clinton*, 8:212.

10. l'Hommedieu to Clinton, August 22, 1783, in *Public Papers of George Clinton*, 8:245.

11. Walker, *The Search for a Promised Land*, 7.

12. Carleton to Livingston, April 6, 1783, enclosed in Livingston's letter to Washington, April 15, 1783, Founders Online, National Archives, https://founders.archives.gov/documents/Washington/99-01-02-11068.

13. Livingston to Carleton, April 11, 1783, enclosed in Livingston's letter to Washington, April 15, 1783, Founders Online, National Archives, https://founders.archives.gov/documents/Washington/99-01-02-11068.

14. Carleton to Livingston, April 14, 1783, enclosed in Livingston's letter to Washington, April 15, 1783, Founders Online, National Archives, https://founders.archives.gov/documents/Washington/99-01-02-11068.

15. Daniel Parker to George Washington, April 20, 1783, Founders Online, National Archives, https://founders.archives.gov/documents/Washington/99-01-02-11121.

16. Guy Carleton to George Washington, May 12, 1783, Founders Online, National Archives, https://founders.archives.gov/documents/Washington/99-01-02-11252

17. Clinton to Benson, April 8, 1783, in *Public Papers of George Clinton*, 8:134–135.

18. Egbert Benson's Report to Governor Clinton of his Conference with Sir Guy Carleton, in *Public Papers of George Clinton*, 8:140–144.

19. Clinton to William Floyd, Alexander Hamilton, April 16, 1783, in *Public Papers of George Clinton*, 8:140.

20. Scott to Clinton, April 19, 1783, in *Public Papers of George Clinton*, 8:148.

21. Hamilton and Floyd to Clinton, April 23, 1783, in *Public Papers of George Clinton,* 8:154.

22. "By the United States in Congress Assembled," April 15, 1783, in *Public Papers of George Clinton,* 8:155.

23. Washington to Carleton, April 21, 1783; Carleton to Washington, April 24, 1783, in *Public Papers of George Clinton,* 8:156–158.

24. Elias Boudinot to George Washington, May 9, 1783, Founders Online, National Archives, https://founders.archives.gov/documents/Washington/99-01-02-11236.

25. *Public Papers of George Clinton,* 8:140; David M. Gellman, *Emancipation New York: The Politics of Slavery and Freedom, 1777–1827* (Baton Rouge: Louisiana State Univ. Press, 2006), 204–205.

26. "Substance of a Conference Between General Washington and Sir Guy Carleton, May 6, 1783," *The Writings of George Washington from the Original Manuscript Sources,* vol. 26, ed. John C. Fitzpatrick (Washington, D.C.:Government Printing Office, 1938), 402–406.

27. Guy Carleton to George Washington, May 12, 1783, Founders Online, National Archives, https://founders.archives.gov/documents/Washington/99-01-02-11252.

28. George Washington to Elias Boudinot, May 14, 1783, Founders Online, National Archives, https://founders.archives.gov/documents/Washington/99-01-02-11263.

29. Virginia Delegates to Benjamin Harrison, May 27, 1783, in *The Papers of James Madison,* vol. 7, *3 May 1783–20 February 1784,* ed. William T. Hutchinson and William M. E. Rachal (Chicago: Univ. of Chicago Press, 1971), 85–86.

30. William Stephens Smith to George Washington, May 30, 1783, Founders Online, National Archives, https://founders.archives.gov/documents/Washington/99-01-0-11351.

31. Egbert Benson to George Washington, June 14, 1783, Founders Online, National Archives, https://founders.archives.gov/documents/Washington/99-01-02-11449.

32. Egbert Benson to George Washington, June 18, 1783, Founders Online, National Archives, https://founders.archives.gov/documents/Washington/99-01-02-11473.

33. Egbt. Benson, William S. Smith, and Daniel Parker, Commissioners, to Sir Guy Carleton, June 9, 1783, and Egbt. Benson and Daniel Parker to General Washington, June 14, 1783, Commissioners, to Carleton, June 17, 1783, Papers relative to Great Britain, 1793, GLC08892, The Gilder Lehrman Institute of American History, New York.

34. American Embarkation Commissioners to Sir Guy Carleton, June 17, 1783, in Giunta et al., eds., *The Emerging Nation,* 2:157–158.

35. Washington to Livingston, June 23, 1783, in Giunta et al., eds., *The Emerging Nation,* 2:171.

36. John Hardy, ed., *Manual of the Corporation of the City of New York* (New York, 1871), 817–839. See also Robert Ernst, "A Tory-eye View of the Evacuation of New York," *New York History,* 64, no. 4 (October 1983): 376–394.

37. Fritz Hirschfield, *George Washington and Slavery* (Columbia: Univ. of Missouri Press, 1997), 23.

38. Commissioners of Embarkation at New York to George Washington, January 18,

204 Notes to Pages 68–74

1784, in *The Papers of George Washington*, Confederation Series, vol. 1, ed. W. W. Abbot (Charlottesville: Univ. Press of Virginia, 1992), 50–56.

39. George Washington to John Jay, September 27, 1785, in *The Selected Papers of John Jay*, 4:193.

40. *New Jersey Gazette* (Trenton), June 4, 1783, 2.

41. *Pennsylvania Packet* (Philadelphia), July 22, 1783, 3.

42. *Pennsylvania Packet* (Philadelphia), July 22, 1783, 3.

43. *New York Gazetteer, or Northern Intelligencer* (Albany), October 27, 1783, 1.

44. Ralph Izard to Arthur Middleton, May 30, 1783, in *Letters of Members of the Continental Congress*, vol. 7, ed. Edmund C. Burnett (Washington: Carnegie Institution, 1934), 175–176.

45. Samuel Hazard, ed., *Pennsylvania Archives*, 1st series, 12 vols. (Philadelphia: Joseph Severns, 1854), 10:27.

46. James Madison's Notes of Debates, May 20, 1783, in *Letters of Delegates to Congress*, 20:267.

47. James Madison's Notes of Debates, May 8, 1783, in *Letters of Delegates to Congress*, 20:239.

48. James Madison to Jefferson, May 13, 1783, in *Letters of Delegates to Congress*, 20:247.

49. *Journals of the Continental Congress, 1774–1789*, vol. 25, *Sept. 1–Dec. 31, 1783*, ed. Gaillard Hunt (Washington, D.C.: Government Printing Office, 1922), 959–960, 964.

50. Ibid., 25:361, 364–365; *Journals of the Continental Congress, 1774–1789*, 25:965.

51. Joseph Jones to Washington, May 6, 1783, in *Letters of Delegates to Congress*, 20:230.

52. Robert R. Livingston to the American Peace Commissioners, May 28, 1783, in *The Papers of Benjamin Franklin*, 40:75–77.

53. Boudinot to Franklin, June 18, 1783, in Sparks, ed., *The Diplomatic Correspondence of the American Revolution*, 10:175. Slightly different wordings of this letter are found in the published compendiums of diplomatic correspondence. *DCAR* that was published by the Department of State in 1833 reads: "It has been an ill-judged scheme in the British to retain New-York so long and send off the negroes, as it has roused the spirit of the citizens of the several States greatly" (*The Diplomatic Correspondence of the United States of America*, vol. 1 [Washington, D.C.: Francis Preston Blair, 1833], 8).

54. Adams, Franklin, and Jay to Livingston, July 18, 1783, *The Revolutionary Diplomatic Correspondence of the United States*, 6:570.

55. John Adams, Benjamin Franklin, and John Jay to David Hartley, July 17, 1783, in Sparks, ed., *The Diplomatic Correspondence of the American Revolution*, 10:185–186.

56. George Washington to John Jay, September 27, 1785, in *The Selected Papers of John Jay*, 4:967. See also *Journals of the Continental Congress, 1774–1789*, vol. 28, ed. Worthington C. Ford et al. (Washington, D.C.: Government Printing Office, 1904–1937), 123.

57. *Journals of the Continental Congress, 1774–1789*, vol. 30, ed. Worthington C. Ford et al. (Washington, D.C.: Government Printing Office, 1904–1937), 387–388.

58. Emory G. Evans, "Private Indebtedness and the Revolution in Virginia, 1776 to 1796," *William and Mary Quarterly* 28, no. 3 (July 1971): 349; Thad W. Tate, "The Coming of the Revolution in Virginia: Britain's Challenge to Virginia's Ruling Class, 1763–1776," *Wil-*

liam and Mary Quarterly 19, no. 3 (July 1962): 336. See also Anthony S. Parent, *Foul Means: The Formation of a Slave Society in Virginia, 1660–1740* (Chapel Hill: Univ. of North Carolina Press, 2003); Woody Holton, *Forced Founders: Indians, Debtors, Slaves, and the Making of the American Revolution in Virginia* (Chapel Hill: Univ. of North Carolina Press, 1999).

59. Charles Hobson, "The Recovery of British Debts in the Federal Circuit Court of Virginia, 1790–1797," *Virginia Magazine of History and Biography* 92, no. 2 (April 1984), 176–200. Aaron Tristan Knapp, "Law's Revolutions: Coercion and Constitutional Change in the American Founding" (Ph.D. diss., Boston University, 2016).

60. *Letters of Joseph Jones,* ed. Worthington C. Ford (Washington, D.C.: Department of State, 1889), 108, 111; David John Mays, ed., *The Letters and Papers of Edmund Pendleton,* vol. 2 (Charlottesville: Univ. Press of Virginia, 1967), 133–134.

61. April 11, 1783, *Journals of the Continental Congress, 1774–1789,* 24:240.

62. Maclaine to Hooper, January 17, 1784, in *The State Records of North Carolina,* vol. 17, ed. Walter Clark (Goldsboro, N.C.: Nash Brothers, 1899), 125.

63. Gould, *Among the Powers of the Earth,* 127.

64. *Secret Journals of Acts and Proceedings of Congress,* 4 vols. (Boston: Thomas B. Wait, 1821), 4:189–202 (hereafter cited as *Secret Journals*).

65. April 11, 1783, *Journals of the Continental Congress, 1774–1789,* 24:240.

66. Harrison to Monroe, February 27, 1784, in Giunta et al., eds., *The Emerging Nation,* 2:305.

67. Monroe to Harrison, March 26, 1784, in *Letters of Delegates to Congress,* vol. 21, ed. Paul H. Smith (Washington, D.C.: Library of Congress, 1994), 460–461.

68. Monroe to Harrison, May 14, 1784, in *Letters of Delegates to Congress,* 21:616.

69. Monroe to Harrison, April 10, 1784, in *Letters of Delegates to Congress,* 21:513.

70. Harrison to Monroe, April 2, 1784, in *The Papers of James Monroe,* vol. 2, *Selected Correspondence and Papers, 1776–1794,* ed. Daniel Preston and Marlena C. DeLong (London: Bloomsbury Academic, 2020), 92.

71. "Notes on Debates, May 8, 1783," *The Papers of James Madison,* 7:28, 172n7.

72. "Resolutions on Private Debts Owed to British Merchants, Resolution A, 7 June 1784," in *The Papers of James Madison, Secretary of State Series,* vol. 8, ed. Mary A. Hackett, J.C.A. Stagg, Anne Mandeville Colony, Jeanne Kerr Cross, Mary Parke Johnson, Angela Kreider, and Wendy Ellen Perry (Charlottesville: Univ. of Virginia Press, 2007), 60; "Editorial Note: Resolutions on Private Debts Owed to British Merchants," in *The Papers of James Madison,* 8:58–60.

73. Gordon Wood, "Interests and Disinterestedness in the Making of the Constitution," in *Beyond Confederation: Origins of the Constitution and American National Identity* (Williamsburg: Univ. of North Carolina Press, 1987), 63.

74. *Pennsylvania Packet* (Philadelphia), July 22, 1784, 2.

75. *Virginia Gazette* (Richmond), July 10, 1784, 1.

76. Lee to the Marquis of Lansdowns, March 3, 1786, in Richard Henry Lee, *Life of Arthur Lee,* vol. 2 (Boston: Wells and Lilly, 1829), 167–168.

77. Monroe to Jefferson, July 20, 1784, in *Letters of Delegates to Congress,* 21:733.

78. April 11, 1783, *Journals of the Continental Congress, 1774–1789*, 24:240.

79. Spaight and Sitgreaves to Gov. Martin, March 1, 1785, in Clark, ed., *The State Records of North Carolina*, 17:606.

80. Hamilton to George Clinton, June 1, 1783, in *Letters of Delegates to Congress*, 20:292–296. Hamiliton was particularly incensed by what he viewed as the sophistry of those who excused New York's violations of the treaty's terms on the proposition that the treaty was not in force until both Parliament and Congress had officially ratified it. To illustrate the absurdity of this idea, Hamilton pointed to the burning issue of General Carleton's refusal to hand over the fugitives from slavery. "Suppose the British should now send away not only the negroes but all other property and all the public records in their possession belonging to us on [such a] pretence . . . should we not justly accuse them with breaking faith? Is this not already done in the case of the negroes"? Clearly, in Hamilton's mind, the issues of loyalist property, English creditors, and fugitive slaves were all tightly intertwined. Alexander Hamilton to George Clinton, June 1, 1783, in *The Papers of Alexander Hamilton*, vol. 3, *1782–1786*, ed. Harold C. Syrett (New York: Columbia Univ. Press, 1962), 367–372.

81. *A Second Letter from Phocion to the Considerate Citizens of New-York. Containing Remarks on Mentor's Reply* (New York: Printed by Samuel Loudon, 1784), in *The Papers of Alexander Hamilton*, 3:530–558.

82. *A Letter from Phocion to the Considerate Citizens of New-York On the Politics of the Day* (New York: Printed by Samuel Loudon, 1784), in *The Papers of Alexander Hamilton*, 3:483–497. See also Ron Chernow, *Alexander Hamilton* (New York: Penguin, 2004), 194–196.

83. *American State Papers: Foreign Relations*, 1:224; "An Act for the speedy Sale of the Confiscated and forfeited Estates within this State," New York Laws, 7th sess., chapter 64 (May 12, 1784).

84. "An Act for the speedy Sale of the Confiscated and forfeited Estates within this State," *New York Laws*, 7th sess., chapter 64 (May 12, 1784); "Remarks on the Treaty of Amity Commerce and Navigation lately made between the United States and Great Britain, [9–11 July 1795]," in *The Papers of Alexander Hamilton*, vol. 18, *January 1795–July 1795*, ed. Harold C. Syrett, ed. (New York: Columbia Univ. Press, 1973), 404–454.

85. *Westminster Magazine or, The Pantheon of Taste*, August 1, 1784, 444.

86. *Dunlap's American Daily Advertiser*, February 3, 1794, 1.

87. *Laws of the Legislature of the State of New York, in Force Against the Loyalists and Affecting the Trade of Great Britain and British Merchants and Others Having Property in that State* (London: H. Reynell, 1786).

88. *Laws of the Legislature of the State of New York, in Force Against the Loyalists and Affecting the Trade of Great Britain and British Merchants and Others Having Property in that State*, vii.

89. American Commissioners to the Duke of Dorset, October 28, 1784, in *The Adams Papers: Papers of John Adams*, 16:355–358.

90. John Jay to John Adams, April 13, 1785, in *The Adams Papers: Papers of John Adams*, vol. 17, *April–November 1785*, ed. Gregg L. Lint, C. James Taylor, Sara Georgini, Hobson

Woodward, Sara B. Sikes, Amanda A. Mathews, and Sara Martin (Cambridge, Mass.: Harvard Univ. Press, 2014), 23–24.

91. Gerry to Adams, February 24, 1785, in *Letters of Members of the Continental Congress*, vol. 8, ed. Edmund C. Burnett (Washington, D.C.: Carnegie Institution, 1936), 39.

92. John Adams to Richard Henry Lee, April 29, 1785, in *The Adams Papers: Papers of John Adams*, 17:72–73.

93. John Adams to Elbridge Gerry, April 28, 1785, in *The Adams Papers: Papers of John Adams*, 17:66–70.

94. Read to Washington, March 9, 1785, in *Letters of Delegates to Congress*, 22, ed. Paul H. Smith (Washington, D.C.: Library of Congress, 1995), 256–258.

95. "John Adams' Instructions as Minister to Great Britain, 7 March 1785," *The Adams Papers: Papers of John Adams*, vol. 16, *February 1784–March 1785*, ed. Gregg L. Lint, C. James Taylor, Robert Karachuk, Hobson Woodward, Margaret A. Hogan, Sara B. Sikes, Sara Martin, Sara Georgini, Amanda A. Mathews, and James T. Connolly (Cambridge, Mass.: Harvard Univ. Press, 2012), 548–549; Adams to Jay, May 8, 1785, in Giunta et al., eds., *The Emerging Nation*, 2:569, 622.

96. Adams to Jay, May 30, 1785, in Giunta et al., eds., *The Emerging Nation*, 2:645.

97. Adams to Jay, June 6, 1785, in Giunta et al., eds., *The Emerging Nation*, 2:654.

98. Congressional Resolution on Slaves Carried Off by the British, August 9, 1786, in Giunta et al., eds., *The Emerging Nation*, 3:256.

99. Jay to Congress, January 31, 1786, *Secret Journals*, 3:609.

100. *Journals of the Continental Congress, 1774–1789*, vol. 32, ed. Roscoe R. Hill (Washington, D.C.: Government Printing Office, 1936), 229.

101. *Journals of the Continental Congress, 1774–1789*, 32:379–380.

102. Grayson to Madison, November 22, 1785, in *Letters of Delegates to Congress, 1774–1789*, vol. 23, ed. Paul Smith (Washington, D.C.: Library of Congress, 1995), 24,

103. John Adams to John Jay, May 25, 1786, in *The Adams Papers: Papers of John Adams*, vol. 18, *December 1785–January 1787*, ed. Gregg L. Lint, Sara Martin, C. James Taylor, Sara Georgini, Hobson Woodward, Sara B. Sikes, and Amanda M. Norton (Cambridge, Mass.: Harvard Univ. Press, 2016), 313–315.

104. John Jay to John Adams, November 1, 1786, in *The Adams Papers: Papers of John Adams*, 18:501–504.

105. John Adams to John Jay, May 8, 1785, in *The Selected Papers of John Jay*, 4:79–83.

106. Robert W. Smith, *Keeping the Republic: Ideology and Early American Diplomacy* (DeKalb: Northern Illinois Univ. Press, 2004), 37; Minute of Conversation with Mr. Adams, October 20, 1785, David Hartley Papers, vol. 1, 426, Clements Library, University of Michigan.

107. John Temple to Lord Carmarthen, December 7, 1786, *The Emerging Nation: A Documentary History . . .* , vol. 3, ed. Mary A Giunta et al. (Washington, D.C.: National Historical Publications and Records Commission, 1996), 372.

108. John Adams to John Jay, May 8, 1785, in *The Selected Papers of John Jay*, 4:79.

109. John Adams to John Jay, October 25, 1785, in *The Adams Papers: Papers of John Adams*, 17:541–551.

110. John Adams to John Jay, May 25, 1786, in *The Selected Papers of John Jay*, 4:338.

111. John Adams to John Jay, May 8, 1785, in *The Selected Papers of John Jay*, 4:81.

112. *Secret Journals*, 4:44, 85, 107. The most complete account of Jay's interactions with Congress on the British treaty remains Robinson, *Slavery in the Structure of American Politics*, 347–352.

113. *Journals of the Continental Congress, 1774–1789*, vol. 31, ed. John Fitzpatrick (Washington, D.C.: Government Printing Office, 1934), 867.

114. *Journals of the Continental Congress, 1774–1789*, 31:863–864.

115. "Extracts from John Jay's Report on Violations of the Treaty of Peace, 13 October 1786," in *The Selected Papers of John Jay*, 4:417–433.

116. *Journals of the Continental Congress, 1774–1789*, 31:868.

117. *Secret Journals*, 4:103–104.

FOUR. *The Rope of Sand*

1. Robbie Totten formulates a theory that diplomatic pressures overshadowed the "Critical Period" and were central to shaping the U.S. Constitution. Robbie J. Totten, "Security, Two Diplomacies, and the Formation of the U.S. Constitution: Review, Interpretation, and New Directions for the Study of the Early American Period," *Diplomatic History* 36, no. 1 (January 2012): 77–117.

2. Mary Sarah Bilder, *Madison's Hand: Revising the Constitutional Convention* (Cambridge, Mass.: Harvard Univ. Press, 2015).

3. Max Farrand, *The Framing of the Constitution of the United States* (New Haven: Yale Univ. Press, 1913), 3–4. I've borrowed the phrase "power not powers" from the late great Stanley Kutler, who used it frequently in his constitutional history course at the University of Wisconsin, which I had the privilege of assisting him with.

4. Hamilton to James Duane, September 3, 1780, *The Papers of Alexander Hamilton*, vol. 2, ed. Harold L. Syrett (New York: Columbia Univ. Press, 1961), 400–418.

5. John P. Kaminski, Gaspare J. Saladino, Richard Leffler, Charles H. Schoenleber, and Margaret A. Hogan, eds., *The Documentary History of the Ratification of the Constitution*, vol. 1, *Constitutional Documents and Records, 1776–1787* (Charlottesville: Univ. of Virginia Press, 2009).

6. George William Van Cleve, *We Have Not a Government: The Articles of Confederation and the Road to the Constitution* (Chicago: Univ. of Chicago Press, 2017), 84–87.

7. Robert Morris to the President of Congress, March 17, 1783, in *The Revolutionary Diplomatic Correspondence of the United States*, vol. 6, ed. Francis Wharton (Washington, D.C.: Government Printing Office, 1889), 309–311.

8. Gouveneur Morris to Jay, January 1, 1783, in *John Jay: The Making of a Revolutionary*, vol. 2, ed. Richard B. Morris (New York: Harper and Row, 1975), 485–486.

9. Van Cleve, *We Have Not a Government*, 96–99.

10. Kaminski et al., eds., *The Documentary History of the Ratification of the Constitution*, 1:154.

11. Tristram Dalton to John Adams, December 21, 1784, in *The Adams Papers: Papers of John Adams*, 16:474–477.

12. George Washington to Tench Tilghman, April 24, 1783, Founders Online, National Archives, https://founders.archives.gov/documents/Washington/99-01-02-11161.

13. Many scholars have pointed to international issues as being preeminent among those impelling structural change in government in this period. "Two external issues were especially compelling in the call for the Constitutional Convention. Widespread perceptions of national failure reflected the powerlessness of Congress in the areas of commerce and treaties. What further undermined the country's prestige and effectiveness abroad was the determination of the states to violate not only the Treaty of Peace with Britain, but the treaties with France and Holland as well." Norman A. Graebner, Richard Dean Burns, and Joseph M. Siracusa, *Foreign Affairs and the Founding Fathers: From Confederation to Constitution, 1776–1787* (Santa Barbara, Calif.: Praeger, 2011), 105. Eliga H. Gould concludes, "For the delegates who attended the Constitutional Convention in Philadelphia during the summer of 1787, the need for better relations with nations in Europe supplied one of the main reasons for drafting a new charter to replace the Articles of Confederation." Gould, *Among the Powers of the Earth*, 130. Melvin Yazawa argues that the problem of conflicting state and federal laws and "the barriers they erected against the advancement of a uniform national policy was nowhere more apparent than in the realm of postwar diplomacy," where states as diverse as Massachusetts and South Carolina passed laws shielding their citizens from having to repay their English creditors as the Treaty of Paris required. Yazawa, *Contested Conventions*, 4. Robbie Totten formulated a similar theory that diplomatic pressures overshadowed the "Critical Period" and were central to shaping the U.S. Constitution. Totten, "Security, Two Diplomacies, and the Formation of the U.S. Constitution," 77–117. Finally, in 2018, law scholars David M. Golove and Daniel J. Hulsebosch asserted that international relations were the foremost factor in dumping the government built on the Articles of Confederation and replacing it with the Constitution of 1787. They wrote, "It was the uncertain struggle to ensure that the United States complied with its (or their) treaty obligations and the law of nations that was arguably the most important, and the most consensual, reason for the drafting and ratification of the new Constitution." David M. Golove and Daniel J. Hulsebosch, "The Law of Nations and the Constitution: An Early Modern Perspective," *Georgetown Law Journal* 106, no. 6 (2018): 1593–1658.

14. Henry Knox to George Washington, May 24–28, 1784, in *The Papers of George Washington, Confederation Series*, vol. 1, *1 January 1784–17 July 1784*, ed. W. W. Abbot (Charlottesville: Univ. Press of Virginia, 1992), 403–405.

15. George Washington to Henry Knox, June 2, 1784, in *The Papers of George Washington, Confederation Series*, 1:419–420.

16. *Journals of the Continental Congress, 1774–1789*, vol. 27, ed. Gaillard Hunt (Washington, D.C.: Government Printing Office, 1928), 530; Henry Knox to George Washington, July 26, 1784, in *The Papers of George Washington, Confederation Series*, vol. 2, *18 July 1784–18 May 1785*, ed. W. W. Abbot (Charlottesville: Univ. Press of Virginia, 1992), 10–11.

17. Samuel Flagg Bemis, *Jay's Treaty: A Study in Commerce and Diplomacy* (New York: Macmillan, 1924), 4–10.

18. *Journals of the Continental Congress, 1774–1789*, 28:247–248.

19. Henry Knox to George Washington, May 5, 1785, in *The Papers of George Washington, Confederation Series*, 2:539–540.

20. Henry Knox to George Washington, November 22, 1785, in *The Papers of George Washington, Confederation Series*, vol. 3, *19 May 1785–31 March 1786*, ed. W. W. Abbot (Charlottesville: Univ. Press of Virginia, 1994), 379–380.

21. George Washington to Henry Knox, December 5, 1784, in *The Papers of George Washington, Confederation Series*, 2:170–172.

22. Henry Knox to George Washington, January 31, 1785, in *The Papers of George Washington, Confederation Series*, 2:301–306.

23. Abigail Adams to Elizabeth Smith Shaw, October 15, 1786, in *The Adams Papers, Adams Family Correspondence*, vol. 7, *January 1786–February 1787*, ed. C. James Taylor, Margaret A. Hogan, Celeste Walker, Anne Decker Cecere, Gregg L. Lint, Hobson Woodward, and Mary T. Claffey (Cambridge, Mass.: Harvard Univ. Press, 2005), 372–375.

24. James Warren to John Adams, October 22, 1786, in *The Adams Papers: Papers of John Adams*, vol. 18, *December 1785–January 1787*, ed. Gregg L. Lint, Sara Martin, C. James Taylor, Sara Georgini, Hobson Woodward, Sara B. Sikes, and Amanda M. Norton (Cambridge, Mass.: Harvard Univ. Press, 2016), 485–487.

25. Henry Knox to George Washington, October 23, 1786, in *The Papers of George Washington, Confederation Series*, vol. 4, *2 April 1786–31 January 1787*, ed. W. W. Abbot (Charlottesville: Univ. Press of Virginia, 1995), 299–302.

26. "November 1786," in *The Adams Papers, Diary of John Quincy Adams*, vol. 2, *March 1786–December 1788*, ed. Robert Taylor J and Marc Friedlaender (Cambridge, Mass.: Harvard Univ. Press, 1981), 120–135.

27. James Sullivan to John Adams, December 16, 1786, in *The Adams Papers: Papers of John Adams*, 18:523–525.

28. Benjamin Lincoln to George Washington, December 4, 1786–March 4, 1787, in *The Papers of George Washington, Confederation Series*, 4:418–436.

29. Holton, *Unruly Americans and the Origins of the Constitution*, 218.

30. John Jay to John Adams, November 26, 1785, in *The Adams Papers: Papers of John Adams*, 17:606–607.

31. Louis Ottenberg, "A Fortunate Fiasco: The Annapolis Convention of 1786," *American Bar Association Journal* 45, no. 8 (August 1959): 834–837, 877–882.

32. Egbert Benson, *Memoir Read Before the Historical Society of New York, Dec. 31, 1816* (n.p.: n.d.), Collections of the New York Historical Society, 2nd series, vol. 2, part 2, 77–148, quote on 135.

33. Clinton to Benson, April 8, 1783, in *Public Papers of George Clinton*, 8:134–135.

34. Carson Holloway and Bradford P. Wilson, eds., *The Political Writings of Alexander Hamilton* (New York: Cambridge Univ. Press, 2017), 214–218.

35. Jean Gordon Lee, *Philadelphians and the China Trade, 1784–1844* (Philadelphia Muse-

um of Art, 1984), p. 53; Charles Henry Hart, "Colonel John Nixon," *Pennsylvania Magazine of History and Biography* (Philadelphia) 1, no. 2 (1877), 188; Charles Pettit, "An Impartial Review (1800)," reprinted in *The Magazine of History, Extra No. 23* (New York: William Abbatt, 1913), 5–27; *Autobiography of Charles Biddle* . . . (Philadelphia: E. Claxton, 1883), passim.

36. "Letter to the Committee of the Merchants Traders etc. of Boston from the Philadelphia (Pa.) Committee of Merchants, May 19, 1785," EM. 9328, Thomas Addis Emmet Collection, New York Public Library.

37. "Annapolis Convention. Address of the Annapolis Convention [September 14, 1786]," in *The Papers of Alexander Hamilton*, 3:686–690.

38. Benson, *Memoir Read Before the Historical Society of New York, Dec. 31, 1816* (n.p.: n.d.), 138.

39. Jonathan Elliot, ed., *The Debates in the Several State Conventions on the Adoption of the Federal Constitution* . . . , 2nd ed., vol. 3 (Philadelphia: Lippincott, 1891), 26–27

40. John Adams, *A Defence of the Constitutions of Government of the United States of America* (London: John Stockdale, 1794), 364.

41. Varnum to Collins, April 4, 1787, in Burnett, ed., *Letters of Members of the Continental Congress*, 8:571.

42. *Journals of the Continental Congress, 1774–1789*, 32:124–125.

43. *Journals of the Continental Congress, 1774–1789*, 32:177–184. For a thorough study of the constitutional issues raised in the clash of treaties and states' sovereignty, see David M. Golove, "Treaty-Making and the Nation: The Historical Foundations of the Nationalist Conception of the Treaty Power," *Michigan Law Review* 98, no. 5 (March 2000): 1075–1319.

44. Madison to Jefferson, April 23, 1787, in Burnett, ed., *Letters of Members of the Continental Congress*, 8:589.

45. Charles Pettit to Jeremiah Wadsworth, May 27, 1786, in Burnett, ed., *Letters of Members of the Continental Congress*, 8:368–371

46. *Full and Faithful Report of the Debates in Both Houses of Parliament* . . . (London: S. Bladon, 1783), 20–21.

47. "Letters of Phineas Bond, British Consul at Philadelphia . . . ," in *Reports of the Historical Manuscripts Commission of the American Historical Association*, ed. J. Franklin Jameson (December 30, 1896), 513.

48. Bond to William Fraser, February 4, 1787, "Letters of Phineas Bond, British Consul at Philadelphia . . . ," 519.

49. Bond to Carmarthen, February 21, 1787, "Letters of Phineas Bond, British Consul at Philadelphia . . . ," 521–522.

50. Bond to Carmarthen, May 16, 1787, "Letters of Phineas Bond, British Consul at Philadelphia . . . ," 532–533.

51. Bond to Carmarthen, June 3, 1787, "Letters of Phineas Bond, British Consul at Philadelphia . . . ," 536.

52. Bond to Carmarthen, May 1, 1787, "Letters of Phineas Bond, British Consul at Philadelphia . . . ," 528–530.

53. Benjamin Franklin to David Hartley, September 6, 1783, in *The Papers of Benjamin Franklin*, 40:582–583.

54. Benjamin Franklin to Richard Price, August 16, 1784, in *The Papers of Benjamin Franklin*, vol. 43, *August 16, 1784, through March 15, 1785,* ed. Ellen R. Cohn (New Haven: Yale Univ. Press, 2018), 12–15.

55. "On the Settlement of Disputes between States by Judicial Means," in *The Papers of Thomas Jefferson*, vol. 6, *May 21, 1781–March 1, 1784,* ed. Julian P. Boyd (Princeton: Princeton Univ. Press, 1952), 505–507.

56. "Lies Respecting the Americans," in *The Papers of Benjamin Franklin*, 43:74–77.

57. Benjamin Franklin to Charles Thomson, May 13, 1784, in *The Papers of Benjamin Franklin*, vol. 42, *March 1 through August 15, 1784,* ed. Ellen R. Cohn (New Haven: Yale Univ. Press, 2017), 243–245.

58. *The American Museum* (Philadelphia), May 1787, 343–349; Gould, *Among the Powers of the Earth*, 127.

59. *The American Museum*, May 1787, 349–352.

60. *The American Museum*, May 1787, 353–354.

61. *The American Museum*, May 1787, 364.

62. *The American Museum*, March 1787, 187–188.

63. Madison to Randolph, February 18, 1787, in Burnett, ed., *Letters of Members of the Continental Congress*, 8:542.

64. Madison to Washington, February 21, 1787, in Burnett, ed., *Letters of Members of the Continental Congress*, 8:545–546.

65. Madison to Pendleton, February 24, 1787, in Burnett, ed., *Letters of Members of the Continental Congress*, 8:547.

66. Madison to Randolph, March 25, 1787, in Burnett, ed., *Letters of Members of the Continental Congress*, 8:565.

67. "Notes on the Sentiments on the Government of John Jay, Henry Knox, and James Madison, April 1787," in *The Papers of George Washington, Confederation Series*, vol. 5, *1 February 1787–31 December 1787,* ed. W. W. Abbot (Charlottesville: Univ. Press of Virginia, 1997), 163–166.

68. George Washington to James Madison, March 31, 1787, in *The Papers of George Washington, Confederation Series*, 5:114–117.

69. Irvine to Wilson, March 6, 1787, in Burnett, ed., *Letters of Members of the Continental Congress*, 8:551.

70. Johnson to Williamson, March 31, 1787, in Burnett, ed., *Letters of Members of the Continental Congress*, 8:568.

71. King to Parsons, April 8, 1787, in Burnett, ed., *Letters of Members of the Continental Congress*, 8:572.

72. Grayson to Short, April 16, 1787, in Burnett, ed., *Letters of Members of the Continental Congress*, 8:581.

73. Grayson to Short, April 16, 1787, in Burnett, ed., *Letters of Members of the Continental Congress*, 8:581.

74. John Jay to John Adams, February 21, 1787, in *The Selected Papers of John Jay*, 4:478–479.

75. *Charleston (S.C.) Morning Post*, January 30, 1786, 2. See also Janet Wilson, "The Bank

of North America and Pennsylvania Politics: 1781–1787," *Pennsylvania Magazine of History and Biography* 66, no. 1 (January 1942), 3–28.

76. Madison to Jefferson, October 24, 1787, in *The Papers of James Madison,* vol. 10, *May 27 1787–March 3, 1788,* ed. Robert A. Rutland, Charles F. Hobson, William M. E. Rachal, and Frederika J. Teute (Chicago: Univ. of Chicago Press, 1977), 205–220. Hamilton used the phrase "excesses of democracy" while arguing for a more powerful Senate and executive during the Constitutional Convention. *The Papers of Alexander Hamilton,* vol. 4, *January 1787–May 1788,* ed. Harold C. Syrett, ed. (New York: Columbia Univ. Press, 1962), 195–202.

77. On Madison's vote on tobacco, see J. Gordon Hylton, "James Madison, Virginia Politics, and the Bill of Rights," *William and Mary Law Review* 31, no. 2 (February 1990): 275–285. Madison to Jefferson, October 24, 1787, in *The Papers of James Madison,* 10:205–220; William Grayson to James Madison, May 28, 1786, in *The Papers of James Madison,* vol. 9, *9 April 1786–24 May 1787 and supplement 1781–1784,* ed. Robert A. Rutland and William M. E. Rachal (Chicago: Univ. of Chicago Press, 1975), 61–66.

78. "The Vices of the Political System of the U. States," *The Papers of James Madison,* 9:345–358.

79. E. H. Scot, ed., *Journal of the Constitutional Convention Kept by James Madison* (Chicago: Scott, Foresman, 1893), 59–60.

80. Charles Pinckney, "Observations on the Plan of Government Submitted to the Federal Convention, in Philadelphia, on the 28th of May, 1787" (May 28, 1787), in *The Records of the Federal Convention of 1787,* ed. Max Ferrand, 3 vols. (New Haven, Conn.: Yale Univ. Press, 1911), 3:120–121.

81. Pinckney's signal contribution to the architecture of the U.S. Constitution has not been popularly recognized. According to Christopher and James Collier, it was James Madison himself who "managed to destroy the posthumous reputation of Charles Pinckney by selective reporting." Christopher Collier and James Lincoln Collier, *Decision in Philadelphia: The Constitutional Convention of 1787* (New York: Ballantine Books, 1987), 81. Mary S. Bilder has thoroughly exposed Madison's massaging of his own original notes in order to burnish his own reputation after those who could contradict him, like Pinckney, had died. Bilder, *Madison's Hand.* Much evidence suggests that the version of Pinckney's plan published officially under the authority of John Quincy Adams in 1819 (and quoted here) is likely what he submitted on May 29. See Collier and Collier, *Decision in Philadelphia,* 64–74; Andrew C. McLaughlin, "Sketch of Charles Pinckney's Plan for a Constitution, 1787," *American Historical Review* 9, no. 4 (July 1904): 735–747; Charles C. Nott, *The Mystery of the Pinckney Draught* (New York: Century, 1908); S. Sidney Ulmer, "James Madison and the Pinckney Plan," *South Carolina Law Quarterly* 9 (1957): 416–443; J. F. Jameson, "Studies in the History of the Federal Convention of 1787," *Annual Report of the American Historical Association* 1 (1902): 87.

82. Charles Pinckney, "Observations on the Plan of Government Submitted to the Federal Convention, in Philadelphia, on the 28th of May, 1787" (New York: Francis Childs, 1787); Jonathan Elliot, ed., *The Debates in the Several State Conventions on the Adoption of the Federal Constitution,* 2nd. ed., vol. 1 (Philadelphia: Lippincott, 1851), 68–69.

83. Max Farrand, ed., *The Records of the Federal Convention,* vol. 1 (New Haven: Yale Univ. Press, 1911), 24–25.

84. Farrand, ed., *The Records of the Federal Convention,* 1:24. The quotes are from the journal of the convention. According to Madison, Randolph boiled his most important points down to two resolutions, the first of which was that "a Union of the States merely federal will not accomplish . . . common defence, security of liberty, & genl. Welfare." The second was scribbled down by James Madison as that "no treaty or treaties among the whole or part of the States, as individual sovereignties, would be sufficient" (33).

85. Farrand, ed., *The Records of the Federal Convention,* 1:39. These quotes are from Robert T. Yates's notes, originally published as *Secret Proceedings and Debates of the Convention* . . . (Cincinnati, Ohio: Alston Mygatt, 1838).

86. Farrand, ed., *The Records of the Federal Convention,* 1:34

87. Farrand, ed., *The Records of the Federal Convention,* 1:30–31.

88. Farrand, ed., *The Records of the Federal Convention,* 1:61, 54.

89. See also William Ewald, "James Wilson and the Drafting of the Constitution" (2008), Faculty Scholarship at Penn Law, 988, https://scholarship.law.upenn.edu/faculty _scholarship/988.

90. See Van Cleve, *A Slaveholders' Union,* 52–56. Emily Blanck documents how the Articles were judged in state courts to restrict states from harboring or freeing fugitives from slavery. Emily Blanck, *Tyrannicide: Forging an American Law of Slavery in Revolutionary South Carolina and Massachusetts* (Athens: Univ. of Georgia Press, 2014).

91. Farrand, ed., *The Records of the Federal Convention,* 1:594, 603–605; Max Farrand, ed., *The Records of the Federal Convention,* vol. 2 (New Haven: Yale Univ. Press, 1911), 95, 442–443, 446, 453.

92. Farrand, ed., *The Records of the Federal Convention,* 2:453, 601–602. Later the Committee of Style wordsmithed this clause to read: "No person legally held to service or labour in one state, escaping into another, shall in consequence of regulations subsisting therein be discharged from such service or labor, but shall be delivered up on claim of the party to whom such service or labour may be due."

93. Blanck, *Tyrannicide,* 151–152.

94. James Madison to Thomas Jefferson, October 24, 1787, in *The Papers of James Madison,* 10:205–220.

95. *Boston Independent Chronicle,* May 22, 1788, quoted in *The Documentary History of the Ratification of the Constitution: Ratification by the States,* vol. 9, *Virginia,* no. 2, ed. John P. Kaminski, Gaspare J. Saladino, Richard Leffler, Charles H. Schoenleber, and Marybeth Carlson (Madison: State Historical Society of Wisconsin, 1990), 843.

96. Kaminski et al., eds., *The Documentary History of the Ratification of the Constitution: Ratification by the States,* vol. 9, *Virginia,* no. 2, 1095, 1107.

97. "Publicola: An Address to the Freemen of North Carolina, March 20, 27, 1788," in *The Documentary History of the Ratification of the Constitution: Ratification by the States,* vol. 30, *North Carolina,* no. 1, ed. John P. Kaminski, Charles H. Schoenleber, Jonathan M. Reid,

Gaspare J. Saladino, Margaret Flamingo, Timothy D. Moore, David P. Fields, Dustin M. Cohan, and Thomas H. Linley (Madison: State Historical Society of Wisconsin, 2019), 114.

98. David Ramsey to Benjamin Lincoln, January 29, 1788, in *The Documentary History of the Ratification of the Constitution: Ratification by the States*, vol. 27, *South Carolina*, ed. John P. Kaminski, Charles H. Schoenleber, Jonathan M. Reid, David P. Fields, Michael E. Stevens, Gaspare J. Saladino, Margaret R. Flamingo, and Timothy D. Moore (Madison: Wisconsin Historical Society Press, 2016), 198.

99. Bond to Carmarthen, July 2, 1787, "Letters of Phineas Bond, British Consul at Philadelphia . . . ," in Giunta et al., ed., *The Emerging Nation*, 3:540–541.

100. Bond to Carmarthen, September 20, 1787, "Letters of Phineas Bond, British Consul at Philadelphia . . . ," in Giunta et al., ed., *The Emerging Nation*, 3:588.

101. Bond to Carmarthen, March 3, 1788, "Letters of Phineas Bond, British Consul at Philadelphia . . . ," in Giunta et al., ed., *The Emerging Nation*, 3:736–737.

102. *State Papers and Publick Documents of the United States*, 3rd ed. (Boston: Thomas B. Wait, 1819), 361–365.

103. Bond to Duke of Leeds, November 10, 1789, "Letters of Phineas Bond, British Consul at Philadelphia . . . ," *Annual Report of the American Historical Association, 1896*, vol. 1 (Washington, D.C.: Government Printing Office, 1897), 627–628.

104. Bemis, *Jay's Treaty*, 43–47; Chernow, *Alexander Hamilton*, 294–295; Douglas Brymner, ed., *Report of Canadian Archives, 1890* (Ottawa: Brown Chamberlin, 1891), 125, 127, 239.

FIVE. *Jay's Treaty and the Politics of Recapture*

1. Bond to Duke of Leeds, March 14, 1791, *Annual Report of the American Historical Association, 1898*, vol. 1 (Washington, D.C.: Government Printing Office, 1899), 474–481.

2. Jefferson was not formally named as secretary of state until a month later, on November 10, at which time Hammond presented his own credentials. Thomas Jefferson to George Hammond, October 26, 1791, in *The Papers of Thomas Jefferson*, 22:234–235.

3. George Hammond to Thomas Jefferson, November 26, 1791, in *The Papers of Thomas Jefferson*, 22:336–344.

4. Thomas Jefferson to George Hammond, November 29, 1791, in *The Papers of Thomas Jefferson*, 22:352–353.

5. George Hammond to Thomas Jefferson, November 30, 1791, in *The Papers of Thomas Jefferson*, 22:356–358.

6. Thomas Jefferson to George Hammond, December 15, 1791, in *The Papers of Thomas Jefferson*, 22:409–412.

7. "Enclosure III: Agreement on Fugitive Slaves, 7 August 1791," in *The Papers of Thomas Jefferson*, 22:408–409.

8. George Washington to Gouverneur Morris, October 13, 1789, in *The Papers of George Washington, Presidential Series*, vol. 4, ed. Dorothy Twohig (Charlottesville: Univ. Press of Virginia, 1993), 179–183.

9. Gouverneur Morris to George Washington, April 7, 1790, in *The Papers of George Washington, Presidential Series*, vol. 5, ed. Dorothy Twohig, Mark A. Mastromarino, and Jack D. Warren (Charlottesville: Univ. Press of Virginia, 1996), 319–323.

10. Gouverneur Morris to George Washington, May 1, 1790, in *The Papers of George Washington, Presidential Series*, 5:362–368.

11. Gouverneur Morris to George Washington, May 29, 1790, in *The Papers of George Washington, Presidential Series*, 5:430–439.

12. *Virginia Gazette and General Advertiser* (Richmond), October 30, 1794, 2.

13. Alexander Hamilton to George Washington, [April 14, 1794], in *The Papers of Alexander Hamilton*, vol. 16, *February 1794–July 1794*, ed. Harold C. Syrett (New York: Columbia Univ. Press, 1972), 266–279.

14. "Enclosure: Points to be Considered in the Instructions to Mr. Jay, Envoy Extraordinary to G B, [April 23, 1794]," in *The Papers of Alexander Hamilton*, 16:319–328. Gellman depicts Hamilton's actions as being more consistently abolitionist during the evacuation and later Jay Treaty controversies, noting that "Hamilton for years had soft-pedaled the significance of the alleged British transgression against American slave owners" and "It is worth noting that Hamilton displayed considerable consistency in his private and public handling of the evacuation issue." Gellman, *Emancipation New York*, 138–139.

15. "Enclosure: Edmund Randolph to John Jay: Private, 16 August 1795," in *The Papers of Alexander Hamilton*, vol. 19, ed. Harold C. Syrett and Patricia Syrett (New York: Columbia Univ. Press, 1973), 150–153; see also Joshua Miller, "The Historical Presidency: The Rendition of Fugitive Slaves and the Development of the Law and Order President, 1790–1860," *Presidential Studies Quarterly* 49, no. 3 (December 2018): 684–697. Charles R. Richeson falsely writes that Jay's instructions contained "no explicit reference to the abducted slaves." Richeson, *Aftermath of Revolution*, 333.

16. Bemis, *Jay's Treaty*, xi–xii

17. Alexander Hamilton to John Jay, May 6, 1794, in *The Papers of Alexander Hamilton*, 16:381–385. Elkins and McKitrick cite this same letter to support their contention that the Washington administration had no interest in pushing the fugitive slave issue. They wrote that Jay would not "let the negotiations be stalled over the issue of slaves carried off. That there was not a word about this in Hamilton's letter of May 6 to Jay is some indication of what they must have said about it in private." Stanley Elkins and Eric McKitrick, *The Age of Federalism* (New York: Oxford Univ. Press, 1993), 401.

18. John Jay to George Washington, August 5, 1794, in *The Selected Papers of John Jay*, vol. 6 *(1794–1798)*, ed. Elizabeth M. Nuxoll (Charlottesville: Univ. of Virginia Press, 2020), 71.

19. John Jay's Objections to Grenville's Draft Treaty Proposals of August 30, in *The Selected Papers of John Jay*, 6:126.

20. *American State Papers: Foreign Relations*, 1:492–493.

21. John Jay to Edmund Randolph, September 13, 1794, in *The Selected Papers of John Jay*, 4:144–145.

22. Gellman, *Liberty's Chain*, 94. See also Jerald A. Combs, *The Jay Treaty: Political Battleground of the Founding Fathers* (Berkeley: Univ. of California Press, 1970), 155; Todd Estes,

The Jay Treaty Debate, Public Opinion, and the Evolution of Early American Political Culture (Amherst: Univ. of Massachusetts Press, 2006), 28; Bemis, *Jay's Treaty*, 236.

23. Edmund Randolph to John Jay, November 12, 1794, *American State Papers: Foreign Relations*, 1:501.

24. Edmund Randolph to John Jay, December 3, 1794, *American State Papers: Foreign Relations*, 1:509.

25. Edmund Randolph to John Jay, December 15, 1794, *American State Papers: Foreign Relations*, 1:510.

26. John Jay to Edmund Randolph, November 19, 1794, *American State Papers, Foreign Relations*, 1:504.

27. John Jay to Edmund Randolph, February 6, 1795, in *The Selected Papers of John Jay*, 6:273. See also Wendy H. Wong, "Diplomatic Subtleties and Frank Overtures: Publicity, Diplomacy, and Neutrality in the Early American Republic, 1793–1801" (Ph.D. diss., Temple University, 2014).

28. *New York Magazine, or Literary Repository* (New York) 6, no. 6 (June 1795), 381.

29. *Weekly Museum* (New York), January 24, 1795, 3; *New York Magazine, or Literary Repository* 6, no. 2 (February 1795), 125.

30. *Annals of Congress*, Senate, 4th Congress, 2nd Session, 859–860.

31. *Annals of Congress*, Senate, 4th Congress, 2nd Session, 861–862.

32. Annals of Congress, Senate, 4th Congress, 2nd Session, 861–862; also see *Treaty of Amity, Commerce, and Navigation . . .* , 2nd. ed. (Philadelphia: Lang and Ustick, 1795), 28.

33. Elkins and McKitrick dismiss this episode as a "distraction," and though they report the votes on other last-ditch amendments, they curiously neglect to note that this one only fell two votes short of passage. Elkins and McKitrick, *The Age of Federalism*, 419. Note that not all senators were present for every vote.

34. *Treaty of Amity, Commerce, and Navigation*, 865.

35. One of the first historians to recognize the popular anger Article 7 aroused because of its silence on the question of compensation for slave fugitives was David N. Gellman, who observed of the Jay Treaty controversy, "The attacks on the treaty's handling of slavery at first revealed the potent hostility that even indirect emancipationist policies aroused, not just in the South but in New York itself." David N. Gellman, *Emancipating New York: The Politics of Slavery and Freedom, 1777–1827* (Baton Rouge: Louisiana State Univ. Press, 2006), 136.

36. *Weekly Museum* (New York), 8, no. 374 (July 11, 1795), 3.

37. *Philadelphia Gazette*, July 28, 1795, 1–2; July 29, 1795, 1.

38. "Address of the Citizens of Portland, New Hampshire, agreed upon at a meeting held July 17, 1795," in *Treaty of Amity, Commerce, and Navigation*, 159–160.

39. *Treaty of Amity, Commerce, and Navigation*, 160–161.

40. *Providence (R.I.) Gazette*, July 25, 1795, 1.

41. "Letters of Stephen Higginson, 1783–1804," in *Reports of the Historical Manuscripts Commission of the American Historical Association* (December 30, 1896), 704–708.

42. Stephen Higginson to Timothy Pickering, July 14, 1795, "Letters of Stephen Higginson, 1783–1804," 787.

43. Stephen Higginson to Timothy Pickering, July 14, 1795, "Letters of Stephen Higginson, 1783–1804," 788.

44. Richmond, Va., Citizens to George Washington, July 30, 1795, in *The Papers of George Washington, Presidential Series, vol. 18*, ed. Edward G. Lengel (Charlottesville: Univ. of Virginia Press, 2008), 473–479.

45. Caroline County, Va., Citizens to George Washington, August 11, 1795, in *The Papers of George Washington, Presidential Series*, 18:531–535.

46. Amelia County, Va., Citizens to George Washington, August 28, 1795, in *The Papers of George Washington, Presidential Series*, 18:600–604.

47. *American Minerva*, August 3, 1795, 2.

48. *City Gazette* (Charleston, S.C.), July 23, 1795, 2, and August 4, 1795, 1; *The American Remembrancer: Or, An Impartial Collection of Essays, Resolves, Speeches, &c. Relative, or Having Affinity, to the Treaty with Great Britain*, 3 vols. (Philadelphia: Mathew Carey, October 24, 1795), 2:5–21.

49. *The American Remembrancer*, 2:271–272.

50. George Washington to Alexander Hamilton, July 3, 1795, in *The Papers of Alexander Hamilton*, 18:398–400.

51. Alexander Hamilton to George Clinton, June 1, 1783, in *The Papers of Alexander Hamilton*, 3:367–372.

52. "Remarks on the Treaty of Amity Commerce and Navigation lately made between the United States and Great Britain, [9–11 July 1795]," in *The Papers of Alexander Hamilton*, 18:404–454.

53. Edmund Randolph to George Washington, July 12, 1795, in *The Papers of George Washington, Presidential Series*, 18:312–326. Oliver Wolcott Jr. sent Washington his comments on the treaty on June 30, but was silent as to the issue of the "carried off." Though there is evidence that both William Bradford and Timothy Pickering also submitted their opinions, these have not been found. Oliver Wolcott Jr. to George Washington, June 30, 1795, in *The Papers of George Washington, Presidential Series*, 18:276–277.

54. *Connecticut Courant* (Hartford), August 3, 1795, 2.

55. *American Minerva*, July 20, 1795, 2.

56. Estes, *The Jay Treaty Debate, Public Opinion, and the Evolution of Early American Political Culture*, 22.

57. "Juricola No. 2," reprinted in the *American Remembrancer*, 2:77, 78.

58. "Extracts from John Jay's Report on Violations of the Treaty of Peace, October 13, 1786," in *The Selected Papers of John Jay*, 4:424.

59. Bergman and McCarroll, eds., *The Negro in the Continental Congress*, 73–75.

60. *Greenleaf's New York Journal*, July 29, 1795, 2.

61. Curiously, standard histories of this congressional debate largely overlook the issue of fugitive slaves. Todd Estes's chapter on the House debate, "The Final Push: The Debate in Congress and Out-of-Doors," contains not a single reference to the fugitive slave issue. Estes, *The Jay Treaty Debate, Public Opinion, and the Evolution of Early American Political Culture*.

62. Benjamin Franklin Bache, ed., *Debates in the House of Representatives of the United States during the First Session of the Fourth Congress upon the Constitutional Powers of the House with Respect to Treaties* (Philadelphia: Benjamin Franklin Bache, 1796), 138.

63. Bache, ed., *Debates in the House*, 146.

64. Bache, ed., *Debates in the House*, 34.

65. Bache, ed., *Debates in the House*, 39–40.

66. Bache, ed., *Debates in the House*, 40–41.

67. Bache, ed., *Debates in the House*, 83–84.

68. Bache, ed., *Debates in the House*, 92.

69. David F. Ericson, *Slavery in the American Republic: Developing the Federal Government, 1791–1861* (Lawrence: Univ. of Kansas Press, 2011), 93; *A Brief Memoir of the Life, and Revolutionary Services, of Major William Hazzard Wigg, of South Carolina* (Washington, D.C.: L. Alexander, Printer, 1860).

EPILOGUE

1. Alan Taylor, *The Internal Enemy: Slavery and War in Virginia, 1772–1832* (New York: Norton, 2013); Quarles, *The Negro in the American Revolution*; Frey, *Water from the Rock*; Gilbert, *Black Patriots and Loyalists*; Van Buskirk, *Standing in Their Own Light*.

2. Matthew Mason's extensive survey of the popular press of this period concluded that the war drove Americans "to choose nationalism over antislavery. In a transatlantic debate that involved the very nature and reputation of America's republican institutions, many Americans North and South saw the defense of their country as of primary concern." Matthew Mason, *Slavery and Politics in the Early American Republic* (Chapel Hill: Univ. of North Carolina Press, 2006), 93.

3. Monroe wrote: "It is equally proper that the negroes taken from the southern states should be returned to their owners, or paid for at their full value. It is known that a shameful traffic has been carried on in the West Indies, by the sale of these persons here, by those who professed to be their deliverers. Of this fact the proof that has reached this department shall be furnished you. If these slaves are considered as non-combatants, they ought to be restored; if as property, they ought to be paid for. The treaty of peace contains an article which recognises this principle." Monroe to American Plenipotentiaries at Gottenburgh, January 28, 1814, *State Papers on the Peace and Negotiations with America* (London: Sheerwood, Neely and Jones, 1815), 18.

4. Charles Francis Adams, ed., *Memoirs of John Quincy Adams, comprising portions of his diary from 1795 to 1848*, 12 vols. (Philadelphia: Lippincott, 1874), 3:26–27.

5. Adams, ed., *Memoirs of John Quincy Adams*, 3:92.

6. Adams, ed., *Memoirs of John Quincy Adams*, 3:96.

7. John Quincy Adams to Edward Perkins, April 6, 1816, in Adams, ed., *Memoirs of John Quincy Adams*, 6:2.

8. *American State Papers: Foreign Relations*, 3:735.

9. Andrew Jackson to John Lambert, March 13, 1815; Andrew Jackson to John Lam-

bert, February 26, 1815; John Lambert to Andrew Jackson, March 19, 1815; John Lambert to Andrew Jackson, March 18, 1815 (quoted); Andrew Jackson to John Lambert, March 24, 1815 (quoted), all in *Andrew Jackson Papers, 1775–1874,* Series 1, General Correspondence and Related Items, 1775–1885, Library of Congress.

10. John Clavelle to the American Commissioners, February 23, February 24, April 15, 1815, *American State Papers: Foreign Relations,* 4:109.

11. Thomas Newell to Brigadier General Floyd, March 16, 1815; Cockburn to Newell and Spalding, March 11, 1815; Spalding to Cockburn, March 13, 1815, all in *American State Papers: Foreign Relations,* 4:109, 112, 113.

12. Thomas Spalding to the Secretary of State, May 1815, *American State Papers: Foreign Relations,* 4:113.

13. Monroe to Augustus Neale, June 17, 1815, in *The Papers of James Monroe,* vol. 7, *Selected Correspondence and Papers, April 1814–February 1817,* ed. Daniel Preston and Marlena C. De-Long (New York: Bloomsbury Academic, 2020), 393. For a thorough narrative of the freed community's migration to Nova Scotia, see Taylor, *The Internal Enemy,* chapter 11.

14. Taylor, *The Internal Enemy,* 387.

15. James Madison to James Monroe, April 5, 1815, in *The Papers of James Madison, Presidential Series,* vol. 9, *19 February 1815–12 October 1815,* ed. Angela Kreider, J. C. A. Stagg, Mary Parke Johnson, and Anne Mandeville Colony (Charlottesville: Univ. of Virginia Press, 2018), 140–141.

16. Adams, ed., *Memoirs of John Quincy Adams,* 3:204.

17. Adams, ed., *Memoirs of John Quincy Adams,* 3:255–256.

18. Adams, ed., *Memoirs of John Quincy Adams,* 3:257.

19. Adams, ed., *Memoirs of John Quincy Adams,* 3:398; Taylor, *The Internal Enemy,* 432. See also Fehrenbacher, *The Slaveholding Republic,* 93–94.

20. Mason, *Slavery and Politics in the Early American Republic,* 49.

21. Alan Taylor noted that Virginians "began the war as champions of the Union" and "ended it with powerful new doubts." Taylor, *The Internal Enemy,* 315.

INDEX

abolitionism, 34–35

Adams, Abigail, 106–7

Adams, John, 7, 33, 36–39, 44, 61, 80, 84–92; appointed as ambassador to the U.K., 85–86; doubts about congressional power, 91–93, 116–17

Adams, John Quincy, 108, 176–78, 182–83

African Americans: in colonial armies, 2; reenslaved after patriot service, 18–23; patriot dreams of banishment of, 4. *See also* fugitives from slavery

American Flag Riot of October 1783, 65–66

American Museum, The, 122–24

Annapolis Convention, 110–16

Arabas, Jack, 21–22

Armistead, James, 22

Articles of Confederation, 7–9; lack of powers in, 96, 98, 100, 102–3, 108–10, 115–16, 126; amendments to taxing powers in, 100–101

Article Seven of the Treaty of Paris: American interpretations of, 46–48, 61, 65, 72–73, 78, 89, 94–95, 166–67, 169–73; British interpretations of, 45–46, 57, 61; debate after adoption of the U.S. Constitution, 142; debate over ratification, 53–54, 60–61; de-

fined, 8, 33; diplomatic negotiations over, 44–46, 67–68, 143–48, 150–55; drafting of, 35, 39–41, 44–45. *See also* Paris, Treaty of

Bache, Benjamin Franklin, 161, 163, 169

Bailyn, Bernard, 42

Barbé-Marbois, Francois Marquis de, 15

Bassett, Burwell, 78

Beckwith, Lt. Col. George, 139–41

Benezet, Anthony, 23

Benson, Egbert, 58–59, 61, 62; and Annapolis Convention, 111–16

Berger, Caspar, 20–21

Biddle, Charles, 114

Biddle, Nicholas, 114

Bland, Theodore, 70

Bloodworth, Timothy, 160

Bond, Phineas, 119–21, 138–39, 142

"Book of Negroes," 67, 158

Boudinot, Elias, 60, 73

Brown, John, 78, 160

Burke, Aedanus, 164

Burke, Edmund, 43, 153

Burr, Aaron, 158–59, 160

Burroughs, John, 22

Butler, Pierce, 28, 133, 160

www.ingramcontent.com/pod-product-compliance
Lightning Source LLC
Chambersburg PA
CBHW030303100426
42812CB00002B/550